Six Sigma
and the Quality Toolbox
for Service and Manufacturing

John Bicheno and Philip Catherwood
with contributions from Rob James

PICSIE Books

ISBN 0 9541 2442 1

In memory of Big Chris

Contents

Six Sigma

Introduction	7
What is Six Sigma	7
Evolution	8
The Approach	9
Philosophy	11
Roles and Responsibilities	12
Six Sigma as a Metric	16
Cost of Poor Quality	17
Six Sigma Caveat and Sustainability	20

The Gurus

Deming	25
Juran	27
Crosby	30
Feigenbaum	31
Ishikawa	32
Garvin	34
Shingo (and Failsafing)	35
Taguchi	36
Kano	38
Grönroos	40
Shainin	40

Improvement Cycles

DMAIC	43
PDCA	44

Define

Project Charter	47
SIPOC	47
Voice of the Customer	48
Critical Path Analysis	49

Measure

Data Representation	52
Measures of Central Tendency and Variation	53
Sampling	54
Measurement System Analysis and Guage R+R	55
The 7 Tools of Quality	57
Cross Impact Analysis	64
Process Capability	65
Statistical Process Control	67

Analyse

Sampling Distribution	74
Hypothesis Testing	76

Improve

Regression Analysis	82
Design of Experiments	83
Failure Mode and Effect Analysis	87
Error Proofing	88

Control

Control and Sustainability	90
Standard Work	91
Window Analysis and Johari	93
Total Productive Maintenance	95
Six Sigma Control Plan	95
Story Board	96

7 Wastes

The 7 Wastes	98
New Wastes	101
Service Wastes	101

'New' Tools

Affinity Diagram	103
Interrelationship Diagram	104
Tree Diagram	105
Contingency Chart	105
Matrix Analysis	106

General Tools

5S	110
5 Whys and Root Causes	112
Honest Men	113
Benchmarking	113
Best Demonstrated Practice	116
Brainstorming	117
Cusum Charts	117
Force Field Analysis	118
Importance – Performance Matrix	119
Kaizen	120
Market Surveys	122
Nominal Group Technique	123
Quality Function Deployment	125
Single Point Lessons	128
Supplier Partnerships	129

Service Quality Concepts

Cycle and Service Mapping   133
Moments of Truth   134
Service Blueprints   135
Customer Loyalty   137
Service Gaps and SERVQUAL   140
Service Profit Chain   141
Service Recovery and Retention   142
Zone of Tolerance   144
Value Demand and Failure Demand   145

Systems

ISO 9000   147
EFQM Excellence Model   149

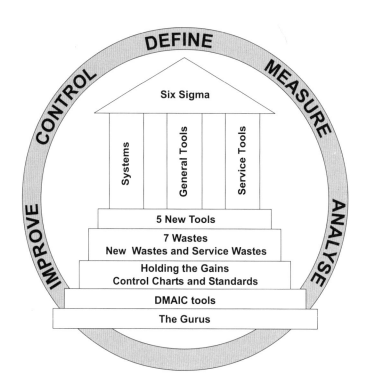

Six Sigma

Introduction

The term 'Six Sigma' has been around since 1986 when Motorola set out to improve its quality by X100. In the 1970's, the U.S. consumer electronics market came under threat from the Japanese who began eroding Motorola's market share. Six Sigma was a company wide response to this competition. In the early years it was a quality initiative rather than the rigorous methodology that exists today.

History of Six Sigma at Motorola

After 20 years Six Sigma is fully embedded in relatively few organisations. Its early adoption was in US companies such as Texas Instruments and Kodak, and then General Electric and Allied Signal dedicated increasing resources to introduce the methodology. Other organisations such as Raytheon, Bombardier and Johnson & Johnson have identified Six Sigma as the way forward for their companies and as success stories have been reported, other U.S. companies have followed. The fact that many of the U.S. companies are multinational has resulted in its adoption in many countries. In the UK, there are many companies who are now claming to be 'doing' Six Sigma, although this often refers to training being undertaken and to projects being tackled as opposed to the actual quality levels attained. Companies such as General Electric, Johnson & Johnson and Bombardier have continued to roll-out the methodology in their UK plants and other blue chip companies such as Ford, Land Rover, Sony and Black & Decker are also well into implementing their Six Sigma programmes. Today, Six Sigma is widely adopted in the automotive sector in the UK, and the service sector (for example, BT, Citibank, Lloyds TSB) is recognising the benefits and the applicability to their processes.

This book aims to strike a balance between the several pocket guides that are available and detailed books on the topic.

What about the benefits of Six Sigma? Motorola developed the approach to raise quality levels but the approach has undergone Continuous Improvement in itself. Six Sigma is now a recognised approach to improving Quality, Cost and Delivery (QCD). It delivers superior customer satisfaction and supports the retention of existing business. It supports a culture change to making decisions based on fact and arms the organisations' key players with a world class Project Management skill-set. It is the logical partner to Lean operations and Supply Chain Development.

Why is this important? Many key employment sectors such as consumer electronics and automotive are under extreme pressure to reduce costs to maintain market share in the face of ever increasing competition, both at home and from overseas. If the costs of not getting things right first time are not reduced, uncomfortable choices such as reducing salaries or cutting back the workforce will become necessary in order to survive. Cost avoidance of poor quality is the most cost-effective, least capital-intensive route to improving QCD and sustainability.

What Is Six Sigma (6σ)?

There is no one standard definition of Six Sigma although a literature search will offer a number of alternatives. A simple, easy to remember, statement explaining what Six Sigma is about is offered by Air Academy Associates:

'The relentless and ruthless pursuit of the elimination of variation'.

This statement is by no means all-embracing of the Six Sigma subject area but it does demonstrate the importance of variation. This is a key concept within Six Sigma and is a defining property when comparing and contrasting Six Sigma with other concepts such as Lean.

A notional goal of Six Sigma is 3.4 defects per million but Six Sigma is much more than a quality target; it is a rigorous methodology to improve processes, increase customer satisfaction and reduce the Cost Of Poor Quality (COPQ) in a highly structured manner, focussing on process variation.

It is about understanding how process inputs affect process outputs. Once the input variables are understood, then there is sufficient knowledge to optimise a process using robust designs. Six sigma promotes a 'management by fact' philosophy utilising powerful statistics (where appropriate). Process improvements are measured using standard metrics, the most important one being financial impact.

The actual term Sigma is a Greek letter, represented by the symbol σ, and is used in the field of mathematics to denote variation.

The terms 'dispersion' and 'spread' are also used, but the most commonly used term is variation. When Sigma is calculated, it is commonly referred to as 'standard deviation' and this is a measure which represents the degree of variation within a distribution of data.

$$6\sigma$$

Six Sigma is a term that is a measure of process capability. It is a comparison of the process distribution against the customer defined specifications. Put another way, it is the relationship between the Voice Of the Customer (VOC) and the Voice Of the Process (VOP).

If the process distribution is such that there are six standard deviations between the mean of the process and the customer specification, then the process is deemed as being Six Sigma capable.

So, Six Sigma is about process capability. (It is worth noting that Six Sigma does not refer to the process control limits that contain 99.73% of all process data.)

Evolution to Six Sigma

The evolution of Six Sigma has evolved from a number of preceding quality philosophies which include:

- Inspection
- Quality Control
- Quality Assurance
- Total Quality Control
- Total Quality Management
- Six Sigma

The precision with which the ancient pyramids of Egypt were built is an early demonstration of a grasp of the quality concept. Such precision was apparent in Babylon around 575 BC when there were strict controls for weights and measures.. Prior to the concept of interchangeable parts and Henry Ford's moving assembly line, much of manufacturing and assembly depended upon each part being made to fit. Interchangeable parts and standardisation changed the way in which products were made. The importance of quality was now clear, although the consequences of poor quality were less clear.

The quality *modus operandi* at the time of Henry Ford was **Inspection**. If a part was out of specification, it was rejected. Inspection of completed products is referred to 'sort-and-salvage'.

Inspection evolved naturally to **Quality Control**. A feedback loop was introduced so the production department were informed of the end product quality and given the opportunity to take corrective action.

Quality Control gave way to **Quality Assurance** (QA). With QA, Quality was built into the process. The emphasis was on prevention rather than inspection. Inspection activity was now directed towards process inputs such and manpower and methods. Assurance involved auditing the process inputs. There was a trend towards process documentation and third party audits.

Total Quality Control (TQC) followed. Quality was now seen as being integrated into the processes of design and manufacture. TQC was an expansion of QA, taking it into all departments and becoming embedded in all company activities.

In the 1980s **Total Quality Management** (TQM) emerged. TQM built on the earlier contributions but involved a more forward thinking, proactive slant. The concept of understanding internal customers as well as external customers was a basic concern. Leadership and eliminating inter-departmental barriers were pillars of this approach, as was the introduction of TQM facilitators who would observe and coach employees.

The difference between the TQC and TQM approach has been likened to steering a boat. One can observe the wake behind the boat and make corresponding adjustments to the rudder or one can look forward and position the rudder accordingly.

The Quality gurus of the 20th century offer Quality Improvement principles that, if blended and quantified, provide a programme that contains all of the Six Sigma constituent parts. An overview of their contributions follows:

Deming   Focus on variation (special and common causes), Plan Do, Check, Act.

Juran   Quality Planning, Quality Control and Quality Action. Project by Project, improvement. Cost Of Poor Quality (COPQ), prioritisation using Pareto charts.

Ishikawa   Good data collection and use of 7 Quality Tools. In particular the use of the Cause & Effect diagram in Quality Circles to sort sources of variation.

Taguchi   Taguchi Loss Function and cost relationship with degree of inaccuracy, Robust system design, and screening design experiments.

The philosophies and tools of these four Quality Gurus cover much of the Six Sigma approach. We may reasonably pose the question,

"Is Six Sigma new, or just a repackaging of old concepts?"

Six Sigma - The Approach

The scope of Six Sigma is very much in-line with the work of the quality gurus. If other contributions are added such as Dorian Shainin's approach to root cause (involving component search, paired comparisons and designed experiments), and Shigeo Shingo's Poka Yoke approach to the elimination of mistakes, then one could argue that there is little new in Six Sigma. However, the power of the approach comes from taking the best quality contributions from the past and packaging them into a roadmap for process excellence.

It is typical for Six Sigma courses to begin with a list of Six Sigma classifications for example:

Philosophy
Metric
Goal
Benchmark
Methodology
Set of tools & techniques
Culture
Statistical Concept

Those that are fortunate to complete Six Sigma training will concur that the reason Six Sigma succeeds is that it provides a thorough roadmap to translate business intentions (objectives) into actions. Far too often the approach is summarised as a set of tools, or as a measurement of 3.4 defects per million. As Six Sigma has postdated the TQM initiative, it has been said that Six Sigma is a philosophy with the addition of statistics. Six Sigma provides a detailed roadmap for attaining improvement. Six Sigma also provides an approach that is able to attribute effects to causes. Note the use of the plural. It is common for complex problems to be solved when a number of input variables are examined simultaneously for their effect on the output. If this was not the

The Scope of Six Sigma

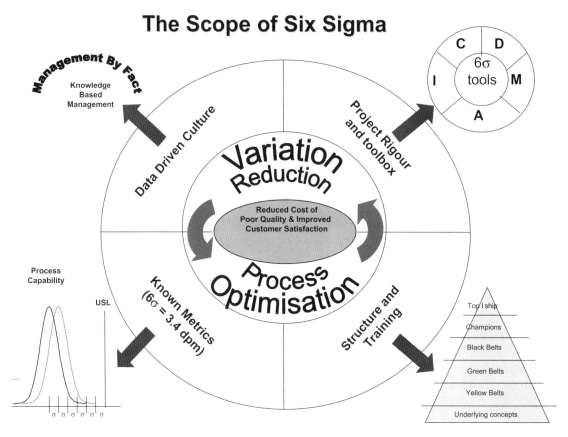

case, then complex problem solving would not be necessary and traditional approaches such as changing one-factor-at-a-time (OFAT) would rule the day.

This ability to solve complex, chronic problems that may have existed for weeks, months, or years, sets it apart from other approaches. Whilst not wishing to decry alternative initiatives, sometimes other approaches merely offer a structure or step-by-step approach. This is a reasonable way forward as long as there is substance behind the steps. There must be content that offers a new way of working. Whilst Deming offered much to the Quality movement, it has been argued that a project step-by-step approach such as Plan Do Check Act is a logical sequence but unlikely by itself to solve chronic quality problems. Six Sigma has the tool kit to gain process knowledge and thus make the breakthrough. The benefit of making breakthrough quality improvements is

wide reaching, reducing internal costs, improving market quality, improving customer satisfaction and increasing profit.

DPMO   Defects Per Million Opportunity
COPQ   Cost Of Poor Quality

Philosophy

One of the key concepts of Six Sigma is 'remove the variation, hit the target'. This echoes Taguchi's approach and his Loss Function proposition. This brings into focus two important, but totally opposed approaches to Quality. On one hand, there is an approach (sometimes referred to as the Old Philosophy of Quality) which states that as long as the process is operating within-specification, there is no loss. The approach goes further at times and suggests that the aim is for the process to be as variable as allowable (within the specifications). This concept proposes that there is a cost associated with hitting the target and that it will cost less to just perform within specification.

Old Philosophy Of Quality

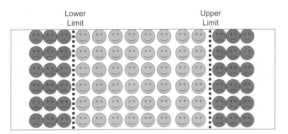

In complete contrast, Taguchi offers the view that it is only when the process is centered on its target value that there is no loss and so no cost of poor quality.

Taguchi's Quality Philosophy

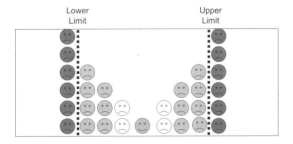

Taguchi gives an equation that suggests that the loss of quality has a relationship with the squared distance from the target value (Taguchi Loss Function),

$$L = k(y-T)^2$$

where L is the financial loss, y is the response value, T is the target value and k is a monetary constant.

This contrast will typically lead to a focus on the position of the specification limits and whether they are really customer specification limits or perceived limits as calculated by the designer to ensure 'conformance to requirements'.

There is a well-publicised example which involved the manufacture of automotive transmissions. A major American automotive company formed a partnership with a Japanese automotive company to make transmissions. Both organisations made the same product to the same specifications. However, the transmissions from the Japanese company had lower warranty costs, ran more quietly and shifted more smoothly than those made by the American company. A detailed investigation was carried out and found that both manufacturers were meeting the design specifications. The key difference was the Japanese transmissions had much less variation. The Japanese were not content to stop improvement when they were 'just-inside' the specification limits.

The Reality

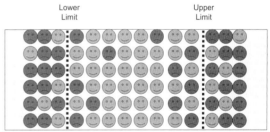

It is common for manufacturers to set specifications where the customer has a 'the more the better' attitude towards value. Consider the number of sweets in a bag or the size of the steak in a restaurant. Exceeding the upper specification is likely to result in greater customer satisfaction but at a greater cost. At the lower specification, there are examples such as excess product packaging that cause customer dissatisfaction. There are some products that are inside the specification limits but, perhaps due to a marketing campaign, raise the expectations of the product e.g. 'the perfect television picture', and as a result are considered unsatisfactory.

Hit the target, remove the variation.
The variation can come from various sources, and the understanding of these sources is vital if Six Sigma is to be implemented successfully.

the people chosen for the training are not always the business 'movers and shakers'. Six Sigma project managers must therefore act as facilitators ensuring a match between problem solving skills and organisational structures and systems. The Six Sigma hierarchy is applied in different ways across businesses but it often takes the following form:

Primary Sources of Variation

Six Sigma Hierarchy

Roles and Responsibilities
One of the potential failures of Six Sigma is that, due to the statistical nature of the problem solving,

The Sigma Black Belt is a pivotal position. To qualify as a Black Belt requires 4 weeks of training, spread over 13 weeks.

Classical Six Sigma Black Belt Training Cycle

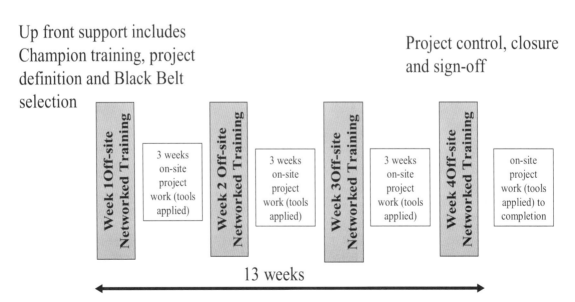

The 13 week cycle typically consists of 1 week off-site training in a classroom environment with other Black Belts, followed by 3 weeks deploying the training on significant business projects. The project is seldom finished within the 13 weeks as the Black Belt candidate must still complete the project. This must be done to the satisfaction of the Champion or the relevant departmental Manager (if different from the Champion) and the Finance Manager. To become a certified Six Sigma Black Belt, it is a typical requirement to complete 2 projects. These projects are presented for scrutiny; (a) verification that the claimed results have indeed been achieved and (b) that a high proportion of the Six Sigma tools have been utilised at the appropriate project stage. It is common that any particular project may not have a requirement for an important tool or set of tools, e.g. Design of Experiments, but two completed projects allow the Black Belt candidate to demonstrate his or her ability over a wider area.

The Six Sigma Champion's role is crucial. Whereas a Black Belt has to undergo a large amount of training, the Champion has to ensure that the wider picture is maintained and that progress and eventual success are achieved. The Champion has a responsibility for Black Belt candidate selection, project selection and supporting the Black Belt in the first stage of the Six Sigma methodology where the detailed problem statements are written and the voice of the customer is understood. The progress of the Black Belt project will often need the input of the Champion to provide adequate resources and to raise the profile. The methodology is delivered through distinct project phases, although reiteration through these phases may be necessary when process knowledge is obtained. It is good practice that these project phases are treated as doors or gates, and that Champion agreement (sign-off) is required before the project may progress to the next phase.

Like the success of any initiative, the importance with which it is treated by senior management is vital for sustainability and success. As people behave in line with the way in which they are measured, it is important that the Champion has

responsibility in the business plan to achieve certain Six Sigma milestones. These responsibilities are recognised in the annual objectives and are likely to be part of a business appraisal system. The objectives may then be broken down into achievable projects for Black Belts, and hence the approach is deployed through to implementation. This approach will depend on the Champion and Black Belt working for each other's success. This dependence is vital. If the Process Manager is different from the Champion, then he or she too will have objectives which should be aligned to the success of the Six Sigma project.

The Green Belt is the next level down from the Black Belt in terms of required training. This may vary from business to business but typically ranges from between 9 days and 15 days. The role of the Green belt is similar in some ways to that of the Black Belt (to manage projects using the Six Sigma methodology) but the role is not seen as full time, and Green Belt projects may form part of a Black Belt project. The Green Belt rarely supports projects outside his or her normal area of responsibility. The accreditation for Green Belt status may be either 1 or 2 successfully completed projects, depending on the tool set utilised and the accreditation process being followed.

It is becoming common practice for organisations to train Project Managers in the Black Belt curriculum but for them to subsequently operate within a Green Belt role.

Below Green Belts in the hierarchy of Six Sigma is the Yellow Belt. This position is often a team member within a project led by a Black or Green Belt. It is common for the training of a Yellow Belt to be 2 days. The training is very much biased towards the practical use of tools. Ishikawa's seven tools of quality (Pareto, Flowchart, Cause and Effect Diagram, Run Chart, Histogram, Check Sheet and Scatter Diagrams) make up a large part of this training. It is proposed by some that this training should be expanded to cover project management and to set targets for Yellow Belts to complete their own projects.

An accreditation process has been introduced for Black and Green Belts. There is a role for a resource to be able to deliver training to all levels of the Six Sigma hierarchy, to provide on-site project support and to determine whether the project manager has demonstrated sufficient application of the methodology and tool set to be accredited as either a Black or Green Belt. This position is commonly referred to as a Master Black Belt. The curriculum for becoming a Master Black Belt is particularly variable, but a full time practising Black Belt is likely to deliver training to colleagues at some stage. Many will agree that if we want to understand a subject, try teaching it.

The most senior level of the organisation is required to give direction to Six Sigma. They need to understand the goals, the route and the implications if Six Sigma is to be taken seriously. In its best case, the lead taken by Jack Welch, former CEO of General Electric was such that Six Sigma now enjoys a higher profile at GE than at Motorola. If Six Sigma is chosen as the appropriate methodology to transform the business, then it is important that the whole organisation is aware of this. This is particularly important with Six Sigma as, to many, its name does not give a lot away, unlike a Cost Down or Winning Business programme. One way to inform the organisation is to hold several presentations and demonstrate the main premise of the approach, namely the removal of variation.

Project Rigour and Methodology

The methodology for managing a Six Sigma project is a 5 phase approach:

Six Sigma Methodology

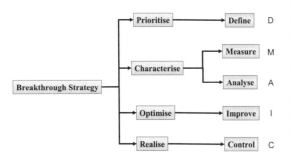

This is known as the DMAIC methodology.

There are some variations on this theme. Some of these variations include the elimination of the Define (with the implication that it is inherent within the Measure phase), the addition of 'Innovate' within the Improve phase, making a $DMAI^2C$ methodology, and the additional 'Transfer' or 'Replicate' phase to the end, to ensure that opportunities to maximise the gain from the improvement project are not missed (DMAICT).

Within each of the phases, there are a number of standard tools. These tools will not always be appropriate for each project, but there is an expectation that a high proportion of tools from the Define and Measure phase will always be employed.

The tools for Six Sigma Project Management are contained within the Project Charter and Tracker.

The importance of a document such as a Project Charter should not be underestimated. The need to be specific in terms of producing a detailed problem statement and having agreement with the Champion and Departmental Manager is vital. The cost-benefit is also calculated (based on assumptions at the initial stage) and this focus should keep the project on track. The tools within each of the 5 phases are listed in the Tracker and are required to be ticked off as they are used. This provides clarity to the Black Belt or Green Belt should they fall behind during the training.

One of the success criteria for any training is the ability to apply the lessons as soon as is practically possible. This is a strength of Six Sigma as all Black Belt and Green Belt training is geared towards the delivery of a successful project which is worked on throughout the duration of the training cycle.

Should the Black Belt not have the opportunity to work on the project during the intervals between the networked training weeks, then this will be apparent as the deliverables on the Project Tracker will be incomplete. This situation is covered in the section 'Six Sigma Caveat'.

Six Sigma - Project Charter & Tracker

Project Name		Project Owner		Champion
Project Code	Start Date	Department		Manager
Estimated Savings (Annualized)	Date Completed	Estimated Improvements (Annualized)		
Project Description				

Checkboxes:
- ☐ Master Blackbelt
- ☐ Blackbelt
- ☐ Greenbelt
- ☐ Yellowbelt

DEFINE

Date Started:
Date Completed:

Tools Utilized
- ☐ Project Charter
- ☐ SIPOC
- ☐ VOC Plan
- ☐ Kano (VOC)
- ☐ CTQ(VOC)
- ☐ Pareto
- ☐ Project Gantt chart

Deliverables
- ☐ Project plan (time & resource)
- ☐ Project Charter
- ☐ Detailed Problem Statement
- ☐ COPQ (involve finance)
- ☐ dpu, dpmo, s-level, yield
- ☐ Process Performance Scorecard (appropriate metrics)
- ☐ Project Team
- ☐ Goals

MEASURE

Date Started:
Date Completed:

Tools Utilized
- ☐ Process Map
- ☐ Cause & Effect with CNX/SOPs
- ☐ Partitined variables
- ☐ Prioritisation matrix
- ☐ FMEA
- ☐ Pareto of Defects
- ☐ Measure/Track Y's: Run Charts
- ☑ Frequency plots of Y s and X s
- ☐ Gauge R & R (MSA)
- ☐ Data Collection Plan
- ☐ Check sheet
- ☐ Process Capability

Deliverables
- ☐ Process Map
- ☐ Performance Measures (Y s)
- ☐ Customer Specs on Y s
- ☐ Sources of Variation (X s)
- ☐ PF/CE/CNX/SOP
- ☐ MSA (%GR&R and P/Tol)
- ☐ Cpk, Cp, Ppk, Pp
- ☐ Revisit Improvement Target
- ☐ Goals

ANALYZE

Date Started:
Date Completed:

Tools Utilized
- ☐ Scatter & Correlation
- ☐ Confidence Intervals
- ☐ Sample Size Determination
- ☐ Hypothesis Tests-t test, F test
- ☐ R.of T for shifts in avg, std dev
- ☐ ANOVA & Multi vari
- ☐ Control Charts (set I.D. Variable)
- ☐ Stratification (box/dot/Pareto)
- ☐ Pareto Analysis
- ☐ Regression Analysis
- ☐ Screening DOEs
- ☐ Process Capability

Deliverables
- ☐ Identify/Quantify KPIVs that: affect average of KPOVs affect s of KPOVs
- ☐ Cpk, Cp, Ppk, Pp
- ☐ Process Performance Scorecard (compare to Measure results)
- ☐ Revisit Improvement Target
- ☐ Goals

IMPROVE

Date Started:
Date Completed:

Tools Utilized
- ☐ FMEA
- ☐ Error Proofing
- ☐ New Standards
- ☐ Screening DOE
- ☐ Modelling DOE
- ☐ Taguchi Designs
- ☐ Robust Design
- ☐ Multiple Response Surfaces
- ☐ Tolerancing
- ☐ Process Capability

Deliverables
- ☐ DoE report to include: models relating Y s to X s optimal settings for X s variability in Y s at optimal
- ☐ Cpk, Cp, Ppk, Pp
- ☐ Process Performance Scorecard (compare to Analyze results)
- ☐ Solution Geneation
- ☐ verification & new Process Map
- ☐ Goals

CONTROL

Date Started:
Date Completed:

Tools Utilized
- ☐ Control Plan
- ☐ Control Chart
- ☐ Visual Management
- ☐ FMEA Revisited
- ☐ Reliability
- ☐ Total Productive Maintenance
- ☐ Spec Setting Analysis on X s
- ☐ Standardisation
- ☐ Error proofing in Supply Chain
- ☐ Error Proofing in Design

Deliverables
- ☐ Control Plan (inc. training)
- ☐ Cost Savings/Avoidance
- ☐ Evidence of finance dept.
- ☐ Process Documentation
- ☐ New process Capability
- ☐ Project Handover
- ☐ Process Performance Scorecard
- ☐ Opportunities to translate improvements to other areas
- ☐ Goals

Six Sigma as a Goal and a Metric

Six Sigma is a statistical capability metric which may not sound thrilling to non-statisticians, but the idea of a metric is very powerful. We know from sport that both practice and keeping score are important. Six Sigma performance is quoted as 3.4 defects per million opportunity (dpmo). The table below shows how dpmo changes with the different Sigma capability indices.

Six Sigma as a metric

σ Process Capability	Defects per million opportunities
2	308,537
3	66,807
4	6,210
5	233
6	3.4

A complication is that processes drift over a period of time and that short-term variation provides a different capability to long term variation. Consider a rugby example. The goal kicker will strive to kick the ball mid way between the posts. One might argue that unlike Taguchi's Loss Function, there is no cost associated with variation away from the mid point as the effect of the output is constant whilst the kicks are inside the posts (3 points for a penalty – England rarely have a conversion). However, in a game where a goal kicker may take as many as 10 kicks on goal, a 100% success rate does not mean that the performance is infallible. If the position of the kicks between the posts was fitted into a distribution and an expected success rate was calculated, there may well be a number of failures. The point is that the observed defect rate is not the same as the expected failure rate. If the process mean was to shift, then a higher number of failures would result. In rugby, the distribution of kicks may not be perfectly centred, perhaps because of wind.

In such a case, it can pay to be more consistent. If there is a process change in one of the conditions, (say wind) the process is sufficiently robust to deal with that change. Also, there is a possibility of changing customer specifications. In the rugby analogy, it may be that the kick is taken from an off-centre position offering a reduced spread for a successful kick. In business, there may be market pressures which reduce the specification limits. In such cases, the processes with the higher capabilities will stand the better chance of exploiting the changes.

Note the diagrams indicate a process mean shift by 1.5 sigma to account for changing process conditions. Why 1.5 sigma shift? Simply because this figure was quoted by Motorola. The relationship between sigma capability and defects per million opportunity has taken this shift into account. The reader needs to be aware that every process will shift by different amounts at different times.

6σ process (centred) = 0.002 dpm

6σ process after a 1.5σ shift = 3.4 ppm

Why Six Sigma?

Every process aims to achieve high consistency. However, variations within the process and by the input variables may be extremely difficult to control. The process variation is measured in standard deviations (sigma) from the mean. 99.73% of the values lie between +3 and –3 sigma

3σ process (centred) = 2,700 dpm

3σ process after a 1.5σ shift = 66,807dpm

about the mean when the distribution of the results is in the form of a normal distribution. If the specification limits are placed on the +3 and –3 sigma points, then approximately 2,700 parts per million (ppm) will fall outside the specification limits. Is this level of ppm acceptable? It is certainly not defect free, although traditionally, many might think that 99.73% quality is very good. If the process in question is likely to have a severe consequence when a defect occurs, then this level of defects is not acceptable. Common quoted examples of processes which require much higher quality levels are airport runway landings, the accuracy of surgical operations and carrying new born babies. (Defects are not always as obvious as driving too fast when passing a speed camera. But consider how many opportunities there are to exceed the limit. With the addition of more speed cameras, it will not be long before all drivers will have to drive at process levels far in excess of 6σ if they are to avoid penalties.) As Six Sigma becomes more popular in the service sector, there will be more discussion on what constitutes a defect and what constitutes an opportunity e.g. hotel customer service. The ability to think in Six Sigma terms will enable the service sector to apply metrics appropriate for their business and subsequently benchmark their performance against the best in class.

The Cost Of Poor Quality (COPQ)

We have already mentioned the importance of cost and not getting things right first time. The cost benefit of Six Sigma will more often than not be the driving metric within the Six Sigma approach. (This is, however, not always the case

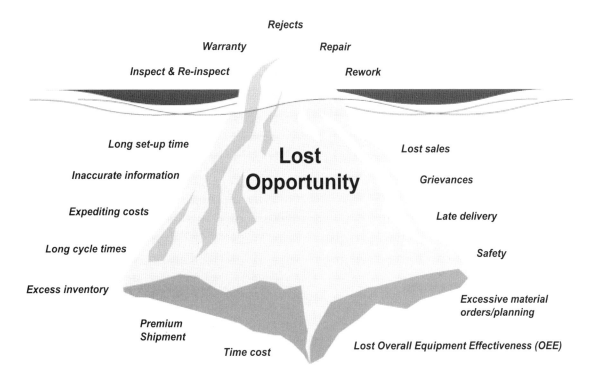

Traditional Cost of Poor Quality (COPQ) – easy to see

Rejects

Warranty   Repair

Inspect & Re-inspect   Rework

Long set-up time   Lost sales

Inaccurate information   Grievances

Lost Opportunity

Expediting costs   Late delivery

Long cycle times   Safety

Excess inventory

Excessive material orders/planning

Premium Shipment

Time cost   Lost Overall Equipment Effectiveness (OEE)

Less Obvious Cost of Poor Quality (COPQ) - hidden

as found in health projects where patient recovery may be more important). The Motorola quoted metrics of 3.4 dpmo and 6σ are a means to achieving more profit. Businesses are generally only interested in business programmes if they are going to have a positive impact on the bottom line. So how much are businesses wasting on COPQ? Some figures estimate that as much as 40% of business turnover is wasted. Figures such as 20% are common. A business around the six sigma level will be wasting fewer than 5% of its sales revenue on COPQ. If your competition are not doing this, then it is clearly a competitive advantage to be spending less on poor quality.

Where do these costs manifest themselves? The obvious costs are those that are easy to see and easy to measure. The cost of the 4 Rees:– Reject, Rework, Repair and Re-inspect, and 'warrantee' claims fall into this category. Unfortunately, there are often larger costs which are not as prominent. Late delivery and lost production can lead to lost sales both in the short and long term. A lost sale is an opportunity for a competitor to become a lifelong preferred supplier. The warranty claims from poor market quality can lead to grievances and the knock on effect of a dissatisfied customer sharing the experience with others may do widespread harm. Lost production can arise through many wastes such as process breakdowns, changeovers, idling stoppages, reduced speed of operations and yield losses (measures of Overall Equipment Effectiveness). How often are these losses converted into COPQ?

There are many other costs of poor quality, some of which are shown on the previous illustration.

Misplaced or incorrect paperwork deserves a special mention for its ability to bring a process to a standstill and absorb an incredible about of human resource in expediting and reconciliation. Consider the time it takes from an order being received to payment being made. How much of that time is spent producing the product, and how much time is spent processing the order?

A typical categorisation of COPQ include costs associated with:

- Internal Failure Costs – (the "hidden factory", scrap, rework)
- External Failure Costs - warranty/returns/ goodwill/legal/field repairs
- Prevention and Appraisal Costs – QA Process validation, Tests, Calibration, Evaluation, SPC
- Lost Opportunity Costs - lost customers

As a closing note on COPQ, consider how much it costs automotive companies to recall models from the marketplace when a safety threatening fault is found.

Profound Knowledge

What is fundamentally different about the Six Sigma approach?

The Six Sigma approach has a very high degree of project rigour, with its DMAIC structure and its coloured belts hierarchy. But that could be aligned to any approach with little difficulty. What separates Six Sigma from many others is that it provides process knowledge that would be extremely unlikely to be obtained through common sense approaches.

There is a limit to the improvement that can be made by applying logic and intuition. There is a limit to how much improvement you can squeeze out of your supply chain before the supply will deteriorate. There is only so much improvement that will result from the application of basic quality tools which often only serve as a way of sequencing and partitioning our subjective observations.

The power of Six Sigma is that it contains and assembles the tools that are the key to step improvements. What Six Sigma delivers is an understanding of how process inputs affect the process output. Some inputs may not have any effect on the output and so require no effort to control. Other process inputs are very sensitive, called key process input variables (KPIV), where the smallest variation may cause a significant change in the output. There may also be process settings that will make the process output insensitive to changes in the input variables, again eliminating the need for tight control of some inputs. The results from such knowledge may be to maximise an output parameter, minimise a defect level, or to hit a particular target, whilst finding a combination of settings that will minimise process variation. It is this knowledge that can deliver against stretch goals, typically achieving greater than single digit percentage improvements.

Without such knowledge, performance improvements may rely on working harder and not smarter.

Better Business
Once the process is understood and the distribution of the output can be controlled, both in terms of hitting the target and eliminating variation, we are less susceptible to the probability that our key output variables will deteriorate at the most unfortunate time. When a process such as a production line is operating with a high level of variation, then the distribution of the output, whether it be quantity or quality, will be wide. This equates to some good performances and some bad performances. So when the manager reports a good week at the management meeting, in all likelihood this will be followed by a not so good week. Unfortunately, Murphy's Law suggests that the good and bad weeks will not be random as the bad weeks will coincide with the visit of the vice president or the key account customer. The coach of the Boston Red Sox Baseball Team once said that there is no such thing as a one game winning streak. You can hit the target once by chance, but to hit it repeatedly requires the removal of variation and an understanding of the process inputs and their effect on the outputs.

Further Reading:
Pete.Pande and Larry Holpp, *What is Six Sigma?*, McGraw-Hill, New York, 2002.
Peter S. Pande, Robert P. Neuman, Roland R.Cavanagh, *The Six Sigma Way*, McGraw? Hill, New York, 2000.
Mikel J. Harry, *The Vision Of Six Sigma*, Sigma Publishing Company, Fourth Edition, Arizona, 1994.
Brian L. Joiner, *Fourth Generation Management,* McGraw-Hill, 1994.

Six Sigma y = f(x) Statistical Concept

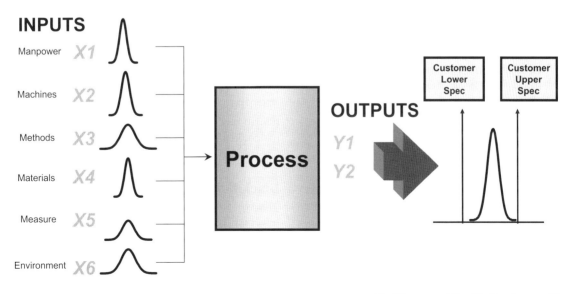

Six Sigma Caveat

There are several success stories of how companies have transformed their business performance through implementing Six Sigma. Examples are Motorola, GE and Allied Signal / Honeywell.

However, there are numerous examples where the business performance has been below inital expectations.

Why do results fall short of expectation?

There are numerous reasons for this, and typically the answer is likely to be due to a combination of the following factors.

The Role of the Champion

A key reason for achieving below expectation results may lie with the role of the Six Sigma Champion. There are examples of deployment when the Champion believes that by training a Six Sigma Black Belt, the result will be similar to taking a magic pill. Unfortunately, Six Sigma, like any other initiative, requires senior management commitment and involvement.

The role of the Six Sigma Champion includes:

- Development of Implementation Strategy
- Accountable for success, not cheerleading
- Obtain & allocate resource
- Selection of projects
- Selection of BBs and GBs
- Develop training plan
- Project review gates and progress tracking
- Basic understanding of all tools
- Lead change
- Political survival skills
- 80% leadership, 20% specialist

A critical point is that the Champion takes responsibility for the success of the Six Sigma activity. The action of agreeing to send a manager on 4 weeks of training over 3 or 4 months and signing off the purchase requisition will not guarantee success.

At the start of the process, organisations should be clear on what their expectations are, and how such an initiative will fit within their current structure and strategy. The GE success is not based on isolated, opportunist successful projects. All managers are expected to be trained to a minimum of Green Belt. The Black Belt, two year full time role is seen as a reward for high performance and is seen to be a route for fast tracking managers to senior positions.

Contrast this with young, immature Six Sigma companies who may wish to 'test the water' and send one manager on a Six Sigma programme. This person may have no colleagues to share experiences with and no or little support from the Champion. The Champion and Black Belt (and Process owner, if different) must work for each others' success. Project success must not be seen solely as the Black belt success but as the team's success.

The Champion should hold regular review meetings with the Black Belt and Project team. The DMAIC methodology provides a framework which encourages this approach. Each phase should not take more than one month, so a monthly review is good practice. If there are problems with the availability of resources to achieve progress, the Champion must be responsible for such matters.

Project Selection

The selection of the projects to be addressed is vital and needs to be aligned to business needs. It is becoming more common for the Champion to have a major input in the Define stage and producing the initial Project Charter. The business will not be transformed by Six Sigma if the selected projects are undertaken in the business 'back water'. See Project Charter section.

Black Belt Selection

This is of similarly high importance to that of project selection. The GE model of selecting high performing managers is considered best practice where the size of the organisation allows the practice. If Black Belts are chosen because they are expendable from the main stream activities, then they may not have sufficient power or respect to drive major projects. If, on the other hand, the Black Belts are the current business 'movers and shakers' (senior managers), there is a high possibility that the organisation will drag them back into their day management role, particularly if additional resource has not been made available and authority delegated. A typical scenario is that one project is completed and the senior manager then returns to his / her old daily routine.

Another failure mode is when the Black Belt candidates are taken from more of a craft role (below graduate or equivalent). This has been seen to fail to meet expectation when the Black Belt struggles with the nature of the statistical tools and their application. The new role has to be carefully monitored by the Champion to ensure the Black Belt understands how he / she is to spend their time.

There is not one model which is guaranteed to deliver success when selecting Black Belts, but the over riding message is that there must be a high level of Champion involvement. The Project Charter has been designed to support the project review process. The way an organisation judges the importance of a management initiative will be influenced by the calibre of people who are assigned to the initiative. The models of Black Belt selection outlined above can be simplified in to the following matrix:

Leadership Competence & Organisational Power

	LOW	HIGH
LOW	HIGH RISK CANDIDATE	ISSUES TO ADDRESS — Grasping statistical concepts and software
HIGH	ISSUES TO ADDRESS — Sponsor support, team authority, local Mgt Buy-in	IDEAL

(vertical axis: Technical / Analytical Competence)

If the Black Belt candidate does not possess both power and analytical competence then at least one of these attributes will be necessary for business success.

Is Six Sigma full time or part time?

There is a general understanding that Black Belt roles are full time and Green Belt roles are part time. The reality of Six Sigma implementation currently in the UK suggests that there are many companies who enable Black Belt training but do not allow the manages to delegate their current roles. This leads to Six Sigma projects becoming a bolt-on activity and is the first casualty when there is a peak in work load.

This can be particularly obstructive if the Black Belt is going through the 4 weeks training programme. The statistical tools can be very powerful but, if unfamiliar to the trainee, the need to use the tools soon after the training block is crucial. If this is not the case, the project enters a state of catch-back and the trainees find themselves learning a new set of tools whilst still not having used the training from the previous training block. This is a strong symptom of poor application. In this environment, the Black Belts present activities to their peers which do not contain the underlying methodology or appropriate application (i.e. opportunist and not thorough). This often results in the application of the 7 basic tools (the level of Yellow Belt training). When one considers that classical Black Belt training consists of 20 days training over a period of 3 to 4 months, then there are few development opportunities one receives in a career which offer such potential for personal and organisational advancement. Not to maximise the opportunity and give the Six Sigma training and application the focus it deserves is a missed opportunity indeed. So, 'Carpe Diem' (Seize the Day).

Choice of Tools

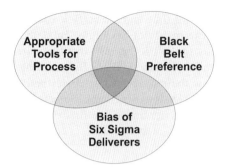

Not only is the choice of tools influenced by the personal preference of the Six Sigma Black Belt, but also by the bias of the delivery from the trainers, whether this is through external consultants or internal Black Belts / Master Black Belts. The style and content of the delivery can vary from what appears to be a statistics course to a repackaged delivery of quality tools (with a Six Sigma stamp included as an afterthought).

It would be interesting to conduct a Measurement Systems Analysis on gauging how different Black Belts, with their own preferences and with the bias of different training providers, approach the same project. It is ironic that the Six Sigma approach spends much of its time eliminating variation but there exists considerable variation in the training programmes themselves.

There are other factors which will influence the choice of tools even when there is a standard for Black Belt candidate level, quality of training and curriculum:

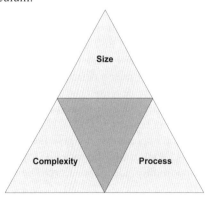

The organisations that have large resources and that can train large numbers of Black Belts and Green Belts, such as Motorola and GE, will continue to dedicate a focus on this activity. Can small and medium sized enterprises afford to copy the same model and is it appropriate? Should the training curriculum be standard when different functions (design, production, sales, finance, logistics) make use of different tools, as do complex processes from basic ones. A problem is that unless the Black Belt is aware of all the tools, how is he/she to know which is appropriate? Against this is the Pareto principle may show 20% of the tools are delivering 80% of the benefits and so why have such an expensive, resource intensive approach when a significant amount is redundant?

Sustainability

Even when Black Belts deliver successful projects which are in line, or exceed the organisations (and customers) expectations, there remains a challenge for the now fully trained Black Belt to continue to deliver projects. The sustainability of the approach must involve the Champion once again. The business goals, the departmental goals and the personal objective plans must be reflected if it is to be sustainable. There is also a need for the Black Belts to meet with peers and to have refresher activities, whether internal or external to the organisation. Six Sigma networks which facilitate refresher training, additional training in appropriate tools, sharing presentations of successfully completed projects, and a demonstration from senior management that the approach is still an important engine of business transformation are likely to improve the sustainability of the approach.

The New Six Sigma

A Customer-Focused Six Sigma Forum held in London in February 2004 highlighted a number of recurring themes, and it was evident that Six Sigma leaders Motorola and GE have both had to modify their Six Sigma programmes to realise their expectations. This does not necessarily point to past mistakes; more that the approach adopted initially is not appropriate for the current and future business conditions.

The most popular recurring theme of the Forum was Six Sigma Alignment to business objectives. The Balanced Scorecard tool appears to be enjoying a resurgence in ensuring that the performance of the Six Sigma activity is delivering against the targets established for the Balanced Scorecard.

This approach is emphasised by Motorola, and their 4-phase approach:

• Align
• Mobilise
• Accelerate
• Govern

The Align phase is absolutely vital for Six Sigma to deliver a business transformation, and not just provide a number of cost-benefiting projects.

The Align phase is backed up with Mobilise (putting the appropriate resources in place), Accelerate (a 60 day target for a degree of visible improvement is suggested as necessary to maintain team enthusiasm and motivation) and Govern (a top-down rigour to see that it happens).

It is interesting that Motorola are re-energising the Six Sigma approach which will be 20 years old in 2006. The fact that they see the need to continuously improve and follow Shewhart's Plan-Do-Check-Act shows that they recognise that to stand still is to go backwards and what works today may not be appropriate for tomorrow.

Finally, of course, Six Sigma is not "the only answer". Even Motorola has experienced several "ups and downs" in company performance since introducing Six Sigma. So, variation applies at the corporate level also!

Further Reading
Peter S. Pande, Robert P. Neuman, Roland R. Cavanagh, *The Six Sigma Way*, McGraw Hill, New York, 2000.
Matt Barney and Tom McCarty (Motorola University), *The New Six Sigma*, Prentice Hall PTR, New Jersey, 2003.

Philip Catherwood, *What's Different About Six Sigma*, IEE Manufacturing Engineer, pp186-189, August 2002.
Roger W. Hoerl, *Six Sigma Black Belts: What Do They Need To Know?*, American Society for Quality - Journal of Quality Technology, Vol 33, No.4, October 2001.
Jiju Antony, Fragkiskos Foutris, Ricardo Banulas and Andrew Thomas, *Using Six Sigma*, IEE Manufacturing Engineer, pp10-12, March 2004.

For an excellent critique of what has gone wrong with Six Sigma, and the future of the methodology see:
Keki Bhote, *The Ultimate Six Sigma*, AmaCom, 2002.
See also the Motorola website.

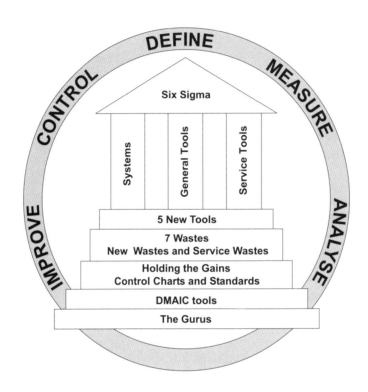

The Gurus

Deming
Juran
Crosby
Feigenbaum
Ishikawa

Shingo
Taguchi
Kano
Grönroos
Shainin and Bhote

Garvin

The Gurus

The field of Quality Management has been strongly influenced by a number of "Gurus". Any choice of which Gurus to include would certainly include the first four given below, but beyond that opinions differ. In any case, it would be a mistake to concentrate solely on the views of one Guru. All have useful things to say. The reader has to distil out those views that are most appropriate to his or her organization.

Deming

Dr. W. Edwards Deming (1900-1993) is probably the most revered figure in quality management. In the 1950s, Deming taught quality to the Japanese by insisting that top management attend his courses. They did, and prospered. Originally Deming taught statistical process control (SPC) to the Japanese and has always maintained that management must have an appreciation of statistical variation. Today Deming is mainly associated with quality management theories, particularly his "14 point" plan, the "Deming Cycle" and his "deadly diseases".

In his *System of Profound Knowledge* Deming has four interrelating theories: The *Theory of Systems* recognises that everything is interconnected. A holistic approach is necessary. The *Theory of Variation* recognises that variation is endemic. Management's failure to account for variation in managing everything was one of Deming's great criticisms. The *Theory of Knowledge* studies the way in which we experiment and learn. *The Theory of Psychology* is considered by Deming to be fundamental to understanding people and teams. What is amazing is that these four are amongst the most fashionable ideas in management today - 40 years plus after Deming - but are still usually treated in isolation.

Appreciation of statistical variation begins with the concept that very little in life is absolutely consistent, and that chance will account for a certain amount of "natural variation". So, for example, a salesman cannot sell exactly the same amount every month. He would have good and bad months, and the differences between good and bad are mainly explained by chance rather than by variations in the salesman's skills. Therefore merely to reward him for the good months, and to penalize for the bad could be de-motivating and poor management. On the other hand truly superior performance can produce sales which are significantly and consistently better. Here, special reward would be justified as would penalties in the case of consistently poor performance.

To illustrate the point, Deming used to do a famous experiment - the "red bead game". Five players are picked from the audience. Each is given a paddle with slots into which coloured beads fit. The players are asked to dip the paddles into a bowel containing a mix of white and red beads. The object is to get as few red beads (representing defectives) as possible. Of course, it is nearly impossible to get zero red. But the numbers of red beads varies between the players. Deming commends the player with the smallest number of reds and admonishes the player with the most reds. This is typical management behaviour according to Deming. More rounds are played, sometimes resulting in one of the players getting "fired" and others where the raise awarded to the best players "goes to his head". The audience quickly grasps the futility of paying for performance when the process is not under the player's control. The messages are that management must understand variation, and that improving the process, not motivation, is critical for success.

Common causes are inherent in the process but special causes are not, and these special causes need to be identified. Poor sales is one example but the same would apply to many other areas of both human-based and machine-based performance. (For machines, this is the basis of SPC.) Moreover, true performance improvement is very seldom within the sole power of an operator or salesman or supervisor. For example, a machine has natural variation and may be producing a certain percentage of defects. The operator can do little about it. Without management action or support significant improvement can seldom be made. Deming's rule of thumb is that perhaps 85% of improvement requires management effort, while only 15% is actionable solely by front line employees. So, mere exhortations and incentives to produce better quality will have only limited results. "Be guided by theory" was a favourite saying.

Defining Quality

Deming said that quality can only be defined in terms of customer satisfaction. Thus there is no absolute measure - two customers may perceive a product or service quality differently. Hence it is management's task to translate the future needs of customers into quality products and services.

The 14 Points

It is sobering to realise that many ideas which are regarded as new and fashionable today were recommended by Deming over 30 years ago. These include continuous improvement (Kaizen) (see point 5 of the 14 points and the PDCA cycle), business process reengineering (see point 9), supplier partnership (point 4), self directed work teams (point 7), and Hoshin (point 1). Perhaps there are more ideas whose time is yet to come! Deming's 14 point plan is a complete philosophy of management, not just quality management. Books have been written on the subject. Here we attempt a brief summary.

1. There should be a consistent message about quality, throughout the organization. It should not vary by department, by pressure of work, by time of the month, or by customer. Usually a clear statement is required from management, with actions that demonstrate that it means what is says.

2. The new age of quality requires a commitment continuously to improve. The competition is doing this; so must you in order to survive. Customers have increasing expectations about quality.

3. Switch from defect detection to defect prevention. Rather inspect the process than the product. Work to understand and reduce the natural variation in processes. The less the variation, the better.

4. In dealing with suppliers, end the practice of awarding business on price. Move towards quality of product, reliability of delivery, and willingness to cooperate and improve. In other words build partnerships with suppliers. There should be advantages for both parties.

5. Constantly improve. Use the PDCA cycle. (See separate section). Improvement is not confined to products and their direct processes, but to all supporting services and activities also.

6. Train in a modern way. Let employees understand the concept of variation, basic SPC, improvement, and the total approach to quality. The idea is to make everyone responsible for their own quality.

7. Supervision must change from chasing to coaching and support.

8. "Drive out fear" of improvement. Management must create the environment which removes all possibility that improvement in quality will somehow penalize operators, through more work, loss of jobs, financial loss, or whatever.

9. Remove any organizational barrier that prevents quality improvement. This means improved visibility between sections and also easier communications. Aim to remove any barrier that prevents the requirements and reactions of the customer being moved rapidly and without distortion to the point where action can be taken.

10. Don't have slogans that mean nothing. Don't have unrealistic targets. Remember, management has most of the power to make real improvements.

11. Deming's eleventh point maintains that work standards and numerical quotas should be eliminated. This is controversial, unless interpreted with the understanding of natural variation. Natural variation says that no standard or quota can be exact and without variation. If the natural variation is understood, the quotas and standards that are beyond the control of employees should not be penalized (nor rewarded for undeserved performance.)

12. Remove barriers that prevent employees having pride in their work. These barriers may include unrealistic quotas and time pressure, short-term requirements for profit rather than quality, lack of investment in the right machines or tools, individual incentive schemes based on output rather than group based schemes based on quality and improvement, and lack of management support or consistency.

13. Train and educate. This follows from point 6 but emphasises that education must be widely based and continuing. Despite being point number 13, it is usually the starting point, after point 1.

14. Create an organizational structure that will support all the previous points. This is important because the 14 point plan is not a short term implementation, but rather a long term philosophy.

The Deming Cycle (or PDCA cycle)

The Deming Cycle is a powerful concept that has picked up several variations. This important topic is described in a separate section.

The "Deadly Diseases"

The seven "deadly diseases" of quality, as Deming terms them, amount to a severe criticism of Western management and organizational practices. The first five are closely related. They are worth pondering, and re-pondering:

1. "Lack of constancy of purpose" is a disease that appears in Deming's 14 point plan. It is a reminder about inconsistent policy on quality, particularly as the end-of-period rush begins! A twin point is,

2. "Emphasis on short term profits" is a reminder to take a more consistent view, without being influenced by the end-of-period financial performance. And this may be brought about by the next point.

3. Overemphasis on performance appraisal and merit rating, particularly when judged solely on financial performance. In an earlier section the issue of variation was discussed. If variation is not understood, appraisal can be literally destructive. He said that America had become great through teamwork, not competition. Deming was particularly worried by the emphasis on short term results rather than on coaching and helping staff to develop their potential. This is made worse by the next two diseases.

4. Too much staff mobility, where managers do not get to learn the real problems and requirements of an organization.

5. Overdependence on figures, particularly financial, which can be massaged to look good in the short term, while the longer term suffers.

6 and 7. The last two points relate to excessive medical costs and excessive legal costs, which Deming believes are paralysing competitiveness. Some would regard these as being typically American problems, but they may be a foretaste of problems to come for others.

Further reading on Deming:

W Edwards Deming, *Out of the Crisis*, Cambridge University Press, 1982

W Edwards Deming, *Quality, Productivity, and Competitive Position*, MIT Centre for Advanced Engineering Study, 1982

W.J.Latzko and W.J. Saunders, *Four Days with Dr. Deming*, Addison Wesley, Reading, MA, 1995

Web sites:

www.deming.org

www.deming.eng.clemson.edu

www.michiganquality.org

Juran

Like Deming, Dr. Joseph Juran is given credit for developing Japanese quality in the 1950s. His books on quality since then have had a profound influence around the world, and are so wide ranging it is difficult to highlight particular contributions from the many that have been made. Perhaps the best known Juran concepts are his definitions of quality, the concepts of "breakthrough" and the "internal customer", and the "quality trilogy". Juran also was responsible for "Pareto analysis" as applied to problem solving, for work on the costing of quality, and for the idea of a "Quality Council" within the organization. Juran has now retired from public lectures, although he continues writing. Juran's centenary was celebrated in 2004.

Juran believes that there are two dimensions to quality, an external one concerned with matching customer requirements, and an internal one concerned with building the product or service correctly. Juran has proposed the well known definition of quality as "fitness for use". This is not as simple as it sounds. One needs to ask, "for whose use?", and "what is the real use?". There may be many possible customers, both internal and external, who may use the product in different ways. (More on external customers later.)

So quality begins with a close understanding of who the users will be and how and where the product will be used. Without this customer orientation, good quality is not possible.

Using some JURAN concepts

And what is an "internal customer"? Each person along the chain, from product design to final user is both a supplier and a customer. Also, of course, the person will be a "process", carrying out some transformation or activity. The process is subject to all the concepts of process control. Taking them together, this is what Juran refers to as the "three role model", that is, each stage is a supplier, a process, and customer or user. So the customer orientation mentioned earlier applies internally as well. At each stage there is opportunity to improve the product, perhaps making it easier to handle, or fit together, or maintain, or update.

Juran emphasises the necessity for ongoing quality improvement. He maintains that this is only achieved through "project by project" improvement, in other words by a succession of small improvement projects carried out throughout the organization. Projects

may be suggested by management, by operators (perhaps through quality circles), by quality specialists or by Pareto analysis of existing problems. Juran was the first to name the Pareto principle and to describe it as a universal problem solving methodology. The Pareto principle simply sets out to identify the "vital few" as opposed to the "trivial many" or the "useful many". This is the well known phenomenon that there will always be a relatively few processes or people or defects or problems that somehow take up most of the time or effort or cost. Hence it makes sense to identify these and to tackle them first. (Pareto analysis is one of the 7 tools - see that section for more detail.)

Improvement projects can also be identified through costs, and Juran was responsible for suggesting that quality costs (or the costs of not getting something right first time) should be recorded and classified. Money is the prime language of management, so that if the costs of poor quality are known this not only gets management attention but helps home in on where effort should be made. For Juran, it is necessary for middle managers in the quality area to be able to translate the language of things into the language of money and vice versa. To do this we need a classification system, and Juran suggested that quality costs could be grouped into failure or appraisal or prevention costs. See the section on Cost of Quality.

Juran emphasized that management needs to attack the "chronic" underlying poor quality that is often not even recognised. He says that there is a tendency to tackle only "sporadic" quality problems that surface from time to time. Breakthrough is needed. The way to tackle chronic quality problems is "project by project improvement". This is perhaps similar to the Deming cycle, and leads straight into the quality trilogy. The quality trilogy, according to Juran comprises quality planning, quality control, and quality improvement. These can be seen as being parallel to the financial processes of budgeting, cost control, and cost reduction. Good quality management requires the quality actions to be planned out, improved, and controlled. So the process can be seen as achieving control at one level of quality performance, then planning to be better, project by project using the tools and techniques discussed, then eventually achieving "breakthrough" to an improved level, and then once again controlling at the new level. This series of actions will not take place by chance or by a series of uncoordinated actions. Rather, they must be organized in a systematic way. This is where the "Quality Council" comes in. This body, typically comprising senior managers, has the responsibility for coordinating the quality improvement actions and projects. They would, for example, set goals, identify needs, establish training, ensure measurements (such as costs of quality), undertake coordination, and in general liaise between quality projects and top management.

In another parallel with the Deming cycle, the Juran breakthrough sequence sees the improvement process as taking two "journeys" - the "journey from symptom to cause" and the "journey from cause to remedy". The first journey moves one from the problem to the "diagnosis" and may be seen as parallel to the "P" and "D" stages of the Deming cycle. Here we are concerned with identification, using for example Pareto, and with the generation of and testing of hypotheses to find the contributing causes. The second journey moves one from the "diagnosis" to the "solution" and may be seen as parallel to the "C" and "A" stages of the Deming cycle. Here one makes the selection of the appropriate cause, implements the necessary actions, and then replicates the improvements where possible in other areas.

Juran has also written on product design. His "Road Map" has 9 junctions : identify customers, determine the needs of those customers, translate those needs into company language, develop a product that can respond to those needs, optimise the product's features to meet both company needs and customer needs, develop a process that is capable of producing the product, optimise the process, prove that the process can produce the product under operating conditions, and transfer the process to operations.

More recently, Juran has spoken about "Big Q". This is to emphasize that quality is not just the concern of production or even of total quality within the organization, but extends further into the linkage between organizations, and includes all service organizations and operations. Under Big Q the concept

of "customer" extends beyond those immediately involved with producing and using the product or service, to include stakeholders who have a legitimate concern such as legislators and consumer groups. Juran states "In many companies there is only a dim awareness that the scope of the customer has widened, so there is no longer a consensus on who is the customer".

Finally in his last (edited) fascinating book covering the history of quality, Juran expresses his views on the future of managing for quality. He sees a parallel with the field of finance and accounting where, for example, the field is organised into distinct processes such as auditing, standard reports have been developed which are widely read and used by top managers, key terms are in widespread use, there are professional examinations, national indexes have been developed, awareness of the importance of the area will be recognized by legislators and economists, and the subject is taught in school.

The publication of this edition coincides with Juran's 100th birthday. Long may he survive. His ideas certainly will.

Further reading:
Joseph Juran and A. Blanton Godfrey, *Quality Control Handbook*, Fifth edition, McGraw Hill, 1999. (The bible on quality!)
Joseph Juran, *Juran on Planning for Quality*, The Free Press, 1988
J.M. Juran, *Juran on Leadership for Quality*, The Free Press, 1989
J.M. Juran (ed), *A History of Managing for Quality*, ASQ Quality Press, 1995
John Butman, *Juran : A Lifetime of Influence*, Wiley, New York, 1997
Web site (The Juran Institute, containing news and recent articles) : www.juran.com

Crosby

Like Juran, Phil Crosby has been a prolific writer on quality. Unlike Juran, some of whose works contain much quantitative and statistical techniques, Crosby concentrates on quality philosophy, particularly relating to management. Crosby's dynamic speaking style and stimulating writing style have gained him a large following.

Crosby is perhaps best known for his "four absolutes" of quality, his phrase "quality is free", his 14 point plan (different from Deming's 14 points), and his down to earth common sense on a wide range of quality topics.

Crosby's "four absolutes" are :

1. "The definition of quality is conformance to requirements". This very specific definition of quality leaves very little open, which is probably what Crosby intends. According to Crosby, once the requirements are specified then quality is judged solely on the criteria of whether they are met or not; aesthetics or feelings don't come into it. It is then the duty of management to specify those requirements very clearly, to say what they want. This, Crosby believes, is one of the major failings of management. Of course, if management does not decide what is needed then by default, operators are going to have to make that decision for the company!

2. "The system of quality is prevention". In other words, prevention is better than detection or appraisal. This is very much in line with the philosophy behind SPC and failsafing; understand the process, look at what can go wrong, and take preventative actions.

3. "The performance standard is zero defect", or "ZD" as Crosby calls it. Here Crosby is stating that nothing less than perfect quality has to be the aim. Setting targets below 100% is the start of a downward spiral. Of course, traditional quality management has taken zero defects to be uneconomic, and there should be a trade-off between prevention costs and failure costs. The Crosby view is now supported by a developing view that prevention costs, particularly where "total quality" is in place, do not necessarily rise massively as one approaches zero defects, but in fact rise by no more than failure costs fall. In other words, zero defect may well be optimal from a cost point of view. But again it comes back to getting the requirements right in the first place.

4. "The measurement of quality is the price of nonconformance". Like Juran, Crosby believes in costing quality as a prime motivator for management. Crosby classifies costs into "PONC" - the price of nonconformance" (all the costs involved in not getting the product or service right) and "POC" - the price of conformance (what it costs to do things right; prevention, detection, etc.). Here Crosby's famous phrase "quality is free" is appropriate. (It is also the title of his first book.) As he says, "it's not a gift, but it's free" or in other words if you put effort into improving quality it will more than pay for itself through improved productivity, reduced rework and claims, and improved customer satisfaction.

The problem with quality, according to Crosby, is not that people disagree with it, but what they think they know about it, namely that workers are sloppy, customers are unreasonable, close checks will find problems earlier, and that there are "trade-offs" in quality. In 1995 Crosby concluded that, after a brief period of improvement, these ideas are once again gaining ground.

Crosby, like Deming, has a 14 step plan for quality improvement. Deming's 14 points are more of a philosophy of quality management, whereas Crosby's are more a specific action plan for implementation. In that respect, the two 14 point plans can easily be seen as reinforcing one another. The 14 steps will not be spelled out in detail here, but they begin with management commitment and the establishment of a team. The next stages deal with measuring quality through "POC" and "PONC". These figures are often much higher than expected, which aids in the next steps to do with creating awareness and planning out what is to be done. Education of employees follows, with a "ZD" day to launch the program. Then employees become involved in detail goal setting as to what can be done in specific sections of the company. With the goals set, identification of the causes of defects can begin in earnest at all levels. Improvement results and recognition must then be given. Now "quality councils" allow quality managers and others to get together and review what has been achieved and how and where else these achievements can be transferred to. This is not the end. Quality is an ongoing process, so the last step is to do it all over again.

Writing years later, Crosby now regrets putting forward his 14 point plan, making the point that many take it as a recipe for quality when what is really required is appropriate thought ("searching for specific procedures among ideas is the sign of a lazy mind"), but that such frameworks should be added to through experience, study and reflection.

Crosby's "Quality Vaccine" is perhaps more closely related to the Deming 14 point plan than the Crosby 14 step process. In typical stimulating style, Crosby's "vaccine" is preventive medicine for management against poor quality. The vaccine comprises practical advice on 21 areas, subdivided into five sections. The quality vaccine is in fact a succinct summary of what is needed for total quality management.

* The first section deals with integrity. This is really about taking quality seriously, from chief executive to every employee. If quality is taken as "first among equals" - the others being marketing, finance, operations, and so on, then everyone understands that their own future and the future of the company will be determined by performance on quality.
* The second section deals with systems - for quality costs, for education, for quality performance, for review and improvement, and for customer satisfaction. All of these must be designed and put in place.
* The third section deals with the need for communication and for communication systems that will make clear the requirements and specifications, and which will communicate improvement opportunities within the organization. Crosby often emphasises the importance of listening - to customers, and to those front line employees who often know what is needed but perhaps have never been asked.

Also external communications, in advertising, letters, and product information must convey a consistent message.
* The fourth section deals with operations, including working with and developing suppliers. Processes must be prepared prior to use and made capable, and process improvement must become the norm.
* And last, Crosby maintains that policies must be made clear and consistent throughout the organization.

Crosby also has a "Quality Management Maturity Grid" passing through the stages of uncertainty, awakening, enlightenment, and wisdom and certainty. During this transition the reported typical cost of quality as a percentage of sales, starts unknown, rises to 8%, then declines to 2.5%. But the actual costs of quality declines from 20% to 2.5%.

In recent years Crosby has been critical of ISO 9000 and of quality awards such as the Baldridge or EQA, saying that they are old fashioned, merely providing a living for consultants, and a recipe for managers who don't want to think about what quality really is! Phil Crosby died in August 2001.

Further reading on Crosby:
Phil Crosby, *Quality is Free*, McGraw Hill, 1979
Phil Crosby, *Quality Without Tears*, McGraw Hill, 1984
Phil Crosby, *Let's Talk Quality*, McGraw Hill, 1989
Phil Crosby, *Quality is Still Free*, McGraw Hill, 1995

Feigenbaum

Armand Feigenbaum, an American engineer, was the originator of "Total Quality Control", now often referred to simply as total quality. In the 1950s, he defined total quality as follows :

"Total quality control is an effective system for integrating the quality development, quality maintenance, and quality improvement efforts of the various groups in an organization so as to enable production and service at the most economical levels which allow full customer satisfaction."

Feigenbaum has a particularly good definition of quality: "The total composite product and service characteristics of marketing, engineering, manufacture and maintenance through which the product and service in use will meet the expectations of the customer."

Feigenbaum referred to the "industrial cycle" which is the ongoing sequence of activities necessary to bring products from concept to market. Included in this cycle are marketing, design, engineering, purchasing, manufacturing, production, inspection, packaging and shipping, installation, and service. In all these stages quality has requirements to be met. Feigenbaum was the first to point out the folly of regarding quality professionals as being solely responsible for the quality function. The cycle begins and ends with the customer, but in between many people and functions must play a role; in fact everyone has a role and the responsibility must be shared. On the other hand Feigenbaum sees the quality professionals playing a central role and coordinating the entire process. He does not appear to agree with the view of quality improvement being a required role for all employees. As one moves through the cycle, there are requirements to be met at each stage, and these different requirements must be defined and communicated. This is where the quality professionals have a prime role. The total cost of quality (or non quality) accumulates through all these stages, and a total view of quality being managed through all the stages will lead to a lower overall cost.

Feigenbaum has a 40 point plan for quality which is far more detailed and specific that those of Deming or Crosby. (See the web site for a full listing). In general he has 3 steps to Quality : quality leadership, modern quality technology, and organisational commitment.

Feigenbaum is also known for his concept of the "hidden plant". That is that in every factory a certain proportion of its capacity is wasted through not getting it right first time. Feigenbaum quoted a figure of up to 40% of the capacity of the plant being wasted. At the time this was an unbelievable figure; even today some managers are still to learn that this is a figure not too far removed from the truth.

Further reading:
A.V. Feigenbaum, "Total Quality Control", *Harvard Business Review*, November 1956
Armand Feigenbaum, *Total Quality Control*, (Third Edition, revised) McGraw Hill, 1991

Web sites: www.generalsystemscompany.com

Ishikawa

The late Kaoru Ishikawa is regarded as the leading Japanese contributor to quality management. His contributions are extensive but perhaps the most noteworthy are his development of the total quality viewpoint, his work on statistical quality control, his emphasis on the human side of quality, and his invention of the Ishikawa diagram and the use of the "7 tools". Perhaps most noteworthy is the fact that he is widely regarded as the "father" of quality circles, since it was he who furthered the concept of circles and popularized their practice in Japan.

Ishikawa extended the total quality view of Feigenbaum by suggesting that operators, and employees in general, have a greater role to play in all the stages suggested by Feigenbaum. In fact, Ishikawa believed that although the total quality view was invented in the West, its potential was limited there due to over-reliance on quality professionals and insufficient attention to the contribution that everyone can make. This leads directly onto quality circles and to his classification of statistical tools for quality control.

Ishikawa classified statistical quality control techniques into three groups of increasing complexity. The first group is the classic "7 tools" (dealt with in a complete separate section), which require minimal statistical knowledge. (The 7 tools include the Ishikawa or fishbone diagram, which is described in that section.) Ishikawa believed that the 7 tools should be known widely, if not by everyone, in the company. They are certainly not the preserve of experts, and are simple enough for everyone to use for ongoing improvement. More specifically they should be used by quality circle members in analysing problems and devising improvements. Used together, they form a powerful set. The next group ("intermediate statistical methods"), are for use by quality specialists but also by some managers who have responsibilities for quality in their sections. Not all these managers need to know about all these methods. They include sampling surveys and sampling inspection, statistical estimation and hypothesis testing, sensory tests, and basic experimental design. These methods do require some prior knowledge of statistics but can and should be learned by relevant managers. Lastly there are some "advanced statistical methods" which are primarily for the use of specialist quality staff and consultants. These include advanced experimental design, multivariate analysis, and operations research techniques. (Note: this would include "Taguchi" methods which are discussed in a later section.)

The classification is a useful "Pareto" type of listing. First, it provides general guidance on how an educational program for quality may be set up. Second, Ishikawa believed that most quality problems - perhaps 90% or more - could be solved by the use of the 7 tools category, and that therefore they should be known to all, from company chief executive right through to operator. Ishikawa has perhaps been more instrumental than anyone in the now widely held Japanese view that without at least some knowledge of statistics, quality management is not possible. Going back to Deming's view on variation, one can notice the similarity.

Ishikawa insisted that "total quality" implies participation by everyone in the organization. Moreover, it is achieved through everyone participating in teams rather than as individuals. In this respect he talks about quality being a "thought revolution". He is critical of heavy dependence on Taylorism which he believed dehumanizes the workplace and destroys much of the opportunity for improvement. (Quality is based on "respect for humanity".) It takes time to build the necessary

widespread human commitment and, according to Ishikawa, too rapid implementation of systems such as total quality and just-in-time is the reason why they have often not been a success. Quality is not a "miracle drug" but rather a "herb medicine". Despite Ishikawa's heavy inclination towards people involvement, this should not be misread as a willingness to avoid quantitative data. On the contrary, Ishikawa is adamant that collection and analysis of the hard facts and data is the essence of quality control. Hence everyone must be trained in basic tools and statistical techniques.

Ishikawa believed that quality begins with the customer. The essence is to understand customers, their requirements, what they can afford, and what their reactions are likely to be. Absolute clarity of specification is needed, and this means specifying exactly what is needed under what conditions, of for example temperature and humidity. He believed that customer complaints are a vital quality improvement opportunity, and that they must be managed. In this respect Ishikawa was the pioneer of the fashionable idea that customer complaints must be actively encouraged.

Ishikawa's quality philosophy is summarised in his 11 points which are :

1. Quality begins and ends with education.
2. The first step is to know customer requirements.
3. The ideal state is when inspection is no longer necessary.
4. Remove the root cause, not the symptoms.
5. Quality is the responsibility of all.
6. Do not confuse means with objectives.
7. Put quality first to achieve long term profits.
8. Marketing is the entrance and exit of quality.
9. Top management should not be angered by facts shown by subordinates.
10. 95% of problems can be solved with simple tools.
11. Data without variability is false data.

On the perennial question of whether quality pays, Ishikawa believes that it does, provided one defines the relevant system wide enough. In other words if quality is equated with inspection then perfection may not be worthwhile. But if quality incorporates the total process, from customer to design and through process control and eventually back to the customer, then it certainly pays.

Finding the root causes of problems was important to Ishikawa, and of course his famous Ishikawa diagram assists in this respect.

As noted, Ishikawa is regarded as the "father" of quality circles. Of course he has extensive advice on how to conduct circles, but a few points are noteworthy. Primarily, circle activities must be part of a wider total quality effort. Managers must first understand both total quality and the functioning of circles before circle activities begin. Those supervisors in whose areas circles are in operation require special training. Members of a circle must be volunteers, but on the other hand everyone in a section has a role to play in quality. So it is an all or nothing affair. Circle members must be trained in appropriate tools, but must also learn to appreciate wider aspects of quality throughout the organization. The organization must cater for these requirements. A problem solving methodology must be learned by team members (Ishikawa's has 9 steps, but can be seen as similar to the Deming cycle.) Effective evaluation of circle efforts must be made. Perhaps one can summarize the Ishikawa approach with his well known axiom - that management must conduct their programs with a "belief in humanity".

Further reading:
Kaoru Ishikawa, *Guide to Quality Control*, Asian Productivity Association, 1976
Kaoru Ishikawa, *What is Total Quality Control? The Japanese Way*, Prentice Hall, 1985

Garvin

David Garvin, a professor at Harvard Business School, has contributed to the concept of quality as a strategy, and to our understanding of just what is meant by quality. Garvin identifies eight "dimensions" of quality, which he maintains cover the various meanings of quality that managers, operators, and customers have. The important idea is that a product

or service does not usually compete on all eight, but usually targets only a select few. Likewise customers may have different perceptions as to what combination of the dimensions really add up to a "quality" package. This implies that management must seek to understand customer perceptions, so that quality efforts will be focused. Also there may be opportunities to compete on different or additional dimensions that are not offered by competitors. The eight dimensions are:

1. **Performance:** the primary operating characteristics of the product or service. Examples would be size, speed, power, sound.
2. **Features:** the "extras" that supplement the main performance characteristics. The "sunroof and spotlamps".
3. **Reliability:** what may go wrong and how often it is likely to.
4. **Conformance:** the closeness of match between the design specification and what is actually produced (or the match between what is advertised and what is experienced by customers).
5. **Durability:** how long the product may last, and its robustness in operating conditions. How often service is needed is also relevant.
6. **Serviceability:** the ease, speed, cost and friendliness of service. Whereas reliability is concerned with mean time between failures (MTBF), serviceability is concerned with mean time to repair (MTTR).
7. **Aesthetics:** the appearance, style, "class" and impression.
8. **Perceived Quality:** the "feel", the "finish", and perhaps the reputation. Also the friendliness and the manner in which the customer is served.

Not all dimensions are applicable in the service sector and often other dimensions may be added or substituted. These could include friendliness, helpfulness, clarity of communication, knowledge, safety and security, decision making ability, and response time.

The dimensions are useful because they help understand the breadth of the challenge which is involved in managing quality. In marketing, there is the well known "marketing mix", the point being that product, price, place, and promotion need to be made compatible as a single package. There is apparently also a "quality mix" which requires the same degree of care in its formulation.

Of late, Garvin has become a Guru on the fashionable topic of organisational learning - surely a field closely related to continuous improvement.

Further reading:
David Garvin, *Managing Quality*, The Free Press, 1988

Shingo:
Failsafing and Source
Inspection

The late Shigeo Shingo is strongly associated with Lean manufacturing and may not be classified as a quality guru by all. Nevertheless his work on so-called "pokayoke" or fail-safe devices and on "source inspection" is very significant and is already widely implemented. For this reason he is bound to be considered as one of the "greats" sooner or later.

Shigeo Shingo did not invent failsafing ("pokayoke" in Japanese, literally mistake proofing), but developed and classified the concept, particularly in manufacturing. More recently failsafing in services has developed. Shingo's book *Zero Quality Control : Source Inspection and the Pokayoke System* is the classic work.

A failsafing device is a simple, often inexpensive, device which literally prevents defects from being made. The characteristics of a failsafing device are that it undertakes 100% automatic inspection (a true pokayoke would not rely on human memory or action), and either stops or gives warning when a defect is discovered. Note that a pokayoke is not a control device like a thermostat or toilet control valve that takes action every time, but rather a device that senses abnormalities and takes action only when an abnormality is identified.

Shingo distinguishes between "mistakes" (which are inevitable) and "defects" (which result when a mistake

reaches a customer.). The aim of pokayoke is to design devices which prevent mistakes becoming defects. Shingo also saw quality control as a hierarchy of effectiveness from "judgment inspection" (where inspectors inspect), to "informative inspection" where information is used to control the process as in SPC, and finally to "source inspection" which aims at checking operating conditions "before the fact". Good pokayokes fall into this last category.

According to Shingo there are three types of failsafing device: "contact", "fixed value", and "motion step", and two actions, control or warning. This means that there are six categories, as shown in the figure with service examples.

The contact type makes contact with every product or has a physical shape which inhibits mistakes. An example is a fixed diameter hole through which all products must fall; an oversize product does not fall through and a defect is registered. The fixed value method is a design which makes it clear when a part is missing or not used. An example is an "egg tray" used for the supply of parts. Sometimes this type can be combined with the contact type, where parts not only have to be present in the egg tray but also are automatically correctly aligned. The motion step type automatically ensures that the correct number of steps have been taken. For example, an operator is required to step on a pressure-sensitive pad during every assembly cycle, or a medicine bottle has a press-down-and-turn feature for safety. Other examples are a checklist, or a correct sequence for switches which do not work unless the order is correct.

Shingo further developed failsafe classification by saying that there are five areas that have potential for failsafing : the operator (Me), the Material, the Machine, the Method, and the Information (4 M plus I). An alternative is the process control model comprising input, process, output, feedback, and result. All are candidates for failsafing. According to Grout (see website), areas where pokayoke should be considered include areas where worker vigilance is required, where mispositioning is likely, where SPC is difficult, where external failure costs dramatically exceed internal failure costs, and in mixed model and

JIT production. Chase and Stewart list four types of pokayoke: Physical (a part can only be used one way), Sequencing (unless the correct steps are carried out it will stop), Grouping (e.g. egg boxes), and Information (e.g. alarm clocks, heijunka boards, automatic counts).

Shingo says that pokayoke should be thought of as having both a short action cycle (where immediate shut down or warning is given), and also a long action cycle where the reasons for the defect occurring in the first place are investigated. John Grout makes the useful point that one drawback of pokayoke devices is that potentially valuable information about process variance may be lost, thereby inhibiting improvement.

Richard Chase has extended Shingo's work to Services. He discusses stages of failsafing by both the provider and the customer. The service provider's work should attempt to be failsafed at the task stage (doing the actual work), at the treatment stage (the interaction with the customer - for instance customer greeting), and with the tangibles (the physical appearance, cleanliness etc). On the Customer side, failsafing could be attempted at three stages, equivalent to Vandermerwe's Pre, During, and Post stages of customer service. (See page 99).

	Control	Warning
Contact	Parking height bars Armrests on seats	Staff mirrors Shop entrance bell
Fixed Value	French fry scoop Pre-dosed medication	Trays with indentations
Motion Step	Airline lavatory doors	Spellcheckers Beepers on ATMs

after: Richard Chase and Douglas Stewart,
Mistake-Proofing: Designing Errors Out, Productivity, 1995

A systematic way to consider failsafing is to construct a Cycle of Service diagram (see separate section), and then for each Moment of Truth consider how it may be failsafed.

Source inspection is simply the concept of responsibility for quality at the point of value adding. As a manufactured product progresses defects become more and more imbedded and so more costly to rectify. Hence the sensible thing is for the human operator to do self inspection, or at worst inspect the previous process. So source inspection is about moving away from dedicated inspectors and towards point of action inspection. The prime rule is "never knowingly pass on a defective". Note that this happens in service also - a typist should self check a letter before handing it on for signature.

Further reading:

Shigeo Shingo, *Zero Quality Control : Source Inspection and the Pokayoke System,* Productivity Press, 1986
Richard Chase and Douglas Stewart, "Make Your Service Fail Safe", *Sloan Management Review*, Spring 1994, pages 35-44
Hroyuki Hirano, *Poka-Yoke: Improving Product Quality by Preventing Defects*, Productivity Press, 1989
Web site on Shingo
The Shingo prize for Lean and Quality. Details at http://www.shingoprize.org
An impressive site with numerous examples and pictures is at: http://www.campbell.berry.edu/faculty/jgrout/pokayoke.shtml

Taguchi

Genichi Taguchi is a Japanese statistician and engineer whose concepts only began to make an impact in the West during the 1980s. His principal contributions have been to our understanding of what product specification really means for quality and how such specifications can be translated into cost effective production. Quality through design could be a short summary.

Taguchi has been critical of the conventional view of quality acceptance, which is that there are specification limits within which a product is acceptable and beyond which it not. This black-and-white or perfect and defective is not the way most customers see quality, nor is it effective in a design or engineering sense, argues Taguchi. For instance, a meal served in a restaurant is not suddenly defective on one side of a particular temperature and perfect on the other. Nor would part dimensions which when changed by a fraction of a millimetre suddenly become defective. Taguchi argues instead for a continuous decline in utility as one moves further away from the target or optimal value. Taguchi refers to this as the "loss function". The function is called this because, Taguchi maintains, any deviation involves a "loss to society" over the lifetime of the product. He maintains that the loss is approximately proportional to the square of the deviation from the target value. That is, as the distance away from the target value doubles, the "loss" will increase by four times. Another interesting view is that there are "customer tolerance limits" rather than engineering or designer specified limits. So although there may be no sharp cutoff of acceptability as far as the design specification is concerned, there will eventually be limits beyond which a customer finds the product or service unacceptable.

Acceptance of the loss function has an important implication for quality improvement. Instead of crossing the limit to achieve acceptance and then ceasing further improvement effort, the loss function would suggest that improvement must be ongoing until the target perfection is achieved. Specification limits become superfluous. This ultimate goal is virtually impossible (there will always be a new magnitude of accuracy to challenge) so the improvement effort must never cease. Perhaps this would explain the apparent Japanese devotion to improvement (in Japan the Taguchi view is more well established) in contrast to more relaxed behaviour elsewhere.

Taguchi believes that it is preferable to design a product which is robust or insensitive to variation in the manufacturing process than it is to attempt to control all the many variations during actual manufacture. Instead of taking measures to control factors which degrade the performance of a product ("noise"), he believes in reducing their influence. Taguchi is fond of quoting an example from tile making where, instead of trying to control all the

factors, such as temperature and pressure, and human error, which have an influence on tile dimensions, by altering the tile mix the process becomes much more robust to changes in these factors.

Some TAGUCHI concepts

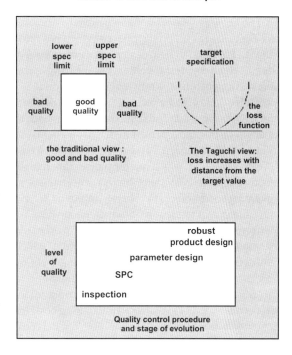

Quality control procedure and stage of evolution

Like many great ideas, this is beautifully obvious. The trick is to put it into practice. This is where Taguchi's ideas on parameter design and the control of experiments come in. Design of Experiments is a well established body of knowledge in the field of statistics and was not invented by Taguchi. But Taguchi has made these concepts more usable and practical for the quality professional. In traditional statistical analysis, often scores of experiments have to be carried out to identify the sensitive parameters. This often puts their practical use out of bounds, but with Taguchi's methods the amount of work is drastically reduced. The object of the experiments is to identify the design parameter settings that minimise the effect of "noise", by systematically varying the design parameters and the noise factors and observing the outcome. Whilst it is true that Taguchi methods are probably beyond the statistical abilities of most operators, they can be appreciated by managers and used by designers. With the Taguchi view, design is the principal determinant to the final product cost, over its lifetime. A distinction is therefore made between "off line" quality control, which includes sensitivity tests and reliability tests, and "on line" quality control which is concerned with control during manufacture.

As Taguchi sees it, product development has three stages. The first, "system design", is a non statistical stage which brings together engineering and marketing/customer knowledge to produce a prototype design. In the second, "parameter design", the relationship of desirable product performance to changing parameters is explored. This amounts to finding a robust design, in other words the most cost effective way in which performance can remain good irrespective (within limits) of changes in operating conditions. The "secret" of this is to use the non-linear effects of product parameters on performance characteristics. (Refer to the tile example). The third stage is "tolerance design" which now sets tolerances around the target settings, not by the usual engineering techniques relating to "tolerance stackup", but by finding the right trade-off between society loss and manufacturing cost. All this sounds terribly complex. It is not, but it is also not simple. There are now thousands of successful examples.

We can view Taguchi methods along a continuum, being that inspecting the process (SPC) is superior to inspecting the product (SQC). And reducing the sensitivity of parameters is an advance on SPC because the process does not have to be so tightly controlled. And best of all is robust design where product performance remains good in spite of changes in operating characteristics.

Further reading:

Genichi Taguchi, *System of Experimental Design*, UNIPUB Kraus, 1985

Glen Stuart Peace, *Taguchi Methods : A Hands-On Approach*, Addison Wesley, 1993

Kano

Dr. Noriaki Kano is a Japanese academic who is best known for his excellent "Kano model". The Kano Model has emerged as one the most useful and powerful aids to product and service design and improvement available.

The Kano model relates three factors (which Kano argues are present in every product or service) to their degree of implementation or level of implementation, as shown in the diagram. Kano's three factors are Basic (or "must be") factors, Performance (or "more is better") factors, and Delighter (or "excitement") factors. The degree of customer satisfaction ranges from "disgust", through neutrality, to "delight".

A Basic factor is something that a customer simply expects to be there. If it is not present the customer will be dissatisfied or disgusted, but if it is fully implemented or present it will merely result in a feeling of neutrality. Examples are clean sheets in a hotel, a station tuner on a radio, or windscreen washers on a car. Notice that there may be degrees of implementation: sheets may be clean but blemished. Basic factors should not be taken for granted, or regarded as easy to satisfy; some may even be exceptionally difficult to identify. One example is course handouts which a lecturer may regard as trivial but the audience may regard as a basic necessity. If you don't get the basics right, all else may fail - in this respect it is like Maslow's Hierarchy of Needs : it is no good thinking about self esteem needs unless survival needs are catered for. Market surveys are of limited value for basics (because they are simply expected). Therefore a designer needs to build up a list by experience, observation and organised feedback.

A Performance factor can cause disgust at one extreme, but if fully implemented can result in delight. This factor is also termed "more is better" but could also be "faster is better" or "easier is better". Performance factors are usually in existence already, but are neutral, causing neither disgust nor delight. It is not so much the fact that the feature exists, it is how it can be improved. The challenge is to identify them, and to change their performance. Examples are speed of check in at a hotel, ease of tuning on a radio, or fuel consumption. Performance factors represent real opportunity to designers and to R&D staff. They may be identified through market surveys, but observation is also important, especially in identifying performance features that are causing dissatisfaction. Creativity or process redesign is often required to deliver the factor faster or more easily, and information support may play a role as in the "one minute" check-in at some top hotels. The Cycle of Service (see separate section) is a useful starting point to identify performance factors.

THE KANO MODEL

To test if a characteristic is basic, performance or delighter, ask two questions :
1. how do you feel if (the characteristic) is absent ?
2. how do you feel if (the characteristic) is present ?

if 1 = bad, 2 = neutral, it is a basic
if 1=neutral, 2 = good, it is a delighter
if the answer is "it depends", it is a performance

Finally, A Delighter is something that customers do not expect, but if present may cause increasing delight. Examples are flowers and wine awaiting guest arrivals in some hotel rooms, or a radio tuner that retunes itself when moving out of range of a transmitter. By definition, market surveys are of little use here. Once again, it is creativity, based on an appreciation of (latent) customer needs that can provide the breakthrough. But we need to be careful about Delighters also : a true Delighter is provided at minimal extra cost - it would certainly cause

customer delight to give them all a complimentary car, but would be disastrous for company finances. Therefore, perhaps a more appropriate hotel Delighter would be to give guests a choice of sheet colour, pillow type (English or German), and sheet type (linen, satin, or cotton).

We should also note that the Kano factors are not static. What may be a Delighter this year may migrate towards being a Basic in a few years time. And also, what may be a Delighter in one part of the world may be a Basic in another. Thus it is crucial to keep up to date with changing customer expectations. Benchmarking may be a way to go. From Kano we also learn that a reactive quality policy, reacting to complaints, or dissatisfiers, will at best lead to neutrality but proactive action is required to create delight.

The Kano Model works well with Quality Function Deployment. Basics should be satisfied, and delighters can be explicitly traded off in the "roof" of the QFD matrix (for example fuel consumption may suggest a lighter car, but safety suggests a stronger one - so the quest is to find material that is light, strong, and inexpensive.)

Further reading:
Special Issue on Kano's Methods: *Center for Quality of Management Journal,* Vol 2, No 4, Fall 1993 (Several artices, including administering Kano questionnaires).
 Hofmeister, Walters, Gongos, "Discovering Customer WOW's", *Annual Quality Congress,* ASQC, May 1996, pp759-770.
Joiner, B.L., *Fourth Generation Management,* McGraw Hill, New York, 1994
Lou Cohen, *Quality Function Deployment,* Addison Wesley, Reading MA, 1995, pp 36-41

Christian Grönroos and the Finnish School

Christian Grönroos is Professor of Service and Relationship Marketing at the Hanken Swedish School of Economics and Business, Finland. Grönroos is considered a Guru of service quality not only for his own contributions but because he has been a stimulant for much innovative thinking in the service area. The following are a few of the excellent contributions made by Grönroos and his associates.

Service Dimensions

Like Garvin's dimensions of product quality and Zeithaml's SERVQUAL dimensions for service (see separate sections) Grönroos has produced a list of the "seven criteria of good perceived service quality". These are Professionalism, Attitudes, Trustworthiness, Servicescape, Credibility, Accessibility, and Recovery. (The acronym is PATS CAR). "Servicescape" is a phrase from Mary Bitner relating to the physical environment. An excellent checklist, perhaps more meaningful than Zeithaml's RATER dimensions.

A Framework for Service Quality Relationships.

Grönroos' Finnish associate Holmlund perceives service interactions taking place in a hierarchy of acts, episodes, sequences, and relationships. An act is the smallest transaction between a provider and a customer. Examples include handing over cash to be deposited at a bank and greeting a guest at a hotel (basically, a "moment of truth"). A series of acts constitute an episode: the entire visit to the bank; a full meal at the hotel. Over time episodes repeat to form a sequence: several visits to the bank; a complete stay at the hotel. Sequences may build into relationships. Ongoing relationship with the bank; repeat visits to a hotel. The customer's perception of the quality of an act builds expectations of episodes and sequences. Experience of relationships and sequences feeds back to expectations of episodes. This model helps understanding of the way in which customer relationships are formed, and aids understanding of the dynamics of service quality.

Expectations

Quality is closely linked to expectations. Grönroos' group has usefully distinguished three types of expectation. *Explicit:* These expectations can be articulated by customers, but may be realistic or unrealistic. A management task is to help customers adjust unrealistic to realistic. *Fuzzy:* where customers are not able to define or formulate clear expectations but which nevertheless impact satisfaction. What do you expect from a theme park visit? Answer: Don't know, but quite a bit. Management has a role to translate these fuzzy expectations into explicit expectations. *Implicit:* These expectations are taken for granted. It is management's task to build understanding, because these factors are easily overlooked. What is an obvious need to a customer may simply not be recognised by the service provider.

Note the overlap with the Kano model. Implicits are Basics. Explicit may be Performance factors. Fuzzy and unrealistic factors, if managed correctly, have the potential to be Delighters. Like Kano, the model is dynamic. Fuzzy becomes explicit. Unrealistic may become realistic.

Further reading:
Christian Grönroos, *Service Management and Marketing*, Second edition, Wiley, Chichester, 2000

Shainin and Bhote

The late Dorian Shainin, who died in 2000, is a "forgotten" guru of Quality probably because he did not seek publicity but worked as a consultant for a large number of companies many of whom were unwilling to share his remarkable methods. "Shainin Methods" are a powerful family of analytical and statistical tools which help identify what he termed the "Red X" (the root problem or dominant cause) as opposed to the "Green Y" (the field or total problem) and the "Pink X" (the second most important cause). Shainin extended design of experiments (DOE), and suggested improvements in SPC. His methods are a considerable advance on the "7 Tools" of Quality but require more advanced understanding. (Bhote is dismissive of the "7 Tools" calling them Kindergarden Methods). Shainin methods have wide application in manufacturing and service.

Keki Bhote worked for Motorola and using Shainin methods helped that company win the Baldridge award and to establish the Six Sigma methodology. Later, working as a consultant, he has done much to popularise Shainin methods. His books *World Class Quality* (first and second editions) describe Shainin methods in detail.

The Shainin / Bhote tools form a powerful set leading from problem identification through implementation and onto control. In other words PDCA, but far more specific than PDCA. Bhote divides the family of tools into four sections: Defining and measuring, Clue generation, DOE, and Transition to SPC. Many of the individual tools are briefly described in this book. Here we attempt an overall summary.

Defining and Measuring: This comprises a set of questions aimed at clarifying the problem area and making subsequent analysis more effective. For instance Bhote suggests looking at the history, at quantification, at which stage the problem is detected (can this be done earlier?), and at clarifying whether the problem is a reliability problem or a quality problem. Measurement requires examination – is the measurement system itself capable?

Clue Generation: The idea of this stage is to reduce a large number of possible causes to a much smaller number. The Multi-vari chart is a prime tool. The Concentration chart is a form of measles chart. Components Search is an efficient procedure used in assembly operations and involving disassembly and reassembly in different configurations. It helps to home in on which assembly step is possibly the "Red X". Paired Comparisons has wide application in service and manufacture and involves looking at successive pairs of items, one good and one bad, and noting the differences until a trend emerges. A more involved method is called the Tukey Test that is used where there is a parameter, say a dimension, that is thought to have an influence in whether the item is good or bad. When ranked by the parameter, if it turns out that performance is good, good, good, bad, bad,

bad this is more significant than if good, good, bad, good, bad, bad. The Product Process Search is a related technique used where it is unclear if variation is as a result of the product (material) or the process. Here, identify the potential process variables. Take samples, measuring each variable, until eight good and eight bad are accumulated. This is usually sufficient data to home in on the Red X, using the earlier and later techniques.

DOE Stage. Following the short list of candidate causes, this stage homes in on the Red X. A Variables Search is used where there are 5 to 20 variables. It is described as similar to the algorithm for finding any number between 1 and 1000 by halving and asking which half over and over again. Full Factorial is used for 4 or less variables and involves the orthogonal array procedure described in a separate section. (Taguchi orthogonal arrays have been criticised by Bhote on clue identification, validity, cost, and effectiveness grounds). Thereafter comes "B vs. C" or better v. current to ensure that the chosen solution is truly better. This is done by alternating between the proposed and current methods, thereby ensuring that the "Hawthorne effect" (where the productivity gains were more to do with the effect of being observed than the variables themselves) does not happen.

Transition to SPC. The final stage is concerned with "holding the gains" through "Positrol" (an extended form of standardisation more or less using the six honest serving men – see separate section), and "Pre Control" (see separate section).

All in all, a hugely powerful methodology.

Further reading:
Keki Bhote and Adi Bhote, *World Class Quality*, (Second Edition), AmaCom, New York, 2000

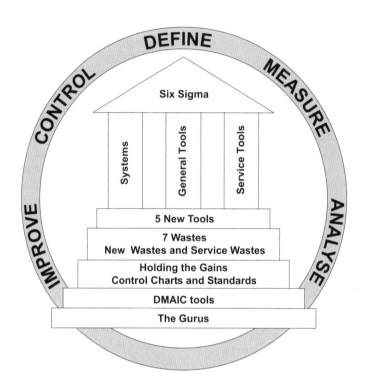

Improvement Cycles

DMAIC and PDCA

The DMAIC Cycle

Six Sigma was introduced in Chapter 1 not as a new approach but a repackaging of quality tools and concepts, with a strong focus on financial results. There are some aspects of the package that could be argued as belonging only to Six Sigma such as the DMAIC cycle and the 1.5 sigma shift.

The DMAIC cycle is an interesting prescription of a route to take because of its similarity with the widely used PDCA cycle. As an alternative way of looking at DMAIC fitting into PDCA, another view is that for each phase of DMAIC, the project team should Plan-Do-Check-Act.

Masaaki Imai, the Japanese guru who originated the Kaizen Process, suggested nine basic steps in PDCA:

Plan	1.	Select the project.
	2.	Understand the current situation.
	3.	Set clear objectives.
Do	4.	Gather information.
	5.	Analyse the facts.
	6.	Develop countermeasure and try out.
Check	7.	Confirm the goals are satisfied.
Act	8.	Officially adopt countermeasures.
	9.	Review project.

Compare this approach to the DMAIC Wheel:

The DMAIC Wheel

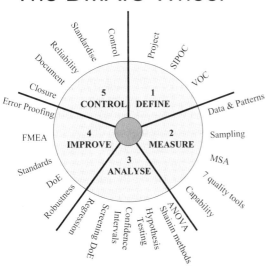

There are similarities but the underpinning power of the DMAIC process is the statistical tools. Some of the tools are common (Ishikawa's 7 quality tools) but others, the 'power' tools such as Gauge R&R, ANOVA and DoE, applied using statistical software packages, are differentiators.

The DMAIC cycle can also be compared to the Industrial Engineer's Method Study process of SREDIM (Select, Record, Examine, Develop, Install, Maintain). This approach looks very similar indeed, but it is not supported with the infrastructure and statistical toolbox that make the Six Sigma approach so successful in delivering financial impacts.

How Prescriptive is the DMAIC cycle?

The cycle is a rigorous process and there is generally no variation in this approach. (One exception is when using Six Sigma for a new product, process or service. The cycle for DFSS (Design For Six Sigma) is DMADV: Define – Measure – Analyse – Design – Verify.)

However, the Six Sigma tools underpinning each phase of the DMAIC cycle are not necessarily going to be appropriate for every project. The tools used on projects in transactional processes may vary from those in production environments although they come from the same toolbox. Does this sound rather opportunist, selecting the tools you want for each project phase? What happens if you choose the wrong tool? The more practice Black Belts and Breen Belts gain in completing Six Sigma projects, the more likely they are to apply the correct tools, in the same way as a professional golf player selects the correct golf club.

The 14 Questions

Air Academy Associates have laid down a template of 14 quality improvement oriented questions managers need to ask. These are a generic set of questions which direct the Project team to select the appropriate tools for each stage of the project:

1. Which value stream are you supporting and who is the recipient of the value, i.e., who is the customer? Who is the value stream owner and who are the players or team members? How well does the team work together?

2. Within the value stream, which process or processes have the highest priority for improvement? Show me the data that led to this conclusion.

   For the process or processes targeted for improvement,

3. How is the process performed? How does the value flow? What activity is value added and what is non-value added?

4. What are the process performance measures, i.e., how will we gauge if a process is improving? Why did we choose those? How accurate and precise is the measurement system? Show me the data.

5. What are the customer-driven requirements or specifications for all of the performance measures? Are the process performance measures in control and how capable is the process? Show me the data. What are the improvement goals for the value stream or process performance measures?

6. What kinds of waste and cost of poor quality exist in the value stream or process and what is the financial and/or customer impact? Show me the data.

7. What are all the sources of variability in the value stream or process and which of those do we control? How do we control them and what is our method of documenting and maintaining this control? Show me the data.

8. Are any sources of waste or variability supplier-dependent? If so, what are they, who are the suppliers, and how are we working together to eliminate waste and variability? Show me the data.

9. What are the key input variables that affect the average and standard deviation of the measures of performance? How do you know this? Show me the data.

10. What are the relationships between the measures of performance and the key input variables? Do any of the key input variables interact? How do you know for sure? Show me the data.

11. What settings or values for the key input variables will optimize the measures of performance? How do you know this? Show me the data.

12. For the optimal settings of the key input variables, what kind of variability still exists in the performance measures? How do you know? Show me the data.

13. Have we implemented a process flow and control system to sustain the gains and continuously improve the process? Show me the data.

14. How much improvement has the value stream or process shown in the past six months? How much time and/or money have our efforts saved the company? Show me the data.

Further Reading:

Stephen R. Schmidt, Mark J. Kiemele, Ronald J. Berdine, *Knowledge Based Management*. Air Academy Press & Associates, Colorado Springs, 1996.

Dana Ginn, Evelyn Varner, *The Design For Six Sigma Memory Jogger*. Goal/QPC Salem, NH, 2004.

PDCA

The Deming Cycle is a universal improvement methodology. The original is PDCA (Plan, Do Check, Act) but there are many variations some with catchy acronyms like DRIVE (Define, Review, Investigate, Verify, Execute). PDCA is the underlying concept of very many concepts in this book.

PDCA and SDCA

Deming originally called the PDCA cycle "the Shewart Cycle" after his mentor and father of statistical quality control, but the cycle has come to be named after Deming himself. PDCA sounds simple and is easily glossed over, but if well done is a powerhouse for improvement. PDCA is considered a foundation of the Toyota Production System. In the West many organisations are apt to just "do" and neglect the P-C-A. Incidentally, Kurt Lewin's ideas on Force Field Analysis (see separate section) and "unfreezing, changing, refreezing" is a variation of PDCA.

Plan. Plan is not just about planning what to do, but about communication, "scoping", discussion, consensus gaining and deployment. Begin with the customer - seek to understand their requirements. It is about setting the time plan. It is claimed that leading Japanese companies take much longer to plan, but then implement far faster and more smoothly. Deming taught that one should think about change and improvement like a scientific experiment – predicting, setting up a hypothesis, observing, and explaining deviations. You need to be clear what the goals are, and how to get there. Attempt to identify constraints beforehand, so force field analysis is a good idea. Try to identify root causes - at least ask the 5 whys. You may have to do some training before proceeding.

Do. An easy stage if you have planned well. It is about carrying out the improvement, often in a test phase.

Check. The learning stage, but too frequently an opportunity lost. Is it working as you predicted? Did it work out as planned? If not, why not, and what can we learn for next time? The US Marines call this "after action review" or AAR. Time needs to be set aside to Check. Like at the end of a meeting, or after completion of a set number of cycles. Keki Bhote refers to B vs. C (Better vs. Current) analysis. This is to see if the improvement is sustained or as a result of the "Hawthorne effect' which ceases when observation ceases. Six Sigma black belts would check the statistical significance – assessing the alpha and beta risks (accepting what should have been rejected, and vice versa). Once again ask about root causes. Also check if there are any outstanding issues.

Act (or Standardise). As Juran says, "Hold the gains". A standard reflects the current best and safest known way, but is not fixed in stone forever. Without this step all previous steps are wasted. So, a vital, but frequently neglected, step. Think about improvement as moving from standard to improved standard. A deviation from standard procedures indicates that something is amiss. (See the section on standardisation). Consider if the new way can be incorporated elsewhere. Communicate the requirements to everyone concerned - this includes people on the boundary of the problem. Give some thought to recurrence prevention - can both the

people and the processes be made more capable? Finally prepare for the next round of the cycle by identifying any necessary further improvements. And don't forget to celebrate and congratulate if gains have been achieved.

The SDCA or standardise, do, check, act emphasises stability. If variability is excessive it is difficult to distinguish between real improvement and chance variation. In this case, stabilise first before planning. (But see also Special and Common causes).

PDCA

Plan	Determine customer needs Identify the concern or problem Set objectives Set out the working plan Collect data and study Seek root causes Train as necessary
Do	Implement the improvement

Check	Were the objectives met?
	Review root causes
	Confirm the results "B vs C" analysis
	       (consider alpha and beta risks)
	After Action Review
	      what was learned?
	      what can be done better next time?
	Is the problem completely solved?

Act	Identify further improvements Write and adopt new standards Communicate the requirements Recurrence prevention Celebrate and congratulate

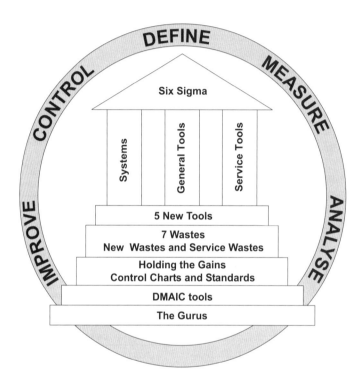

DMAIC Cycle Tools: DEFINE

Project Charter
SIPOC
Voice of the Customer
Project Planning

Define

Project Charter

A crucial element of the Define stage is the Project Charter. This is the contract between the organisation's management and the project team. The purpose of the Charter is to:

- establish the current state, whether it is a problem or an improvement opportunity (project boundary).
- clarify the expectation of the team and goal of the project (what does success look like?
- keep the team aligned with the business objectives.
- state what is the process to be investigated?
- transfer the project from the Champion to the team.
- Track project progress against target, DMAIC methodology and Six Sigma tools.
- Demand Champion involvement; the D-M-A-I-C phases requiring review and agreement before advancement.

For a successful conclusion, it is necessary for the project Champion and Sponsor (if different) to be stakeholders in the process. Therefore, the expectations of the project must be shared and agreed at the outset.

There are many designs of project charters within the Six Sigma umbrella, but there is widespread agreement that there should be a charter, that is understood by the project team and which contains the points above and other important information such as project boundaries, targets and milestones within the DMAIC framework.

The Problem statement needs to cover the justification for the work to follow. The statement should be built around validation of the assumptions made (and initial data) and communicated within the team. The scope of the project should neither be too narrow nor too broad, and a baseline of performance should be established which can be used for future performance comparisons.

It is necessary that project metrics are translated into financial impact and this requires the involvement of the Finance department. This will also help support the project results and dispel the criticism that the project has just played with numbers.

It is common for the Project Charter to evolve during the project life. This does not mean that the first edition is a rough-cut, but that as data is collected and assumptions are more clearly understood, then new information (process knowledge) may require the Charter to be changed accordingly. It is important that changes are first discussed then agreed with all stakeholders, particularly the project champion and sponsor.

Although the Charter contains target milestones and deadlines, just listing these alone will not provide sufficient rigour to succeed. A reporting structure is necessary to maintain dialogue and report progress. An example of a more rigorous Charter template is shown in Fig Project Charter on page 15. This Charter is also used to track the project in detail. A Charter is particularly effective when used on a Training Programme for the Project Manager (Black Belt or Green Belt). Project Managers are required to present to their class colleagues their project progress and the Charter is a pre-requisite opening slide during weeks 2, 3 and 4 of the training. (It would be even more effective to produce this charter pre-training.) The Charter template shown requires tools to be ticked off as they are used, and these tools are then recorded in the Project's Process Notebook.

The SIPOC Diagram

The next tool to be used in the Define stage of DMAIC is the SIPOC diagram.

SIPOC is a Six Sigma term which simply stands for:

Suppliers
Inputs
Process
Outputs
Customer

and is a high-level process map. This tool is a particularly effective communication tool which ensures that the project team share the same understanding of the process and project boundaries. It is useful when presenting the project 'at-a-glance'. The customer will define if the quality of the output is desirable, and the process inputs and process variables are the key to achieving this.

The 'Process' box should not have more than 10 steps at this stage (5 to 7 is typical). Detailed mapping will follow. The sequence for populating the SIPOC diagram is to begin with the Process, and then work from right to left (Customer, Outputs, Inputs and Suppliers). It can be a difficult task to know where to stop adding the detail, and what appears to be a simple task can prove quite troublesome until practised a number of times.

When complete, the SIPOC provides a useful framework, displaying cross functional activities in a simple diagram and maintaining a big picture perspective.

Voice Of the Customer (VOC)

Once a SIPOC diagram has been completed, the process is ready to move on to the Voice Of the Customer (VOC). The VOC is vital for a company to know what products or services to offer and who to sell them to. It is necessary to determine what the customer perceives as good quality and how this requirement is translated into process Critical To Quality (CTQ) characteristics.

The SIPOC lists the process outputs and the customers, but it is necessary to have a greater

understanding of the VOC. A solid starting point for creating a VOC plan is to use Rudyard Kipling's six serving men: (See under General Tools).

Who	are the customers?
What	do they want?
Why	do they want it?
Where	do they want it?
When	do they want it?
How	do they want it?

It is important to list both internal customers and external customers, and establish potential market segments. The affinity diagram can be a useful addition to the VOC roadmap at this point. (See the section in the 'New Tools').

Data Collection
To answer the six questions above, it may be necessary to collect both proactive data (from sampling the population by surveys, observations and interviews) and reactive data (customer feedback, complaints, warranty claims). When collecting proactive data, it is important not to fall into the trap of asking questions which will inevitably deliver a rating of above 90% customer satisfaction. A satisfied customer does not directly lead to repeat business. Proactive data collection plans need to unearth what the customer really values. See Customer Survey section.

"Once you embrace unpleasant news not as a negative but as evidence of a need for change, you aren't defeated by it. You're learning from it." (Bill Gates)

It is worth noting that customer requirements change constantly and what is valued today may not be valued tomorrow. If one considers a the design of a motor car; it is unlikely that such a design would have been acceptable to the market 20 years ago.

The Kano Model
To categorise one's understanding of customer requirements, Dr Noriaki Kano's contribution of basic, performance and delighter factors is useful.

See the reference to KANO in the Quality Gurus.

CTQ Tree

Once a clear understanding of the customer requirements has been established, how are these requirements translated into specific metrics which a process can be measured against?

If a motor car driver wants a smooth gear change, how is the characteristic 'smooth' translated into manufacturing tolerances? If a customer wants a quote for insurance, how is 'good service' translated to Call Centre performance? The CTQ Tree (Critical To Quality) is a tool whose construction facilitates such a translation. It allows the project team to move from high level customer requirements to detailed specifications. This is done by converting high level requirements to Drivers and then further converting Drivers into CTQ characteristics. Caution: when designing specifications, consider Taguchi's Loss Function. It is not always the case that a product is acceptable on one side of the specification limits and unacceptable on the other side.

Call Centre Example

When occasions arise in which it is a complicated process to match operating characteristics to the customer requirements, then the Quality Function Deployment (QFD) approach may be appropriate.

Refer to the section on QFD

Critical Path Analysis

Of course, project management is not unique to Quality Management, but without good project management the implementation of Total Quality or Six Sigma is impossible.

Critical Path Analysis (CPA) is a long established tool for project management. Project Management is a vital part of any quality implementation and is often fairly poorly managed. CPA is useful to schedule resource usage in any environment. Today there is abundant inexpensive software for CPA and its extensions, and you should seldom need to calculate a network. But be warned: DO NOT get carried away by sophisticated software; most features will not be required. And DO use the Contingency Chart in conjunction with CPA.

CPA aims at establishing the time needed for a project, what the critical activities are, and what the expected start and finish times are for each activity. It uses a network of arrows or nodes to establish the logical order of activities. The real value of CPA is in drawing the network, not in the subsequent calculations.

CRITICAL PATH ANALYSIS (CPA)

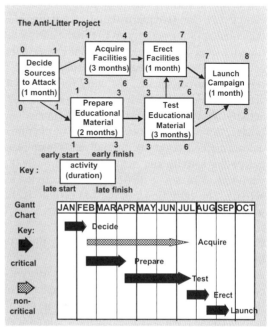

(The method to be described below is known as "activity on node". This is becoming the standard. An older alternative is known as "activity on arrow". In the latter case "dummy" activities are sometimes required. Detail is to be found in numerous textbooks, if you require it.)

Begin by listing all the activities (verb plus noun) that are necessary for the project. Try to keep these at a high level; you can add sub-networks later. Post-it stickers are a good idea for flexibility. Each activity should have an estimated time. Put each activity in a square. Then arrange the activities into logical order by connecting them up with arrows. The rule is : no activity can start before its predecessor activity is complete. If activities can run in parallel do not arrange them in sequence. There should be one start activity and one end activity and no circular loops. Recall that getting the network right (i.e. thinking through the project in advance) is the major benefit. Use a team if possible.

To calculate times, a CPA network requires a "forward pass" and a "backward pass"; both are simple. Begin the forward pass at time 0. This is the "early start" time for the first activity. "Early start" is the earliest time that an activity can start; "early finish" is the earliest time that an activity can be completed by, and is equal to the early start time plus the duration of the activity. Write in the early start time of each activity on the top left hand corner of the activity square, and the early finish time on the top right hand of the square. The early finish of each activity becomes the early start time of the next activity. Where there are two or more immediate predecessor activities, take the greater of the finish dates of the predecessors because all must be complete before the activity can begin. Move through the whole network doing this calculation activity by activity. The early finish of the last activity is the minimum project duration.

Now begin the backward pass. The early finish of the last activity will also be the "late finish" of that activity ("late finish" is the latest time that an activity can finish by whilst not delaying the completion of the entire project. "late start" is the latest time that an activity can start without delaying the whole project.

Write in the late finish on the bottom right hand of each activity square, and the late start on the bottom left of the activity square.) Begin with the late finish time for the last activity. The late start for each activity equals the late finish minus the duration. Now move backwards through the network. The late start of an activity becomes the late finish of its predecessor activity in all cases except where there are two or more immediate subsequent activities. In this case take the smaller of late start dates of the immediate subsequent activities as the late finish for the activity. (Since there are several subsequent activities it is the earliest of the late starts that will govern). At the end of the backward pass you should end with a late start time for the first activity of zero; if not you have made a mistake.

You have now established, for each activity, the "early start". "early finish", "late start", and "late finish". The "slack" or additional free time for each activity equals (late finish - early finish) or (late start - early start). These should give the same result. Some activities, forming a continuous path through the network, will have zero slack. This is the critical path. Any delay along the critical path will delay the whole project; it follows that these are the activities to monitor most closely.

To aid communication, it is a good idea to show the planned early start, early finish and late finish dates on a Gantt chart for each activity.

Gantt Chart

The Gantt chart is a simple bar chart used to time table activities. This can be a most useful visual management tool, particularly if colour coded to illustrate progress.

	April	May	June	July	August
Define					
Measure					
Analyse					
Improve					
Control					

The Gantt chart suffers from its inability to show interrelationships between various activities. It is not possible to see from a Gantt that activity 1 must be completed before activity 2 is able to commence, or to see the bottleneck of a project.

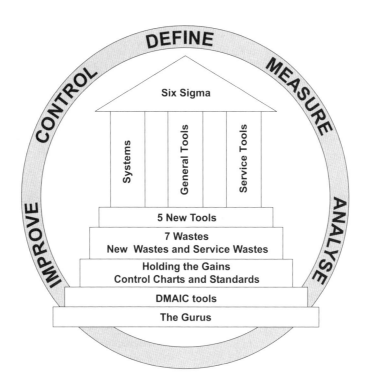

DMAIC Cycle Tools: MEASURE

Data Representation
Measured of Central Tendency and Variation
Sampling
Measurement Systems Analysis and Guage R&R
The 7 Tools of Quality
Sigma Detailed Mapping
Cause & Effect Matrix
Statistical Process Control
Process Capability

Data Representation

Radar Charts

Also known as a web chart or a glyph chart, this type of chart is useful for the display of several performance indicators simultaneously. Deterioration in performance and relative speed of moving towards a goal is easily seen. Some companies display these charts prominently for all employees to see. In a radar chart, the target is at the centre, and the starting position shown near the circumference. Measures are plotted on lines joining the circumference to the centre: the closer to the centre, the better. At Unipart UK these charts are known as "Ten D to Zero" meaning that the target is zero (perfection, at the bullseye) and the starting point is 10.

In the majority of cases, however, the target is the outer circumstamce and the further away from the 'bull' the better.

To draw a radar chart:
1. Decide on the number of measures to be charted. Split these into two groups: those where more is better and those where less is better. These two types of measures are shown above and below the centreline. Further grouping may be desired; for instance, all quality measures together, and all people measures together.
2. Decide the targets, and the present positions of each of the measures. The target values should be shown at the centre. Choose a suitable scale for each measure, with the present situation shown some two-thirds along each line.
3. Arrange the spacing of the measure arms to be uniformly spread. (The angle between measures should be 360 degrees divided by the number of measures in each group + 1).
4. Plot the current status of the measures at regular intervals. Join the plots to form the web.

A sample chart is shown in the figure.

Radar Chart

Chart shows good progress on new customers, poor on customer retention and satisfaction.

Box and Whisker Diagrams, and Numbered Histograms

Variability is important in quality. To quote Ishikawa, "data without variability is false data". Deming agrees, claiming that most managers have very poor understanding of variation and make poor decisions as a result. So this section gives some practical easy ways to show variation.

Box and Whisker

The box shows the limits of half the sample readings.
The whiskers show the extent of the range.

bearing diameter

Sample A is skewed
Sample B has long tails

A   B   C

Box and whisker diagrams are a clear way to show variation on a control chart. Say you have taken a sample of 20 readings. Arrange the readings in ascending order. The box shows the range of the middle 10 readings, and the whiskers show the range of all 20 readings. In other words, the box shows the limits of the first and third quartiles, and the whiskers the minimum and maximum values. Within the box, a line is drawn to indicate the median (i.e. the middle value in a set of readings arranged from lowest to highest). (Where the sample is large, the whiskers may show the extent of 97.5% of the readings, with individual readings beyond this range shown as dots.) Such diagrams are an instant way to appreciate the spread of data; particularly where the data is skewed (i.e. not evenly spread around the median value).

The numbered histogram uses the actual readings to fill in the bars of the histogram. In this way, a reader can get the actual numbers if she wishes or merely gain an overall impression from the bars.

Examples are shown in the figure.

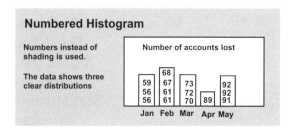

Numbered Histogram

Numbers instead of shading is used.

The data shows three clear distributions

Number of accounts lost

Jan	Feb	Mar	Apr	May
59 56 56	68 67 61 61	73 72 70	89	92 92 91

Manhattan Diagrams

Manhattan Diagrams are a form of stacked bar chart. These can be a very efficient way of showing trends within trends and multiple-dimension quality data.

Take a cricket example. Hour by hour the stacked chart shows total runs made and who was responsible for the runs. Alternatively the bowler responsible for the runs. In a hotel or a plant, total defects for the week are shown by the overall length of bar, and the categories of defect or complaint shown within the bar.

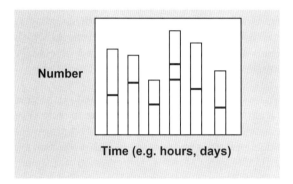

Measures of Central Tendency and Variation

Central Tendency

There are three common measures of central tendency:

- **Mean:** Arithmetic average of a set of values
  — Reflects the influence of all values
  — Strongly Influenced by extreme values
  The most frequently used measure of central tendency, but fraught with dangers. Typically the average calculation does not exist in any of the sample points (average household = 1.2 cars). Beware the flaw of averages (and drowning in a river of average depth 1m)!

- **Median:** Reflects the 50% rank - the centre number after a set of numbers has been sorted from low to high.
  — Does not include all values in calculation
  — Is "robust" to extreme scores
  Often used by political parties and national surveys for statistics such as salaries.

- **Mode:** Most frequently occurring value in a data set. In a histogram this is the largest bar on the chart. Often applied by retail surveys as manufacturers consider the most popular numbers (e.g. prams are made for one baby, fewer for two. There would be little use for a pram built for 0.8 of a baby.)

Variation

There are three common measures of variation:

- The **Range** is the distance between the extreme values of a data set. (Highest - Lowest). This can be very useful, especially when the characteristic under consideration is a minimum or maximum.

- The **Variance** (σ^2) is the Average Squared Deviation of each data point from the Mean. This has a particularly useful mathematical quality that allows components of variation to be added.

- The **Standard Deviation** (σ) is the Square Root of the Variance. This is the most commonly applied measure of variation and takes into account all data points and their distance from the mean.

$$\text{Sample Standard Deviation} \quad s = \sqrt{\frac{\sum_{i=1}^{n} (x_i - \overline{x})^2}{n-1}}$$

When describing a data set, it is necessary to understand both the central tendency and the variation. The graphical representation of the distribution is often the preferred method to describe a data set, but when using numbers only, it is a mistake not to include a measure of the variation. This issue has great relevance to forecasting as events such as customer purchasing patterns rarely occur at an average rate.

Sampling

Sampling is the process by which we select units from a population of interest so that by studying the sample we are able to draw conclusions about the population from which the sample is drawn. Although we have met the words 'sample' and 'population' in other sections of this book, they were not defined. Here are the definitions:

A population is the whole set of measurements or counts about which we want to draw a conclusion. For example this could be a physical parameter of a product, or the level of quality delivered by a service.

A sample is a subset of a population, a quantity of the measurements or counts that comprise the population.

It is apparent that the advantages of sampling can be numerous, as in most instances it is either impractical or even impossible to capture information from an entire population. Sampling can therefore save time, effort and cost and still provide us with the opportunity to draw useful conclusions about the population, provided that we use an appropriate sampling method and sample size.

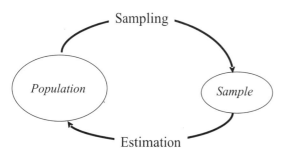

There are many methods available for selecting a sample and they can be broadly categorised into two different types, probability sampling and non-probability sampling. The difference between the two is that non-probability sampling does not involve random selection and probability sampling does.

The following are the most common probability sampling methods:

Simple random sampling
Systematic random sampling
Stratified sampling

A *simple random* sample is defined as one for which each measurement or count in the population has the same chance or probability of being selected. As the name suggests it is technically the easiest method for sampling, but as it requires that we can identify all the objects that comprise the entire population it can sometimes be impractical or expensive to implement, especially in manufacturing processes. Assuming that we can meet those criteria, the sample is chosen using some method such as random number tables or a computer generated random number generator, which ensures equal probability. A common error to be avoided when employing random sampling is basing the selection on a regular time interval, which leads to biasing of the sample and potentially misleading information.

Systematic sampling may be used to reduce the time taken in the actual selecting of the sample. For example, a quality engineer in a manufacturing plant might perform a check on every 50th product on the assembly line. The risk with this method of sampling is that if there is some underlying periodicity in the population, which coincides in some way with the sampling interval, the possible samples may not be representative of the population.

Stratified sampling may be used where it is known that the population is divided into mutually exclusive groups or strata, and then independent samples are selected from each stratum. If this is the case then each stratum effectively becomes an independent population and you will need to decide both the sample size and sample method for each. The sampling method can vary from one stratum to the next and it should be understood that they might have very different distributions for the variable of interest.

The advantage of stratified sampling over simple random sampling is the potential efficiency gain in the number of samples required to gain an accurate estimation of a population variable. For example, if we wanted to get an accurate estimate of the average salary for a given population the most efficient way would be to stratify the subject population by occupation. Then we would only need to select a small sample from each stratum to get a precise estimate for salary within that stratum. These results could be combined to give us an accurate overall picture. If you were to use a simple random sampling strategy in the whole population, without stratification, the sample would need to be much larger than the sum of all the stratum samples. This is to allow for the higher level of variation found within the whole population.

When trying to gain information about the performance of any given process, estimations based on data from sampling is often the only real way of doing so. Careful consideration should therefore be given to the sampling strategy to ensure the accuracy of this information. Remember you may be making potentially costly decisions based on the inferences you draw!

Measurement System Analysis and Gauge R&R

In any process there will be a degree of variability in the actual product or service, but also variability in the way the measurement is taken. There are many sports which involve judges who score the same performance differently e.g. ice skating, gymnastics, boxing. There are also examples when dealing with attribute data where the outcome is not always perceived in the same way e.g. distinguishing Coke from Pepsi.

Variability in measurement is typically present in every process and the variability manifests itself in a number of ways. The aim of Measurement System Analysis (MSA) is to firstly quantify and secondly to reduce the level of variability which exists in the measurement system.

Variable Data
Why is it important to quantify and reduce variability in measurement systems? The following figure shows two distributions:

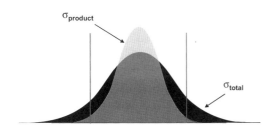

The light shaded area is the distribution illustrating the actual product or service variability, the larger, black distribution represents the combination of actual variation and measurement system variation. The black tails beyond the specification limits represents the proportion of product deemed to be defective, where in fact only the light shaded area is actually defective. This suggests products having acceptable quality characteristics will be rejected, leading to unnecessary costs in rework or scrap. The opposite scenario is also possible where out of tolerance products are deemed in-tolerance. This depends on the bias to either falsely accept or falsely reject products.

Repeatability - the variation in measurements obtained with the same measurement instrument when used several times by one operator while measuring the identical characteristic on the same part.

Reproducibility - the variation in the average of the measurements made by different operators using the same measuring instrument when measuring the identical characteristic on the same part.

There are two key ratios used in MSA:

The Precision–to-total ratio (also referred to as %Gauge R&R) and the Precision-to-tolerance Capability Ration (CR).

Precision-to-total ratio = $\sigma_{measurement}$ / σ_{total}

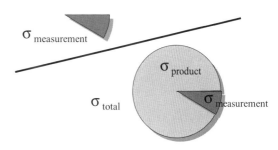

Precision-to-tolerance ratio = $6 \times \sigma_{measurement}$ / tolerance

The relationship between total, product and measurement variation is given by:

$$\sigma^2_{total} = \sigma^2_{product} + \sigma^2_{measurement}$$

and the variability in the measurement system itself can be partitioned into:

$$\sigma^2_{measurement} = \sigma^2 \text{repeatability} + \sigma^2 \text{reproducibility}$$

The rule of thumb for both these ratios is that under 10% is adequate, above 30% is unacceptable and between the two is referred to as the grey area. (Note, if the precision-to-tolerance is below 10%, the precision-to-total is not as important).

It is usual when conducting a MSA with variable data that the true measurement of the product is unknown. For this reason, the accuracy of the system is not measured but the precision of the system is the characteristic of interest. Variability in the system may show itself in a number of ways:

- Repeatability
- Reproducibility
- Stability
- Resolution
- Linearity
- Calibration

MSA is concerned with the measurement system repeatability and reproducibility, hence the term Gauge Repeatability & Reproducibility (R&R).

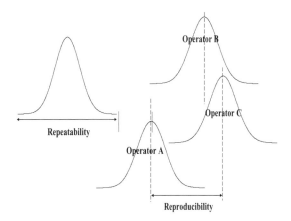

It may be desirable to understand where the measurement error priority is. Statistical software packages such as Minitab are useful additions to the quality management team in pinpointing the source of measurement error and determining an effective course of action.

The Minitab Gauge R&R 'Six Pack' is illustrated in the next column. Together, these allow a comprehensive analysis of the measurement system.

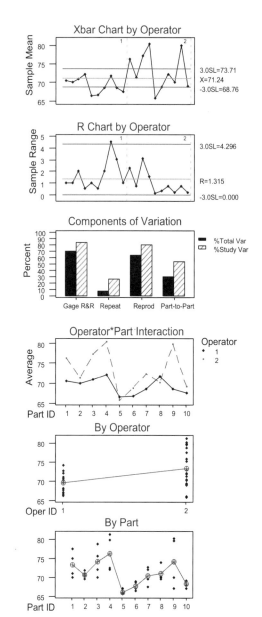

How to conduct a Gauge R&R Study

- Generally 2 to 3 'operators' (people who measure)
- Generally 10 units to measure
- Each unit is measured 2-3 times by each operator
- 'Blindness' is extremely desirable. It is better that the operator not know that the part being measured is a part of a special test. At a minimum they should not know which of the test parts they are currently measuring.

Attribute Data

Unlike dealing with variable data, it is more common to have a known true state for an Attribute Gauge R&R Study. This condition may exist when gauging a product to be defective or non-defective (e.g. the surface quality of a television or motor car), or identifying some other known characteristic (e.g. from which company did the cola drink come from?).

There are alternative Attribute Gauge R&R templates, which may or may not include the condition of knowing the 'true state'. If the true state can be determined with relative ease and small cost, then there are benefits in determining whether operators have a bias towards falsely accepting or falsely rejecting products. It depends on the consequence of out-of-tolerance products reaching the market place as to which bias is the more serious.

Part	True State	OP 1		OP 2		OP 3		
1	R	R	1	R	1	R	1	3
2	A	A	1	A	1	A	1	3
3	A	A	1	R	0	A	1	2
4	R	R	1	R	1	R	1	3
5	A	R	0	A	1	R	0	1
6	R	R	1	A	0	R	1	2
7	R	R	1	R	1	R	1	3
8	A	A	1	A	1	A	1	3
9	A	A	1	A	1	A	1	3
10	R	R	0	R	0	A	1	1
11	R	A	0	R	1	R	1	2
12	A	A	1	A	1	A	1	3
13	R	R	1	R	1	R	1	3
14	R	R	1	A	0	R	1	2
15	R	R	0	A	1	A	1	2
16	R	A	0	R	1	R	1	2
17	A	A	1	A	1	R	0	2
18	A	A	1	A	1	A	1	3
19	R	R	1	A	0	R	1	2
20	R	R	1	R	1	R	1	3
			15		15		18	48

Result Summary

R = Reject
A = Accept
1 = correct response
0 = incorrect response

True State		
A	**R**	
3	2	Op 1
2	3	Op 2
2		Op 3
rejected falsely	accepted falsely	

Results Table

The figure shows a template for a preferred Attribute Guage R&R study. To understand how the Result Summary table has been constructed, consider the Op 1 line which shows 3 in the A column and 2 in the R column. The Op 1 column in the Results Table shows five x 0 entries. This means five incorrect responses have been made, of which 3 are falsely rejected (true state being A) and 2 falsely accepted (true state being R).

The effectiveness of the measurement system can be calculated by dividing the number of parts identified correctly by the total number of opportunities to be correct. Further analysis can be made into whether there is greater probability of an operator falsely accepting or rejecting a product. Falsely rejecting will result in increased rework and internal COPQ. Falsely accepting will result in defective products reaching the market place. The seriousness of each will depend on the effects of the consequences. This analys will illustrate which bias, if any, each operator has.

The "7 Tools" of Quality

The seven tools of quality were originally assembled by Kaoru Ishikawa for use with quality circles. The seven tools, when used together or even individually, are a "first line" attacking force for quality improvement. Today they are regarded as the basic Six Sigma tools relevant to several DMAIC stages. They are taught to a large proportion of operators in Japan and are now increasingly used by operators worldwide. Many people in the service industry will find them equally useful. The tools are presented below in the order in which they are commonly used, although many variations are possible. Remember best used as a set in the order given below!

1.) Mapping

There is a whole variety of mapping tools which are used in Process Reengineering, Lean Manufacturing, and Quality Management. Mapping tools often form a hierarchy. Thus, for instance, Seeing the Whole (Womack and Jones) may be used to map an entire value stream end-to-end across several companies, Value Stream Mapping (Rother and Shook) may be used to map a process wall to wall inside a plant, and process mapping may be used to home in the detail of a particular stage. There are mapping tools which are designed around service - The Cycle of

Service, The Service Blueprint, and the Customer Processing Operation. These are described in the Service section of this book. Here we will concentrate on the process map, which forms one of the classic seven tools.

The Process Map

The process map lists every step that is involved in the manufacture of a product or the delivery of a service. It has long been used by work study officers, who usually use special symbols to indicate "operation", "delay", "move", "store", and "inspect". (See figure). The process chart helps identify waste, (or MUDA) and documents the process completely. Good communication is an important reason to do this. The systematic record helps reveal the possible sources of quality and productivity problems.

It is a good idea to draw the process map using the standard symbols because this aids clarity. The chart can be plotted against a time scale if time is critical. Process charts should also be used to document or standardise a process after it has been changed. This Standard Operating Procedure (SOP) can be used for "auditing" the process - to see if it is still being carried out in the way it was designed.

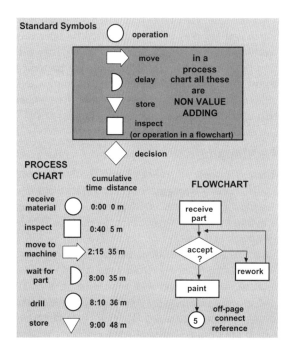

Many companies already have process charts. If they are available, beware! There are often differences between the "official" process charts and the way things actually happen in practice. The team or analyst should take the time to follow through a number of products. "Go to Gemba" (the place of action) and collect the facts; do not sit in the office and collect the opinions or the "normal" situation.

A flowchart is similar to a process chart and is often used when there are decisions involved. The symbol for a decision, a diamond, would lead to branching as a result of different decisions. Flowcharts are often used with computer systems and usually do not include the standard process chart symbols. However there is no reason why these symbols should not be combined.

Once the chart is assembled the individual activities can be classified into those which add value (often a very small proportion), those which are pure waste and which should be eliminated as soon as possible, and those which are necessary non value added - necessary in the short term, but candidates for elimination in the long term.

In process reengineering it is common to draw maps left to right with rows ('swim lanes') to demarcate the organisational boundaries. Of course, a process map usually involves activities in several departments.

A process map is an activity and time based representation. Often it is useful to have a spacial diagram to hand as well. This "Spaghetti Diagram" maps the physical movement of operators.

All maps are best assembled using a team approach, preferably using the people who are "front line". By using the charts the team can begin systematically to document the nature of quality problems and defects. This leads onto the next tool.

Note : There is actually a family of process charts that is used by work study officers and industrial engineers. These are less frequently used by other staff, but they may be useful, particularly for productivity improvement. For instance, the "person-machine" process chart lists, against a time scale, what the person is doing side by side with what the machines that he/she is operating are doing. This enables wasteful time gaps to be identified. Details on these more specialized charts can be found in textbooks on Method Study.

Six Sigma Detailed Mapping

The Six Sigma mapping approach differs from the Standard and Lean mapping approaches in a number of ways, although it is possible to combine the approaches. The first difference was the use of the SIPOC diagram mentioned in the Define stage of DMAIC.

The sequence below shows a six-step approach which builds the map into a detailed state which can be revealing and useful when analysing the variables which affect process outputs.

1. Identify the process steps within the project boundaries
2. Identify Output variables and insert above the appropriate step
3. Identify Input variables and add below appropriate step
4. Partition variables into C,N,X categories
5. Add customer specifications
6. Highlight value adding activities

The C,N,X approach is a useful method employed for partitioning input variables. If there are variables that require holding 'constant' to achieve the desired output or reduce variation, these are labelled 'C'. One would expect these to have a Standard Operating Procedure (SOP) which, as an acronym, is used to double up as 'Something On Paper', but with more information being stored electronically. Those variables which are not currently able to be controlled are labelled 'N'.

Finally, those variables which can be changed to various settings are labelled 'X' for experimental purposes. An 'X' may be come a 'C' following an experiment, such as trying an alternative tea bag.

The example below shows the process steps necessary to make a cup of tea. This is a typical representation of a process having undergone stage 1 above.

What seems a fairly straight forward task which many of us carry out without a second thought can be built up into a useful map for understanding the process, its inputs, outputs and current controls. If the six-step process is completed on this example, then the process owner would see improvement opportunities immediately to reduce variation through the introduction of standards (with adherence audits) and failsafe (poka yoke) designs.

Further reading:
Dianne Galloway, *Mapping Work Processes*, ASQ Quality Press, Milwaukee, WI, 1994

Other Mapping Tools
Details of mapping tools more appropriate to plant-wide and supply chain mapping may be found in:
John Bicheno, *The New Lean Toolbox*, PICSIE Books, Buckingham, 2004
Mike Rother and John Shook, *Learning to See*, Lean Enterprise Institute, Brookline, MA, 1998
See also sections on **Cycle of Service and Service Blueprinting**

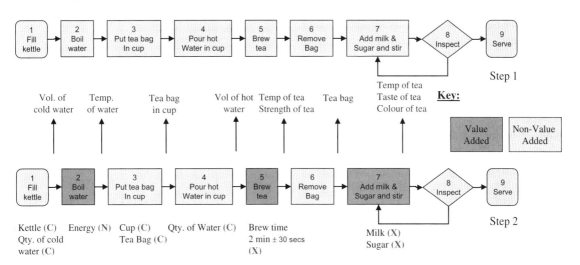

2.) Pareto Analysis

Pareto analysis has been called "the single most powerful management technique of all time" (!). Alternative names are ABC analysis and the "80/20" rule. Pareto analysis gives recognition to the fact that, invariably, a small number of problem types account for a large percentage of the total number of problems that occur. The name "80/20" is representative of this; perhaps 80% of all problems are due to 20% of all the types of problem that occur. (Often 90/10 would be more typical.) The name ABC is also a good one. This suggests that the range of types of problem be classified into A, B, and C categories, designating their importance.

(Pareto analysis is also good practice in many other fields of management; for instance inventory control, forecasting, marketing, and personnel.)

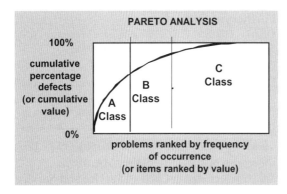

It makes good sense to tackle the most pressing problems first; the "vital few" as Juran calls them. When these are successfully eliminated or reduced, of course, another problem will head the list. So now tackle that one. And so on. Continuing in this way is an effective ongoing improvement methodology.

Pareto analysis begins by ranking problems from highest to lowest. See the example. Along the horizontal axis problems are arranged in order of frequency from highest to lowest. Then the cumulative number of problems is plotted on the vertical axis. It can be seen that the resulting graph rises rapidly then tails off to an almost flat plateau. Now it is easy to pick out how many problems need top priority attention.

Now the team has used the process chart to list and classify the problems, and Pareto analysis to identify the most serious problems. In the next stage the team would begin to explore possible causes and their solution.

3.) The Fishbone Diagram

The Ishikawa diagram, also known as the "Cause and Effect" diagram and the "fishbone" diagram, is used to brainstorm out possible contributing causes of a particular problem or defect. In this respect it follows directly from the Pareto diagram, with the most pressing problem becoming the spine of the "fish". An example is shown in the figure. The name of "fishbone" is clearly representative of the form.

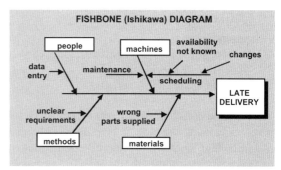

As can be seen, contributing causes are written in on the diagram, arranged in a hierarchy. Hence the name "cause and effect". If some difficulty is experienced in starting off the diagram, use the "6 M's" (men/people, machines, methods, materials, measures, mother nature) as initial "bones". Other alternatives for service operations are to use the "4 P's" (Places, Procedures, People, Policies), or the "4 S's" (Surroundings, Suppliers, Systems, Skills). Usually the diagram is built with one person writing in points on the diagram and a team contributing their ideas.

The beauty of the Ishikawa diagram is the concise and visual way in which contributing causes can be documented on one diagram. It requires literally seconds of instruction in order for any employee to understand.

A variation on the Ishikawa diagram is the "CEDAC"

diagram, originally developed by Fakuda. CEDAC stands for "cause and effect diagram with addition of cards". It is the same Ishikawa diagram except that cards, containing notes and ideas on each particular cause, are added to the diagram. Usually there are slots made for each cause, giving access to a pocket into which cards are placed. This addition is very useful because it allows elaboration on the thinking. The diagram can be kept on display, and as further information or thoughts are acquired, they are added to the pockets. This prevents "reinventing the wheel". Fakuda has developed the CEDAC concept into a complete improvement methodology.

Now with the range of possible causes identified, it seems a good idea to firm up on the information that is available. This is where the next tool comes in.

Further reading:
Ryuji Fakuda, *Managerial Engineering*, Productivity Press, 1983

Note: See also page 64

4.) The Histogram and Measles Chart

The histogram has much in common with the Pareto diagram. It is used to show graphically the relative number of occurrences of a range of events. Using vertical bars, it plots frequency on the vertical axis against events, arranged one after the other on the horizontal axis. (See the figure.)

Following from the Ishikawa diagram, data is collected and classified according to each of the causes suggested. This data is shown on a histogram, from which the most important causes should be apparent. As with the Pareto diagram, it is then clear which are the causes that require further investigation.

Histograms can be used to collect data literally as it happens. Here a flip chart is set up right at the workstation. As problems occur they are written down on the flipchart. When the same problem recurs, a tick is placed next to that problem. In effect this is building up a histogram. (In this case the histogram is lying on its side, but no matter.) The problems with the most ticks are obviously the most frequently occurring and most urgent

problems. Such a "flipchart histogram" has the great advantages of being easy to use, visible for all, and up to date.

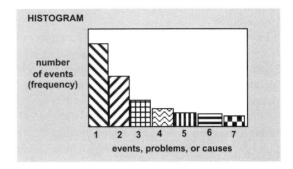

A special form of histogram, with similarities to the flip chart procedure, is the Measles or Concentration chart. Here defects or problems are simply plotted on an engineering drawing, blueprint or map at the location where the problem occurs. The accumulation of marks on the drawing gives an excellent impression as to where the problems lie. It avoids numerical or written description and may lead to the rapid identification of related problems. (A symmetry of the defects may indicate a process problem, but a lack of symmetry may indicate a maintenance or wear problem.) Of course, there are extensions of this technique - times can be written in, or different symbols used for different operators. Measles charts are also used for accident "black spots", and at Ford to indicate which areas are generating the most ideas for improvement. Juran tells the story of how such charts were used to assess damage on WWII bombers raiding Germany. Damage holes were uniformly spread except in some areas. Why? Because hits in those areas proved fatal. This lead to extra armour in those areas, resulting in a reduction in bombers shot down.

5.) Run and Multi-vari Diagrams

Run diagrams and correlation diagrams are used to explore relationships between events and time, and between problems and possible causes,

The run diagram is simply a graph of the number of events plotted against time. It is truly amazing how many organisations ignore this simple but hugely effective tool. For instance, a record can be kept of the number of complaints over time. This may reveal that complaints occur at the beginning of the month or at a certain time of day. If defects produced on a machine are plotted against time, one may discover that most defects tend to occur when the machine has been used for some time (hot?) or just after the tea-break (carelessness?). A common use for a run chart is to detect slow trends (i.e. a gradual increase or decrease). For this, the charts have to be maintained over a long period.

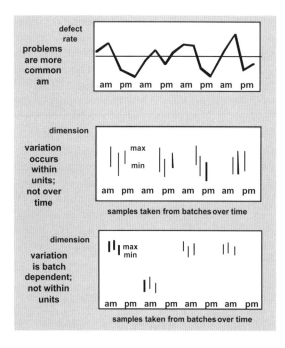

Multi-vari charts extends the run diagram concept to look at variation (a) by time - perhaps by hour, shift, day, week (b) by unit - variation within the same batch or time period and (c) within unit - say operator to operator, machine to machine, or across components within a product

6.) Correlation and Stratification

The correlation diagram is used for more specific experimentation. Usually defect level (or some other measure of performance) is plotted on the vertical axis and the "experimental variable" on the horizontal. An example would be rejects against temperature. (Perhaps as temperature rises rejects fall, but then around a specific temperature rejects begin to increase again.) This could either be found out by a specific experiment involving deliberately varying the temperature, or by simply counting rejects and taking the temperature from time to time in the normal course of operation.

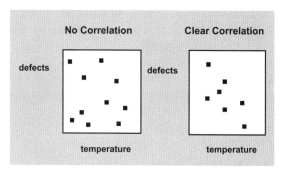

Very often no relationship (or "correlation") is found. So something else has to be tried. Perhaps first temperature, then pressure, then temperature divided by pressure, and so on. (In services, perhaps customer wait time against number of servers, or customer response time against quantity of information displayed on a screen.) Eventually, and with intelligent guesswork, good relationships can be found. This detective work can be a lot of fun, and front line people are often good at it because they have an appreciation of the real factors that make a difference. Normally an attempt is made to hold other factors as constant as possible while one factor at a time is varied.

There is a measure of correlation, called the "correlation coefficient", which can be calculated by formula. This measure is to be found "built in" on many scientific calculators, but is not given here. The reason why it is not given is that it is always preferable to plot the results on graph paper and to judge the relationship visually.

Often both run diagrams and correlation diagrams will be used. First a run diagram is used for more general analysis and to see if time of day or month has an effect. Then follows a correlation study for the specifics. There are other possibilities as well. A common one is the Tally Chart, where, for example, errors are recorded in a matrix which shows operator names along one axis and types of error or time of day along the other axis. This would reveal, perhaps, that different operators are good at different things or have different error-prone periods.

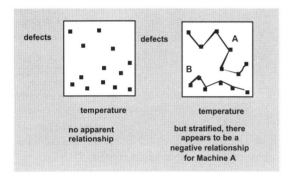

Stratification simply means splitting the data into groups and plotting the results on graphs. For instance, defect data against time may appear to have no particular pattern, but when data for individual operators or machines is plotted the situation may suddenly clarify. Clearly there is often a large number of ways in which data can be separated out; by operator, machine, material, time, batch, product, customer, location are just a few. But once a team knows about stratification they are likely to make good suggestions as to how it can be separated. Of course, this means that care has to be taken in the first place as to how the data is collected. It is a learning process.

Run diagrams, correlation diagrams and stratification have the effect of identifying what are termed "special causes". These are the events or defects which cannot be explained by natural variation of the process. (More on this later.) So having identified and solved some of these problems, it may now be time to set up a more sophisticated control mechanism to bring the process under control and to keep it under control.

7.) Check Sheets and Tally Charts

There are several forms. "Aircraft style" checks would be carried out at the start of every shift or the start of each new batch, as an airline pilot would do before setting out. A process diagram, placed next to the machine or service counter, details what should be done and may advise what action to take in special circumstances.

Yet another variation is the Tally Chart. A typical variation is shown, but other variations include defect type against time, or defect against stage. The latter is sometimes referred to as a "Quality Filter Chart". Costs can also be added.

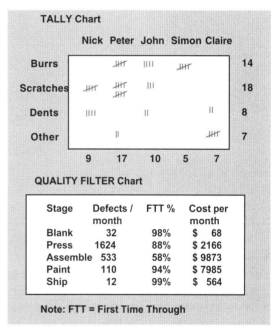

One special form of check sheet, used by Toyota, is related to the "Seven Wastes" and is a sheet containing perhaps 50 questions that ask operators if particular events are taking place. ("Do you have to reach to grasp a control?", "Do you have to take more than two paces to collect parts?".) These are further discussed under the Seven Wastes.

Some Quality Experts regard Standard Operating Procedures (SOPS) as check sheets. SOPS are a vital tool to "hold the gains", but they are not tools for analysis. For this reason they are dealt with in the Control section on page 90.

Cost Impact Analysis

A simple but useful tool to use with all 7 tools is the Cost (or difficulty) Impact Analysis. The matrix is shown below. Its use is obvious. Go for the easy to do "the low hanging fruit" first. The matrix can also be used with any technique that generates several alternatives.

COST IMPACT ANAYLSIS

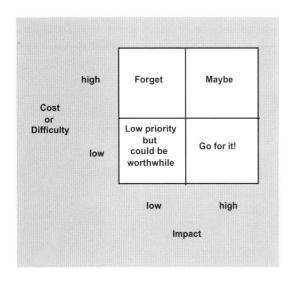

Note: see also Performance Importance Matrix, p119

Cause & Effect Matrix

The Cause & Effect Diagram (Fishbone / Ishikawa) is an important tool in the Six Sigma methodology because it seeks to identify which input variables are having an effect on the output variable.

If there are few input variables for a particular process, then it is not too important in which order the variables are examined. If the process under consideration is large or complex, then a system of prioritising the variables is required. One technique which is effective for this task is the Cause & Effect Matrix.

To construct a Cause & Effect Matrix, the following guidelines have been found useful:

- List the key output variables as the columns.

- Link the output variables to customer requirements. The strength of the relationship is given in the weighting. (10 = relationship cannot be stronger, 1 = little or no strength in the relationship).

- List the key input variables as the rows. The top row is the overall process variable.

- Link input and process variables to output variables: 10 = the input variable has a very strong relationship with output variable.

- Calculate each row on the matrix by multiplying the weighting the input variable by the weighting of the output variable. This process is illustrated in the Figure.

Note:-
This procedure is very similar to that used in QFD. See separate section.

Each row's figures are then added up, and the totals are placed in the right hand column.

These numbers can now be used to decide which input variable or process variable should be investigated further. A logical extension to this process is to apply an FMEA (see FMEA) to the variables which have been identified as of interest. Further analysis of these variables may be necessary by using statistical tools such as hypothesis testing, ANOVA regression analysis and designed experiments.

	Output Variables / Input Variables	Distance (x bar & σ)	Distance from centre	Time constraints	Total
	Weighting	9	9	2	
Process Variable	Catapult set up (x var)	9	1	1	92
Input variable	Position catapult	7	9	5	154
Input variable	Secure	7	5	5	118
Input variable	Achieve angle	9	1	6	102
Input variable	Load ball	6	1	5	73
Input variable	Release (launch)	7	1	3	78
Input variable	Measure output	8	8	7	156

Process Capability

This section will be concerned with the capability of machines to operate within required tolerance limits. However, the concept of capability is wider than just machines. People also need to be capable. Whether we are concerned with machines or people John Oakland points out that we should not be asking, in the first instance, "are we doing the job correctly?", but rather "are we capable of doing the job correctly?". Capability refers to having the clear requirements, appropriate selection of people or machines, adequate training, and adequate measurement.

Being "in control" does not necessarily mean that the process is making good quality products. So there is another requirement. This is referred to as "process capability". Process capability refers to the match between the location of the upper and lower process control limits (UCL and LCL) and the specification limits USL and LSL (also known as tolerance limits UTL and LTL). The location of the process control limits is due to the natural variation of the process that makes the product. The specifications of the product, on the other hand, are given by the designer or manager of the product or service. These are two distinctly separate things, but they must relate in order to produce quality products.

CL= control limit ; TL = tolerance limit

A capability analysis is used to determine how capable a process is of producing a product consistently to the customer requirements. It is the relationship between the Voice Of The Customer (VOC, represented by the upper and lower specification limits) and the Voice Of the Process (VOP, represented by the distribution of process data when only common causes of variation are present). Put another way, it is a measure of how well the process is performing with respect to the output specifications.

A process capability study involves taking periodic samples from the process in a controlled manner and charting the performance characteristics over time.

The primary sources of variation within a typical process are from design, the supply chain and the manufacturing / service process itself. These sources of variation can accumulate and affect the process variation.

A short term study will probably not capture any special cause variation. It may be over a period of minutes, hours or weeks depending on the process cycle time. It should also exclude any other major sources of variation such as machine to machine differences.

A long term study should capture all major sources of variation. Again the period is dependant on the process cycle time.

The Capability measurement statistics include Cp, Cpk, Cm, Pp, Ppk, σ level, σ capability, dpm and dpmo.

Capability analysis should only be used after the process has been verified as being under statistical control. If the process is out of control, the project team must understand that the results from the capability analysis may not be indicative of future performance.

However, it is important to benchmark the process data at an early stage, and this may include measuring the within-subgroup variation.

Within and Overall Standard Deviation
The within-subgroup standard deviation is a measure of the variability within the individual subgroups. This ignores the differences between subgroups. The overall standard deviation measures the variability of the whole data set.

Cp and Cpk are the statistics for measuring capability based on within-subgroup variability. This is also known as Short Term Capability.

Cp is the short term capability potential of a process and assumes the process is centred about its specification limits.

$$Cp = (USL-LSL) / (6x \text{ Std Dev within-subgroups})$$

Cpk is the short term process capability statistic which takes into account the mean value and so is sensitive to process drift.

$$Cpk = \text{lower value of } (USL-mean, mean-LSL) / (3x \text{ Std Dev within-subgroups})$$

In using the above formulae, there are a number of options. The Minitab software offers the user 3 options to estimate short term standard deviation:

1. The average of the sub group ranges
2. The average of the subgroup standard deviations
3. The pooled standard deviation that is the square root of the weighted average of the subgroup variances.

The overall standard deviation is a measure of the total variability and is used in calculating long term capability. The statistics for long term capability are similar to those used for short term capability except that the overall standard deviation is used.

$$Pp = (USL-LSL) / (6x \text{ Std Dev overall})$$

Ppk = lower value of (USL-mean, mean-LSL) / (3x Std Dev overall)

With long term studies, the standard deviation is calculated using the classical formulae.

σ level is the number of std deviations between the centre of the process and the nearest specification limit.

Motorola's σ capability index: 6σ capability = 3.4 dpm.

$$σ \text{ capability} = 0.8406 + sqrt (29.37 - 2.221 \text{ x ln (dpm)})$$

This formula provides the capability chart represented in the opening chapter in this book.

A process that is "six sigma capable" will have the specifications ±6 short-term standard deviations away from the centered process. If a process is in control, it does not necessarily mean that it is a capable process.

Historically, a process with specification limits set on +3 and -3 sigma has been considered capable. As we have seen, the potential capability for such a process is 2,700 defects per million, when the process is centred. Any shift in the process mean will result in a substantial part of the distribution moving outside the specification limit and seriously reducing the yield. A Six Sigma process will have +6 and -6 sigma inside the design width which will deliver a potential yield of 2 defects per billion. Even if this process mean were to shift by 1.5 sigma, the process yield would still be 3.4 defects per million capable. This was Motorola's target with its Six Sigma programme. This would equate to Cp = 2 and Cpk = 1.5 which indicates excellent capability.

Capability Warning
A Motorola 6σ capable process exhibits the same number of defects that a stable and centred 4.5σ level process would exhibit in one tail. So, it can become confusing to know whether a process is actually performing at 4.5σ level (centred) or 6σ capability with a 1.5 σ shift to account for long term process drift. For this reason, some believe it is wise to stay clear of σ level and σ capability and instead utilise the Cp, Cpσ, Pp, Ppk capability statistics.

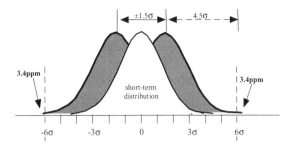

Six Sigma Philosophy of Continuous Improvement

The following four figures demonstrate the Six Sigma philosophy as promoted at Motorola in the 1980s. If we take 80 distances fired by a catapult and examine the capability of the process to perform between the 14 and 15 specification limits, the initial distribution is shown graphically:

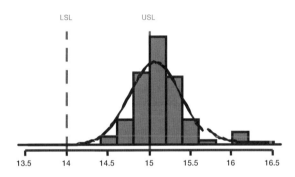

Note that the process is out of control.

The first action is to remove the out of control symptoms:

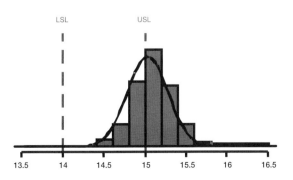

The next action is to centre the process so the actual and potential capability are equal:

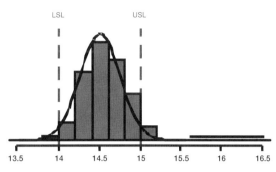

The final, and most difficult stage in this continuous improvement philosophy is to reduce the common cause variation

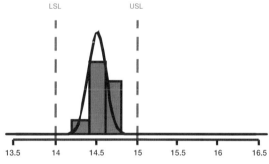

It is this final stage which is often the area of work for Six Sigma Black Belts, and depending on the complexity of the process and the customer specification demands, this is where the more complex tools will be utilised (ANOVA, Multi Vari and DoE).

Statistical Process Control (SPC)

Statistical process control (SPC) aims at achieving good quality during manufacture or service through prevention rather than detection. It is concerned with controlling the process (or machine) which makes the product. If the process is good, then the products will automatically be good. So the process or machine which makes the product is inspected rather than inspecting the product itself. This is really proactive management - inspecting and controlling the process before the event, rather than reactive management - inspecting the product after the event. SPC charts are like the temperature gauge in your car. Things are fine as long as temperature remains in the green zone, but if in the red zone you should stop and investigate.

SPC is not of course the full answer to total quality. A poorly designed product can conform to all manufacturing requirements, but still fail to convince customers that it is a quality product.

Perhaps confusingly at first, the best way to find out what is happening to a process is to take measurements of the products that the process is producing. Of course you do not need to look at every product that is produced. Instead you take samples, and use statistics to judge what is happening to the process. This is why it is called statistical process control. It may seem as if one is inspecting a few of the products coming out of the process, but in fact it is the process that is being inspected and controlled.

SPC is undertaken through the use of charts on which the. performance of the process is plotted. If the process starts to go haywire it can be stopped in good time before many or any defectives are made.

Natural variation of the process

Every process has natural variation. (Refer also to the Measure section). In other words, it is impossible to make any product with absolute consistency. The inconsistency will be caused by chance variations, however small, in, perhaps, the material, tool wear, positioning of the piece, speed of the machine, actions by the operator, and so on. These are called common causes. This variation can be measured and, using statistics, its spread can be predicted. It turns out that the spread follows a particular pattern, known as the normal distribution, irrespective of the type of process, so long as samples are being taken, and there are not "special events" taking place. The special events are "assignable" to unusual or unexpected changes or events, which may cause defects to be produced.

99.7% of normal variation takes place within plus and minus three standard deviations (a standard deviation is a measure of spread, and every normal distribution has this characteristic.) The upper and lower control limits are set at plus and minus three standard deviations. Within this range we say that natural variation is occurring. However if an unusual event or "special cause" takes place, the reading or sample may fall outside of the control limits. Now we would need to stop and investigate. This is just like variation in the temperature gauge in your car. Natural variation occurs when going up a long hill or on a hot day or by hard driving. But the temperature remains in the normal range. If however the fan belt breaks or the coolant leaks, this would soon show up a temperature in the red zone, beyond the "control limit". You stop and investigate. If you do not you are foolish. Likewise you might undertake routine maintenance but it would also be foolish to overreact when the gauge is showing that temperature in within the acceptable zone. So it is important to know where the limits are located.

Control Charts

Control Charts are used to continually monitor the variability of the key performance input variables (those which are sensitive with regards to the process output). The theory behind control charts is based on normal probability and the properties of the Gaussian distribution (named after the German mathematician Karl Frederick Gauss). This distribution is symmetrical around its mean and takes the shape of a bell, to which it is commonly referred.

Three key properties that apply to this normal curve are:

The area under the curve which falls within the boundaries +1 and −1 sigma accounts for approximately 68% of the data within the distribution. Therefore, one can expect 68% all data collected from a normal distribution process to fall within the +1 and −1 sigma boundaries.

The area under the curve bounded by +2 and −2 sigma accounts for approximately 95% of all data within the distribution.

The area under the curve bounded by +3 and –3 sigma accounts for 99.73% of all data within the distribution.

These properties are commonly referred to as: **68 / 95 / 99.73**

Sigma can be calculated using the standard deviation formula, or estimated graphically. One sigma is the distance from the normal distribution's mean to the point to the normal curve's saddle point (point of inflecture) where the shape changes from concave to convex.

These properties of the Normal Distribution are shown in the following figure:

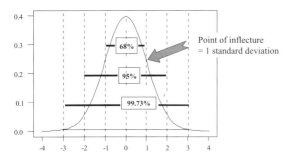

As the distribution shows that 99.73% of all data points lie between the boundaries +3 sigma and – 3 sigma, the probability of a data point being outside these boundaries are 1-0.9973 = 0.0027 (0.27%) when the only causes of variation present in the process are common causes. These boundaries are selected as control limits as they have been found as powerful indicators to guide process operators when to take corrective action and, just as important, when not to. This is the basis for hypothesis testing; demonstrating statistical evidence that a change has occurred and that it is unlikely such an observation would happen by chance. There are 7 conditions for out-of-control used in SPC:

1. One or more points are outside the control limits
2. 7 consecutive points are on the same side of the centre-line
3. 7 consecutive intervals are either increasing or decreasing

4. 2 out of 3 consecutive points are in Zone A or beyond
5. 4 out of 5 consecutive points are in Zone B or beyond
6. 14 consecutive alternate up and down repeatedly
7. 14 consecutive points are in Zone C

The upper and lower control limits are the most commonly used method to indicate when a process is out of statistical control.

If the zones shown in the figure are considered with the super imposed normal distribution curve the 7 conditions can be applied to any set of normal data.

The individual run chart shown in the following example shows 80 distances fired by a catapult.

Statistical software packages can be used to identify out-of-control points and determine which rule has been violated. This example shows three out-of-control points, all in violation of rule 1. (Refer also to the earlier Capabilities section).

Three data points out of control

Types of chart : variables and attributes
There are two main types of chart - variables and attributes. A variables chart measures some characteristic that is variable along a scale, such as length or the number of scratches. It is something that

can be measured. An attribute chart is used where the possibilities are pass or fail, yes or no. With an attribute, a judgement is made rather than a measurement taken.

Selecting the Right Control Chart

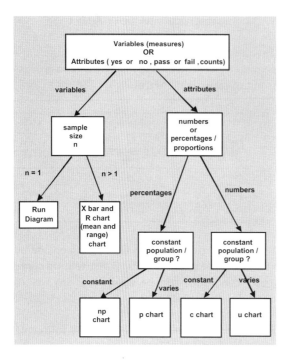

Variables charts : The average and range chart

The main variables chart is the "average and range" chart, also known as the "x bar and r chart". This is actually two charts, one which tracks the average measurement of the sample taken, and the other the range of the sample, that is the maximum minus the minimum value. Both are necessary. For instance the average of a sample of five may be fine, but the range could be unacceptably wide. And the range could be small, but located in the wrong place; that is it has an undesirable average. So typically, at random intervals throughout the day, the operator will take, say, the five most recent products produced and set them aside. This is a "sample". The particular product dimension is measured and the average and range values of the sample calculated. These two results are plotted on the chart, usually by the process operator. The chart indicates if the process is "in control". If it is, work continues. If not, work stops

and investigation begins. Note that it is possible to be out of control and still not be producing defects, and vice versa.

Refer to the figure. Notice that both the average and the range charts have an upper and a lower "control limit". These limits are the bounds beyond which the process is considered "out of control". (See last section).

Setting up the control chart

Charts must be set up for each process - that is for each machine making a particular type of product. (Pre-printed SPC charts are available from some Quality societies or in books, and these make data entry and chart plotting very easy.) When setting up a chart it is important that there is consistency, so samples should be taken over a representative period of time. You will need to decide on a sample size and the number of samples. Typical numbers are a sample size of 5 and at least 20 samples. For each sample calculate the average ("mean") and the range. Refer to the figure. Then calculate the average of the averages, and the average of the ranges. Now you will need to look up the control limit factors for the sample size you have used. (If you have used a sample size of 5, the factors are given in the figure.) Now use the formulas in the figure to calculate the control limits. When these are drawn in you can begin to use the charts for control purposes. You will have to decide a reasonable average interval for samples to be taken. Generally, the higher the "Cpk" value, the less frequent does the sampling have to be. (See the earlier section on capability.)

Attribute charts : p, c and u charts

It is not always possible to measure variables. Some defects, such as scratches, tears, and holes are either there or they are not. The products either pass or they do not. This is where "p" (percentage) and "c" charts come in. p Charts are used where there are batches of product and the percentage that are defective can be determined.

SPC FORMULAS

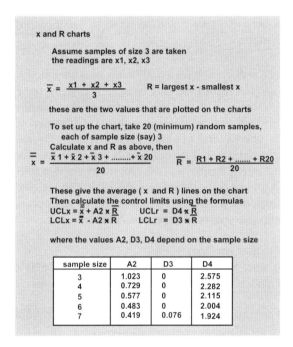

With attributes there is only one chart that is plotted, not two as with the average and range chart. But the basic concepts of controlling variation, of taking samples, of setting up the charts, and of interpreting them remain. Only the formulas are different.

A "c" chart is used to monitor the <u>number</u> of nonconformities per product. Examples are the number of complaints per period, the number of scratches per table top, or the number of errors per processed document. In such cases a percentage figure is less meaningful, so a P chart cannot be used. "c" charts are particularly useful in service situations and are instantly usable because the formula is so easy to remember.

To use a c chart, the number of units sampled should be approximately the same. The control limits for a c chart are at :

$$c +/- 3\sqrt{c}$$

where c is the average value per sample. So if the average number of scratches per sample of 10 tables is 16, then the control limits are at $(16 + 3 \times 4) = 28$ and $(16 - 12) = 4$. Therefore if 30 scratches are detected, the process is out of control. Such an easy to calculate control limit should be known to every service manager to monitor, for example, the number of complaints in a week or the number of nonconformities in a sample of 10 hotel room makeups or the number of late deliveries. Simply find the average number of complaints, take the square root of the average number, and add three times the square root to the average to give the control limit. A significant change has occurred if the number of complaints or nonconformities exceeds this control limit. The only condition to be aware of in using this fast check is that the "population" or units on which this data is gathered is approximately the same. For example, you can use the formula if the hotel occupancy is approximately constant, or the total number of deliveries is about the same. If not, use the following:

Where the number of units is not constant, simply replace "c" by "u" where u = c/n and n is the number of units. The control limit formula is then

$$u +/- 3\sqrt{(u/n)}$$

Chart interpretation

The interpretation of control charts is a skill that can be developed. Particular chart patterns are indicative of particular problems that may be developing. Some indications are given in the figure.

Common Causes and Special Causes

If variation takes place between the control limits we say that the process is in control and common causes are at work. It is stable. If an unusual event takes place (as a result of a change in people, materials, methods, machine, mother nature) the point would plot outside of the control limits and we would say the process is "out of control". Deming was famous for accusing managers of not understanding the difference between common cause and special cause variation. The former should be ignored, but definite action be taken in case of the latter. Of course, a stable process is not necessarily good. For instance, you can have a high level of complaints that nevertheless remain within the control limits. Such a process would be in control but not capable.

STATISTICAL PROCESS CONTROL
Tracing Problems through Charts

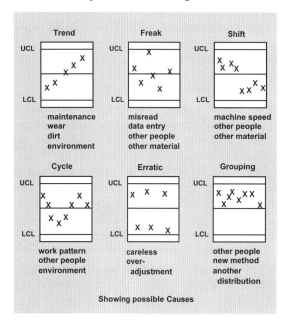

Showing possible Causes

Some Problems with SPC

SPC is a powerful technique, but users must be aware of its limitations and assumptions.

Risk. Since we are dealing with statistical distributions there is a risk of saying it is out of control when it is not and saying a process is in control when it is not. These are known as alpha risk and beta risk respectively. These risks decrease with increasing capability. As noted, control limits are set up at plus and minus three standard deviations corresponding to 99.7% of the full distribution. So when the capability ratio is 1.0 the risk is 0.3% Likewise, a process with a capability ratio of 1.0 will be producing almost 3000 ppm.

Independence. One assumption is that of independent samples. By independent is meant there is no relationship one to another. But if, for instance, there is gradual tool wear then the samples may not be independent. Taking samples at regular intervals is not independent.

Ability to Detect Changes. As noted there are several tests for out of control conditions. One test is for seven successive points on the same side of the mean line. If samples are taken (say) on average once an hour, it may take 7 hours to detect an out of control condition.

SPC was in the news in 2000 when workers at BNFL failed to record the data conscientiously. Nothing was wrong with the process or the product, but the customer noticed some anomalies. The shipment of nuclear fuel had to be sent back, eventually costing the company millions of pounds and several senior managers their jobs. This case illustrates that SPC should never be regarded as mechanical and remote from the product. SPC should be about process improvement not just process monitoring.

Further reading:

Charles Standard and Dale Davis, *Running Today's Factory*, Hanser Gardner , Cincinnatti, 1999.

For a full (and free!) course on SPC see the Autotrain website.

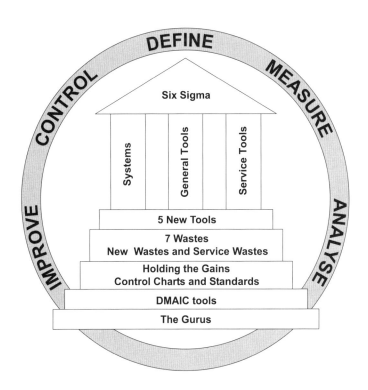

DMAIC Cycle Tools: ANALYSE

Sampling Distributions
Hypothesis Testing
Regression Analysis

Sampling Distributions

Suppose we are taking random samples of measurements of a critical parameter, which is a continuous variable, from our process. This 'parent' population from which we are sampling has a mean, μ, and standard deviation, σ, and may or may not be normally distributed.

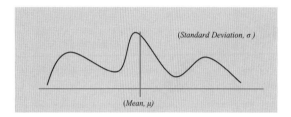

(Standard Deviation, σ)

(Mean, μ)

If we continue this activity, and for each sample we calculate the mean, $\bar{u}$, and as these means are likely to vary, we build up a new 'child' population (so called as it is derived from the 'parent' population) with a distribution which is called the ***sampling distribution of the sample mean***.

It is the properties of this 'child' population, in relation to its 'parent' that are interesting. For reference we will denote its mean, $\mu_{\bar{u}}$, and standard deviation, $\sigma_{\bar{u}}$, to distinguish between parent and child. The relationship can be defined by the three simple rules given below:

1.	The mean of the sample means will equal the mean of the parent. $(\mu_{\bar{u}} = \mu)$
2.	The standard deviation of the sample means will be smaller than the standard deviation of the parent by a factor of √n. $(\sigma_{\bar{u}} = \sigma/\sqrt{n})$
3.	When n is sufficiently large, the sampling distribution of $\bar{u}$ is well approximated by a normal curve, even when the parent population is not itself distributed normally.

(Where n = sample size)

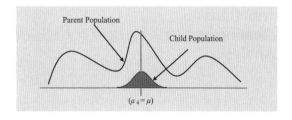

Parent Population

Child Population

$(\mu_{\bar{u}} = \mu)$

The third rule is called the ***central limit theorem***, and it serves as a reminder of the importance of the

role of the normal distribution in our quest for knowledge about our processes. Taken together with the other two rules, this relationship between parent and child enables us to characterise our process, with numbers, from random sampling.

What practical use is this to our goal of process improvement? Given that in a large proportion of the processes we are dealing with we would be unable to capture data about the entire population and are therefore unsure of its true distribution, we can never accurately describe the parameters we are most often concerned with, mean and standard deviation. Application of this theorem enables us to describe them as statistics or estimates and so give us a good understanding of the current performance of the parameter we are interested in.

Confidence Intervals for the Population Means

Referring back to sampling distributions of the sample mean, we can easily relate to how useful it will be in enabling us to characterise our processes with descriptive statistics to help us better manage them and make decisions based on data. For instance, "the sample mean measurement of diameter for a critical component is 231mm and from this we infer that the population mean diameter for the same component is also 231mm". However, because our statistics are derived from a sample of what is probably a much larger population, we might wish to consider the risk of relying on a single-value or point estimate. We might want to give some idea of the precision of the estimate by adding an error term. For instance, "the estimate of the mean diameter is 231mm ± 2mm, meaning that the population mean diameter lies somewhere between 229mm and 233mm". This kind of estimate is termed an interval estimate.

Very rarely in business do we have all of the information required to make 'watertight' decisions, so where there is risk it is always useful to have an understanding of its level. Building confidence intervals about our estimates is a way of doing this.

The range, and therefore the precision of the interval will depend on three factors:

1. **Sample size (*n*).** The larger the sample size, the smaller the error term in the estimate.

2. **Variation (σ).** The larger the variation, the larger the error term in the estimate.

3. **Desired confidence level (%)** How confident do we want to be that the population mean lies within the specified estimate.

It doesn't take too much of a leap of faith to understand how taking a bigger sample gives us a more precise estimate than a smaller sample might. Or, how a higher degree of variation also can have an adverse affect on precision, and the relationship between the two.

In an ideal world we would of course want 100% confidence in any estimates we make, but attaining this level is generally impractical. We therefore have to settle for something less, and this is typically a confidence level of 95%, and calculate a 95% confidence interval for the population mean, μ, using formulae given below. What this means is that on 95% of occasions when such intervals are calculated the population mean will actually be captured. Conversely, on 5% of occasions it will not be captured!

The most commonly used confidence levels are 90%, 95% and 99%, but again it must be stressed the level of required precision is set by you, and we can expect a higher associated cost with attaining a higher level of precision. You must satisfy yourself that these higher levels of cost can be justified, or, can a higher level of risk be tolerated?

The mechanics of actually calculating a confidence interval for the population mean draw on the three rules associated with sample means; they have a distribution with mean μ and standard deviation $\sigma/\sqrt{n}$, and is approximately normal if *n* is sufficiently large, say greater than 30.

It follows from the properties of the normal distribution that 95% of the values of the sample mean lie within approximately 2 standard deviations of the mean of the distribution of sample means, and 99% of the values within approximately 3 standard deviations.

Understanding these factors means that we can use the following to calculate the 95% or 99% confidence interval for μ from our sample data:

$\bar{u}, - 2s/\sqrt{n}$ to $\bar{u}, + 2s/\sqrt{n}$ (95% confidence interval)
$\bar{u}, - 3s/\sqrt{n}$ to $\bar{u}, + 3s/\sqrt{n}$ (95% confidence interval)

Notice that s rather than σ has been used. If we knew what σ was then we would also know the exact value of μ, and would therefore have no need of this tool anyway!

The formula and example above refer to cases where we are able to access a suitably large sample size of 30 or greater, but in real life situations obtaining data from such a sample size could be difficult or costly to achieve, for instance a process that cycles slowly.

Fortunately, a similar formula can be used to calculate a 95% confidence interval for μ from smaller sample sizes. This is done using the percentiles of the *t* distribution, and whilst it is recommended that they be looked up in statistical tables a brief look up guide is also given on the next page.

$$\bar{x} - \text{ts}/\sqrt{n} \ to \ \bar{x} - \text{ts}/\sqrt{n}$$

SAMPLE SIZE	t VALUE
5	2.78
10	2.26
20	2.09
30	2.05
100	1.98

The last question to be addressed relating to building confidence intervals is "how big does my sample need to be?" The answer to this lies with you as the experimenter, and the level of precision you or perhaps your customer requires. It is a function of the level of confidence you want and the size of error term you are prepared to accept, and the formula for calculating sample size for continuous data is given below:

$$n = \bar{}(2\sigma/h)^{2-} \text{ for 95\% confidence}$$
$$n = \bar{}(3\sigma/h)^{2-} \text{ for 99\% confidence}$$

σ in this instance represents our best estimate of the population standard deviation based on previous knowledge.

h is the desired half-interval width or error term (i.e. in our previous cider example for an error term of $\pm$ 1ml h = 1).

Example:

In the cider example, suppose we wanted a 99% confidence interval, with only a 1ml error term.
Using 2.1 as our estimate for standard deviation:

$$n = \bar{}(3\sigma/h)^{2-}$$

$$n = \bar{}(3\sigma2.1/1)^{2-} = 39.69 = 40 \text{ bottle sample required}$$

Hypothesis Testing

Hypothesis tests are the principal method used during the Analyse and Improve phases of Six Sigma for making rational decisions about the reality of the effects we have caused as part of our efforts to improve our processes.

Typically we are testing to determine if any change in a population parameter, μ or σ, has been affected, but because this decision will be made on the basis of information drawn from data with a random component we must try and control the chances of concluding a change has occurred when this is false.

The competing hypotheses are called the **null hypothesis (H_0)**, and the **alternate hypothesis (H_a)**.

The null hypothesis refers to no change, an action had no effect or something is not present. The alternate hypothesis is that some effect is present or that the two parameters do differ.

The explanation of this concept can be helped with a 'legal' anecdote; any person who finds himself or herself in a court of law accused of some felony must be tried by an impartial or unbiased jury. The starting point (null hypothesis), is that the accused is innocent and this assumption can only be rejected if the evidence (data) presented is sufficient to convince the jury of guilt (alternate hypothesis).

Proof of either innocence or guilt is best made with good evidence, or in our case data, but as always with inferential statistics the possibility of error in our conclusion exists.

In our legal anecdote the process can fail and it is possible to falsely convict an innocent person, a most serious error. Because of this the risk of error, if we do make one, is stacked in favour of releasing a guilty man, generally perceived as a less serious failing. And the same is true of statistical hypothesis testing, the risk of rejecting the null hypothesis is minimised. The protocols relating to the types of errors possible in hypothesis testing are given in the table below.

		H_0	H_a
Conclusion Drawn	H_0	Conclusion is correct	Type II error (β)
	H_a	Type I error (α)	Conclusion is correct

α is the risk of finding a difference when there really isn't one.
β is the risk of **not** finding a difference when there really is one.

Ultimately though, you as the experimenter determine the risk you take in rejecting the null hypothesis, and this is referred to as the significance level. The significance level of a test is the risk we are prepared to take in rejecting H_0 in favour of H_a, when in reality H_0 is the correct hypothesis. Typically this value would be 5%, but in practice the significance level depends on the criticality of the test. Such a risk cannot be avoided because we are trying to draw a conclusion about a population using only a relatively small amount of data.

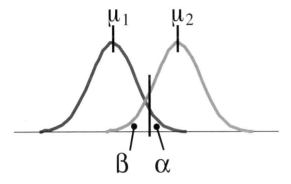

10% Chance we make the wrong decision $\alpha = 0.10$
5% Chance we make the wrong decision $\alpha = 0.05$
1% Chance we make the wrong decision $\alpha = 0.01$

The commonest way to test an hypothesis is to calculate the appropriate test statistic from the data you have collected, from this determine a P-value in accordance with the type of test (derived from statistical tables or software) and then to reject the null hypothesis if the P-value is less than the significance level of the test.

There are a number of options when it comes to which test statistic to use, and this choice is governed by the question you are asking.

The long hand statistics involved can be very daunting, so we recommend that you use any one of the commercially available stats packages if you don't feel comfortable using tables. What is important is that you end up with a P-value, the derivation of which is not so important!

With a P-value we then either reject the null hypothesis or fail to reject the null hypothesis. The wording of the conclusion is important; we do not speak of accepting the null or alternate hypothesis, which serves to remind us that an element of risk always remains.

In summary then, hypothesis testing helps us detect changes in our data, which are statistically significant. This in turn helps us to answer questions about the performance of our processes; are we reducing variation? Are we moving the mean of our measurement under test closer to the desired target? Risk in our conclusions will always be present, but at least through this kind of testing we can understand to what level, and make accordingly better decisions based on data.

Analysis of Variance (ANOVA)

In the previous section describing hypothesis testing we were concerned with testing one sample of data against another, using test statistics such as the t test, to determine if the means of the two different samples were from the same or different distributions. With analysis of variance we are able to deal with several sample populations at the same time and answer the same question, are the means equal or different.

ANOVA is a key tool for the ANALYSE phase, as it deals with the very real life situation that we may need to test different responses for a single factor, two factors, or more. The first two tests will be covered here, with the last being covered in Design of Experiments.

Single-Factor (One-Way) ANOVA

Here we are testing the differences between samples, which have been taken at different levels of a single factor, where factor is a discrete variable that we are concerned with.

If, for example, we wanted to understand the heat absorption ability of five different types of materials we could use one-way anova. The factor would be material type (1, 2, 3, 4 or 5), and the response variable would be the temperature of the material after heating.

The hypothesis we are testing in this example is that the differences in the sample means of the response are large enough to conclude that they are caused by the different factor settings (material type).

One-Way ANOVA Example:

Sample mean from material type 1 = μ_1
Sample mean from material type 2 = μ_2
Sample mean from material type 3 = μ_3
Sample mean from material type 4 = μ_4
Sample mean from material type 5 = μ_5

Hypothesis Test:

H_0: $\mu_1 = \mu_2 = \mu_3 = \mu_4 = \mu_5$

H_a: $\mu_i \neq \mu_j$ for at least one pair

At this point it is wise to just take a quick sense check. Remember we are trying to determine if the means are different with a certain degree of statistical confidence and as part of the experiment we must ensure that we have satisfied certain assumptions before drawing our conclusions.

Some of these assumptions have been covered earlier but a recap may be helpful. Most importantly we need to ensure the experiment samples are independent, which means selecting an adequate size and conducting the trials randomly. Also the assumption that the sample variances are equal must be met. If one or both of these assumptions is not fulfilled then it is statistically unsafe to continue with the analysis.

The calculation of the statistical test itself is beyond the scope of this book, and is such that the use of software is recommended. The benefits of this are that most packages will help confirm that the previously mentioned assumptions have been met and give you both a graphical and a statistical output relating to the hypothesis test itself, all of which enables you to concentrate on interpreting the analysis results rather than worrying about the mathematics involved!

The graphical representation of the analysis of variance will usually take the form of a box plot, dot plot or confidence interval for the mean. Look at the example box plot below, which relates to our heat absorption experiment.

Our software has already confirmed equal variances and we are satisfied with the independence of our data. On the evidence of the box plot alone we can go some way towards rejecting the null hypothesis (no difference in the means). Certainly material types 1 and 4 seem to have higher absorption rates than material types 2, 3 and 5. To be sure though we need to refer to the statistical test and resulting P value.

Refer to the example below.

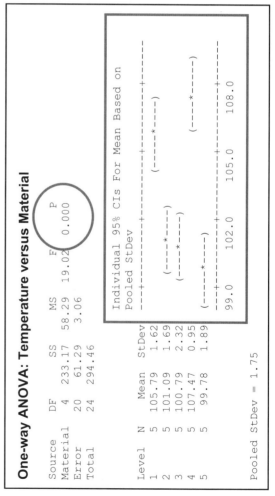

This is a really useful output. It gives us a P value of 0.00, which enables us to reject the null hypothesis (refer to hypothesis testing for P values), and if more proof were needed we have a simple graphic illustrating individual confidence intervals for the mean of each sample.

Reminding ourselves that the higher the temperature the better the heat absorption, we would then want to confirm whether material types 1 or 4 is best suited to our needs, as these have the highest sample mean for temperature. Our anova has helped us conclude that these differences are statistically different from the other materials with 95% confidence.

Two-Factor (Two-Way) ANOVA

We might well have to conduct an experiment with more than one factor, and as the name suggests (two-factor anova), is an efficient and effective way of doing so.

This kind of experiment is really powerful. Not only will you get the same information about each of the factors and the effect of the differing levels on your response variable, but also you will gain information about any interaction between the factors and its effect on the response variable. This element of process knowledge is often overlooked or ignored in traditional process improvement methodologies. Consider this anecdote.

You are suffering with the worst bout of flue you have ever experienced. Needless to say you want effective relief and are considering what will be the most effective strategy. You know from previous experience that medication type A will give a degree of relief, as will medication type B. Considering this is your worst bout of flu ever you feel that taking them alone will not give you the result you are looking for. So based on current experience, which has been testing each factor one at a time, you decide to take both together, reasoning that the combined effect will give you the level of relief you desire! However, we know that these types of medication should not be taken together, and you are now feeling even worse. Taken together the medications act on each other, which has a negative effect on the way you feel. This is the effect of the interaction.

The mechanics of this test are similar to that of the single-factor ANOVA, and again the use of software is recommended for ease of application. The example given below of the statistical analysis output is based on an experiment testing the strength of metal rods. The two factors tested were temperature and carbon content in the rods.

Two-way ANOVA: Strength versus Temperature, Carbon Content

Source	DF	SS	MS	F	P
Temperature	3	166.594	55.531	8.84	0.001
Carbon Content	3	586.844	195.615	31.14	0.000
Interaction	9	91.281	10.142	1.61	0.193
Error	16	100.500	6.281		
Total	31	945.219			

Looking at the P values associated with each of the two factors tells us that both are statistically significant on the rod strength, but that there is little or no interaction between the two factors.

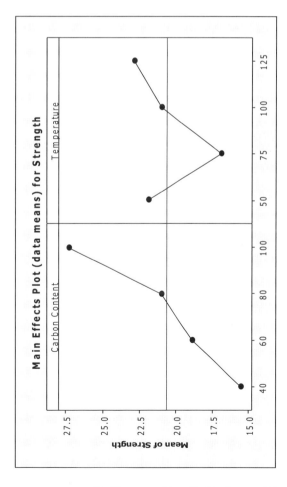

Analysis of the graphical output will help understand to what degree the two factors are having an effect on strength (our response in this case).

The half of the graph relating to Carbon Content is reasonably easy to interpret, as the amount of carbon increases so does the strength. The relationship with temperature is not linear, but if we wished to maximise strength we can see that the optimum temperature setting would be 125 degrees. This would give us an average strength of approximately 27, if we also had the carbon content set to 100.

This type of process optimisation can be carried out in this manner because in this instance we need not worry about any interaction between temperature and carbon content (remember the interaction P value from the statistical analysis summary). What to do when an interaction is present is covered in the section dealing with Design of Experiments.

With the support of the appropriate software, ANOVA is a simple tool to use, and has the potential to uncover information about your process which has previously gone undetected.

Further reading:
A most useful guide to the statistical aspects of Six Sigma is Quentin Brook, *Six Sigma and MINITAB*, QSB Consulting, 2004. See www.QSBC.co.uk

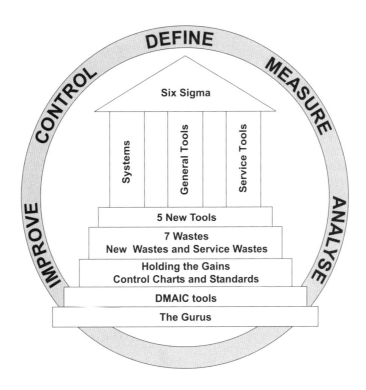

DMAIC Cycle Tools: IMPROVE

Regression Analysis
Design of Experiments
Failure Modes and Effect Analysis
Error Proofing

Regression Analysis

Whilst correlation techniques help us to test the degree of association between two variables, which can be displayed usefully with a scatter plot and represented numerically with the calculation of the correlation coefficient, regression analysis enables us to predict the value of one variable from the value of the other variable. This simple but effective tool is one of the early steps in the Improve phase of the DMAIC cycle.

To continue with the example used regarding correlation, which is a process where temperature has an effect on the number of rejects. Once that association has been established through experimentation or observation of normal operations, then the data gathered can be used to predict the number of rejects we could expect at a given temperature.

Whilst complex relationships, such as quadratic or cubic, may exist between two variables they are outside the scope of this book, we will concentrate on the simplest type, which is **simple linear regression**. This type of analysis typically comprises of three components; a scatter diagram of the data, a regression equation and its graphical representation, a straight line on the diagram (see diagram below).

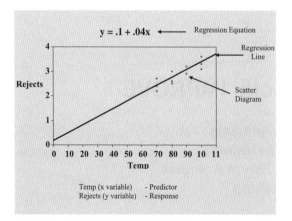

Temp (x variable) - Predictor
Rejects (y variable) - Response

The scatter diagram should be plotted first, with variable that we wish to predict on the Y-axis and the variable we wish to do the predicting on the X-

axis. A judgement should be made as to the nature of the relationship, which we are looking for to be reasonably linear.

The regression equation for y on x can then be calculated. It takes the form of:

$$y = b_0 + b_1 x$$

b_0 represents the y intercept (the value of y where the line crosses the y axis)

b_1 represents the slope or gradient of the line

Determining the coefficient of the equation will not be covered here as it is felt that most practitioners will either rely on the statistical function built into scientific calculators or more likely a statistical software package.

Once you have the equation you can then plot the regression line.

A simplified, non-mathematical approach is recommended initially and will yield reasonably accurate results. This is done by plotting the regression line 'by eye' in such a way that the distance from all the plotted points and the line are minimal. This is often referred to as the 'best fit'.

Given that we now have the requisite components in place it is possible to use either the equation or the line of best fit to predict values of y for given values of x within the range of our data. This is an important caveat, and the temptation to extrapolate the regression line beyond the range of our sample data should be resisted as we can't say with any confidence that the relationship between x and y will still be linear.

Obviously this is not a tool limited to just manufacturing applications; so long as the relationship between the two variables in question is linear, then one can be used to predict another. The application of regression analysis as part of your process improvement can really add a 'wow factor'!

Design of Experiments

Design of Experiments (DOE) is a family of techniques, which enables the Six Sigma practitioner to efficiently home in on the key process input variables during the ANALYSE and IMPROVE stages identified. This is achieved by purposefully changing a number of input factors to a process or activity in order to observe the corresponding changes in the output.

Air Academy Associates claim experimental designs are used as:

1. the most effective method for identifying the key input factors,
2. the most efficient way to gain an understanding of the relationship between the input factors and the response,
3. a method for building a model relating the input factors to the response,
4. a means of determining the settings of the input factors to optimise the process,
5. a scientific method for setting tolerances.

Source: *Understanding Industrial Designed Experiments.*

DOE has a long history with its roots in agriculture, going back to Sir Ronald Fisher in 1930, but in recent years has not been very popular in mainstream business. This can be attributed to two possible reasons; the complexity of the calculations required for all but the very simplest experiments have traditionally made it cumbersome to use, and when it has been employed, the failure to deliver the expected results.

A wide range of software is now readily available which simplifies the whole process and greatly improves accessibility. The fact that DOE is part of the Six Sigma rigour has improved its usefulness. The fault previously lay not with DOE per se but with the lack of groundwork required prior to employing a DOE. The DOE itself should be the last phase of a process, preceded by a large amount of preparation. An appropriate amount of effort should be expended on actually planning and preparing for the experiment rather than taking shortcuts, as this may well contribute to failing to gain the required process knowledge.

Preparation for the experiment should be team based, and follow a process similar to the one given below:

1. Define the problem (should relate to VoC).
2. Establish the objective.
3. Select the response variable(s) to be measured.
4. Select the input factors, which are anticipated to have an effect on the response.
5. Choose the factor levels (or settings).
6. Select the experimental design.
7. Collect the data.
8. Analyse the data.
9. Draw conclusions.
10. Control the process.

Steps 1 – 4 would typically be completed through the early phases of the DMAIC cycle with the use of such tools as cause and effect diagrams and hypothesis testing. Factor levels are the settings at which each factor will be tested. Typically they will be set at a 'high' and 'low' level and should be set as close as possible to actual design settings.

The type of experimental design to be used, and there are many, is largely determined by the number of factors to be tested and the desired level of understanding to be achieved. If we consider an experiment with only two factors each with two levels, to test all possible effects the number of combinations or runs would be just four (number of runs $n = 2^k$ where the base 2 refers to the number of levels and the index k the number of factors). This type of experiment is referred to as a **full factorial**. When more factors are to be tested it can become impractical or expensive to complete a full factorial. A typical training tool on a Six Sigma programme is the catapult, that is likely to have a number of input variables which can be set to different values (ball type, pull back angle, position of ball holder, position of elastic band on arm, position of elastic band on front upright arm, position of pull back arm stopper and operator). If each of these settings had two levels, this experiment with seven factors (2^7) would require 128 runs to complete. If that sounds a lot, a design with eight factors, seven of which have three levels and the remainder having 2 levels, has a total number of runs to cover all combinations of 4,374. Therefore it may be necessary to consider an experimentation strategy which employs the use of designs with a drastically reduced number of runs at the expense of losing information about certain effects. These are **fractional factorial** designs.

Experimentation Strategy:

Regardless of the type of design used the mechanics are broadly the same, and they are best explained by way of an example. The one given here takes the form of a two level two factor full factorial design.

Process	= Taking a shower
Response	= Comfort level (1 –10)
Factors	= 1. Flow of hot water
	2. Flow of cold water
Levels	= 1. Low - High
	2. Low - High

Design Matrix

Run #	Factor 1 Cold Water	Factor 2 Hot Water	Response Comfort
1	Low	High	3
2	High	Low	2
3	High	High	9
4	Low	Low	6

The high and low levels are coded +1 and -1 and multiplying these levels for each run, the product gives the result of the interaction (cold water x hot water).

Run	Cold Water	Hot Water	CW x HW	Comfort
1	- 1	+1	-1	3
2	+1	-1	-1	2
3	+1	+1	+1	9
4	-1	-1	+1	6

	Effect of High setting	–	Effect of Low setting		Effect
Cold Water:	(2+9)/2	-	(3+6)/2	=	5.5 – 4.5 = 1
Hot Water:	(3+9)/2	-	(2+6)/2	=	6.0 – 4.0 = 2
Interaction: (Cold x Hot)	(9+6)/2	-	(3+2)/2	=	7.5 – 2.5 = 5

Graphical analysis is also recommended at this stage. Pareto diagrams and main effects plots will illustrate which factors are significant. This is especially useful in experiments that involve many factors.

Main effects plots for this example are shown below.

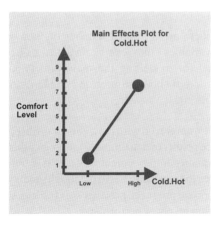

The main effects plots show the effect of hot and cold water taken independently have a relatively low significance with regard to comfort level. However, the interaction between the two factors is significant, shown by the sharp gradient of the line in the main effects plot of the interaction.

The interaction plot shown below also helps to illustrate the fact that an interaction between the two factors, temperature and pressure, is present. The temperature variable 'Hot' is positioned on the x axis at low and high pressures, and the two 'Cold' pressures are drawn as lines showing the effect pressure and temperature have on each other at low and high settings. The comfort experienced in the shower when cold high pressure is matched to hot high pressure is significant. The comfort experienced by having cold low pressure at hot low pressure is not as great, and the comfort level deteriorates at the hot pressure is increased. An important characteristic of the plot is the intersection which is the area of design robustness. The point on the x axis the cold high and low pressure lines intersect, gives the comfort level that remains consistent at this level of hot pressure, regardless of what cold pressure is selected. This is an important aspect of Taguchi's robust design concept. To interpret an interaction graph, the closer the lines are to being perpendicular, the stronger the correlation between the two factors. If the lines plotted were parallel, then this would suggest no interaction. Anything between the two states indicates the presence of a weak interaction.

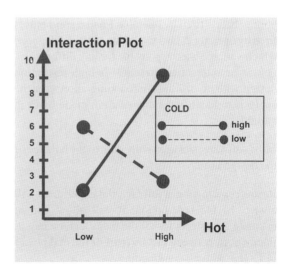

If we wanted to maximise our comfort level our design results tell us to set both hot and cold water to their high settings.

Other factors to consider when setting up an experiment are the randomisation of runs, number of replicates or repetitions of runs to be completed and the balance of the design (orthogonal or non-orthogonal designs).

Conducting the experiment in a random order is essential to compensate for the effects of potentially uncontrolled factors, which were left out of the experiment

To model the variation of a process it is necessary to carry out multiple runs for the same settings. This can be conducted through the use of repetitions or replicates. Completing repetitions means to take multiple responses at the same level without changing the set up. Replication means to take multiple responses at the same level, but repeating the set up each time. From a statistical standpoint replication is preferred as all of the set up variation is captured.

The balance of the design, whether it is orthogonal or not, is an important factor. An orthogonal design allows for the effects of each factor to be evaluated independently. A design which is non-orthogonal will have factors that are confused or confounded (to use DOE terminology), which may well result in the true level of the effects for those factors being disguised. For example, when firing a catapult, if a hollow ball is fired by operator 1 and a solid ball is fired by operator 2, how would the analysis diagnose which variable was responsible for any differences, or was an interaction present? A high resolution design with no or little confounding allows for the analysis to identify the contribution made by each variable.

Most software packages will confirm the balance of the design used.

Resources allowing, a full factorial experiment will always be the best option. It will allow you to estimate the effects for all the main factors and all interactions between factors (part of the real power of DOE), with no confounding.

Where resources are a problem the fractional factorial design can be employed (number of runs $n = 2^{k-q}$ where the base 2 refers to the number of levels and the index k the number of factors and q is some positive integer less than k where q = 1 indicates a half fraction, q=2 a quarter fraction, etc).

Number of Runs Comparison:

Full factorial:	Half fraction factorial:
2 Levels	2 Levels
4 Factors	4 Factors
$2^4 = 16$ runs	$2^{4-1} = 8$ runs

By employing such a half fraction factorial the effect of a three way interaction is lost. We cannot separate the effects of the fourth factor from the effects of the three-way interaction. Seldom are interactions found beyond two way, so time and resources can be conserved.

If an experiment has a large number of factors, then a sensible strategy for process improvement using DOE is to start with a fractional factorial experiment or Taguchi design. Theses are used to screen out insignificant factors with regard to the response. The main effects plots and Pareto charts will support this. This type of application is known as "screening".

Once there are a limited number of 'key process input variables" they can be analysed using a full factorial for modelling the main effects and any interactions for both the mean and standard deviation of the response variable.

If DOE is employed with the rigour described, it may produce results of a magnitude far greater than most other quality improvement tools. It is a core tool, enabling the experimenter to potentially reduce costs and improve products, processes and services to true six sigma levels of performance.

Further Reading:

Keki R Bhote and Adi Bhote, *World Class Quality*, Second Edition, AmaCom, 2000. Reviews traditional DOE and gives a full explanation of Shainin DOE.
Glen Stuart Peace, *Taguchi Methods : A Hands-On Approach*, Addison Wesley, 1993. A very comprehensive treatment of Taguchi.
Larry B Barrentine, *An Introduction to Design of Experiments : A Simplified Approach*. ASQ Quality Press, Milwaukee, 1999. An easy-to-understand introduction - sufficient for most purposes.

Failure Modes and Effect Analysis (FMEA)

Failure mode and effect analysis (FMEA) is a methodology to assess and reduce risk in systems, products or services. It aims to define, identify, prioritise, and eliminate known or potential failures at an early a stage as possible. FMEA is a Pareto type of analysis, homing in on the "vital few" failure modes. It is often used in conjunction with QFD (see separate section). As QFD is deployed from stage to stage, a corresponding FMEA is carried out. Other techniques used with FMEA include flowcharting, cause and effect diagrams, brainstorming / nominal group technique, process capability (Cpk) and design of experiments (see separate sections). The SERVQUAL dimensions are useful in service FMEA. With increasing risk of litigation in connection with products and services, several large companies (eg. Ford) require their suppliers to undertake FMEA analyses. But whether the aim is reduced risk from litigation or improved customer satisfaction, FMEA is becoming a standard procedure to be applied to all new products and services.

FMEA usually begins by assembling a group who are familiar with the product, service or system. If possible the group should include customers (internal or external), marketing and field service. The group will have the task of brainstorming out all the possible causes of failure. In addition to brainstorming, designers and engineers will be able to advise on likely modes of failure and records may show failures in past performance.

The four types of FMEA form a hierarchy, and can be used independently or in sequence. A System FMEA is used at the design stage to analyse overall systems including the interactions between functions so as to minimise failure effects. A Design FMEA is used to minimise design faults before they are passed to manufacturing. The Process FMEA focuses on failures caused in the manufacturing process. Service FMEA focuses on service failures. All four FMEAs use basically the same procedure and analysis sheet, an example of which is shown in the figure.

The first stage is to obtain a sketch or engineering drawing of the system, product or service. Then a flowchart (process chart) of the product or service should be drawn up. Then, using the flowchart, step by step, all possible failure modes should be written down. The team should ask itself how could the process fail, and what might be found unacceptable by the customer. If warranty, field failure, or customer complaints data is available for a similar product or service this should be used. In a process or design FMEA the team should consider, for each step of the chart or component on the drawing, the inputs (parts, supply, testing), the process (manufacture), and outputs (inspection, transport, storage).

Failures		Rankings			Risk Priority Number (RPN)
		Severity (A)	Occurrence	Detection (C)	
potential mode of failure	potential causes and effects of failure	1 = none 3 = slight 5 = moderate 7 = major 9 = serious 10 = hazard	1 = never 3 = v slight 5 = low 7 = mod high 9 = v high 10 = almost certain	1 = certain 3 = high 5 = medium 7 = slight 9 = remote 10 = almost impossible	(A) * (B) * (C)

The effects of each mode of failure is then analysed under three criteria - severity, occurrence, and detection. (This is easy to remember: the mnemonic for the three criteria is SOD. FMEA tries to get to the root of the failure. Around roots are sods of earth.) For each mode of failure, the group allocates a score for each of the three. A 10 point scale is recommended.

Severity indicates the seriousness of a failure, viewed from the perspective of the system or the customer. Occurrence is a rating reflecting the estimated number (or frequency) of failure. Detection reflects the possibility that a fault or problem will be discovered before it is released to the next stage (for system or design FMEAs) or to the final customer (manufacturing or service FMEAs). Like several other techniques much of the benefit of FMEA is derived from the discussions amongst group members as they assign relative scores. Thereafter the "RPN" or risk priority number is calculated by multiplying the three factors (S x O x D).

When all failure modes have been considered, the most critical or highest priority modes are identified by ranking the RPN scores. Clearly a high score indicates reasonable severity, more likely to occur, with reasonable difficulty of detection. Of course suitable actions must now be taken, in priority order. A threshold is usually established, above which action must be taken. For a 10 point scale the maximum RPN score is 1000 points, but the threshold may be as low as an RPN of 10 or 20. Once the threshold RPN number has been decided, the team should assess all modes of failure above the threshold for risk. If risk is small, no action is needed, but if high, action becomes essential.

Further reading:
D.H. Stamatis, *Failure Mode and Effect Analysis,* ASQ Quality Press, Milwaukee, WI, 1995

Error Proofing

Please refer to the section on Shingo: Failsafing and source Inspection (in the "Gurus" Chapter).

Shingo's work on Pokayoke has long been the classic on error proofing or mistake proofing.

Recently, however an excellent text has been added that promises to be the new classic. It is C. Martin Hinckleys *Make No Mistake*.

Hinckley has developed a classification system that enables one to identify the most useful mistake proofing devices.

Also, Hinckley has proposed a framework that is powerful for any quality initiative Six Sigma or otherwise. An adapted version is given below.

	Men (People)	Machines	Method	Material	Measures	'Mother Nature'
Variation						
Mistakes						
Complexity						

A comprehensive quality initiative would involve addressing every cell in the framework whether by Six Sigma, Design for Six Sigma, Lean (including standard work), or Value Engineering.

Further Reading:
C. Martin Hinckley, *Make No Mistake*, Productivity Press, 2002.

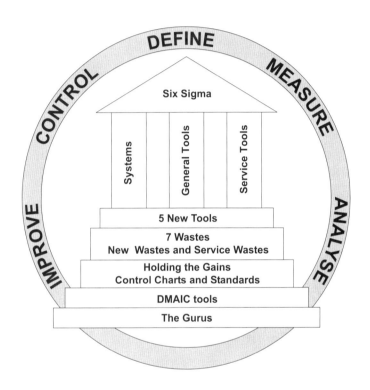

DMAIC Cycle Tools: CONTROL

Control and Sustainability
Standard Work
Windows Analysis
Reliability & TPM
Control Plan
Story Board

Control

The Control stage tool set looks relatively thin when compared to the tool set of the other phases. There are reasons for this. Many of the tools which fit into this stage have been introduced in previous stages and so reference will be made to them rather than duplicate material. However, the importance of this stage should not be underestimated. Process improvements are most vulnerable at the beginning and end of the project, a characteristic similar to the failure rate 'bath tub' curve shown under TPM. Once a process improvement project has been completed (although one can argue that process improvements continuous and are never complete) there has to be a plan to 'hold the gain'.

The Deming Cycle

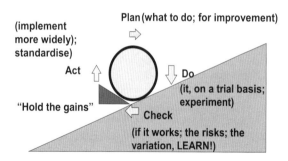

Pande and Holpp refer to organisations as similar to elastic bands, capable of being stretched to new and interesting shapes, but as soon as you let go, the band returns to its original shape. The purpose of the Control stage is to prevent this return. Why do so many improvement projects fail to sustain their new performance level? A managing director at a blue chip consumer electronics factory in South Wales addressed his management team in the late 1990s stressing the definition of insanity was to continue to do the same things but to expect a different result.

Beth Cauldwell claims leaders are very good at whipping up enthusiasm for starting projects. New jargon is introduced to management

meetings and teams are encouraged to participate in this new initiative. Organisations value visionaries who want to 'change'. Change management is rewarded. But all this may result in those same organisations not valuing or rewarding perseverance with a project or programme. As time passes, initiatives that once enjoyed a blaze of publicity are seen as dour and boring. Leaders look for new initiatives to inject fresh impetus and further their own promotion aspirations.

How can organisations sustain their initiatives? The term 'sustainability' is critical to the success of a Six Sigma programme (or any other process improvement / management system initiative). This subject area was introduced in the chapter 'Six Sigma Caveat – Delivery & Deployment' and is explored further below.

One of the main premises of the Six Sigma approach is that the few critical process inputs are understood, $Y = f(X_1, X_2, X_3)$. This makes controlling the process and holding the gains that much easier because it is only these few critical Xs which require constant attention. When processes have many input variables and the effects of these are not understood, process resource allocation difficulties may occur and out-of-control symptoms result.

It was highlighted early on in this book that the deployment of Six Sigma varies from one organisation to the next. Some organisations train Black Belts to be full time Project Managers, roaming around the organisation and helping various departments solve their chronic problems. Other organisations train Green Belts who are expected to employ the Six Sigma methodology to work smarter within their current roles. Whatever model is adopted, it is vital that when Process Owners inherit the result of the Six Sigma project, they understand their process. Project buy-in and involvement are good-practice leadership techniques but this is not always possible due to staff turnover, promotion or rotation. Therefore, there are recommendations that Project Managers should follow at the end of a Project. These include:

- Producing a Process Notebook, containing all the work undertaken as part of the project
- Producing a Story Board
- Producing a Control Plan
- Training the appropriate people responsible for the process.
- Communicating the new Performance Measures
- Communicating the new Standard Operation Procedures (SOPs) and its system
- Recommendations for future work

(adapted from Pande et al, 'The Six Sigma Way')

These actions should be treated as a vital part of the Six Sigma project and the Project Charter should not be signed off by the Champion and Financial Controller until this has taken place. It is tempting for an organisation to pull the Six Sigma experts off a project as soon as the target performance has been achieved but this can result in the elastic band scenario, particularly when the improvements are not pokayoke controlled but rely on human judgement.

Standard Work and Standard Operating Procedures

Standard work is a pillar of the Toyota Production System (TPS). A definition and two useful quotations introduce this vital topic.

A dictionary definition is "a basis for comparison of judgement" (Oxford).

"To standardise a method is to choose out of many methods the best one, and use it. What is the best way to do a thing? It is the sum of all the good ways we have discovered up to the present. It therefore becomes the standard. Today's standardisation is the necessary foundation on which tomorrow's improvement will be based. If you think of 'standardisation as the best we know today, but which is to be improved tomorrow' - you get somewhere. But if you think of standards as confining, then progress stops."
(Henry Ford, *Today and Tomorrow*, 1926)

"In a Western company the standard operation is the property of management or the engineering department. In a Japanese company it is the property of the people doing the job. They prepare it, work to it, and are responsible for improving it. Contrary to Taylor's teaching, the Japanese combine thinking and doing, and thus achieve a high level of involvement and commitment."
(Peter Wickens, Former HR Director, Nissan UK)

Standard and Davies explain that there are 3 key aspects of standard work which need to be understood

1. Standard work is not static, and when a better way is found the procedure is updated
2. Standard work supports stability and reduces variation because the work is performed the same way each time. Moreover variations (defects, deviations, discrepancies) are easily recognised.
3. Standard work is essential for continuous improvement – moving from one standard to a better standard without slipping back.

Standards should cover three aspects: work time, work sequence, and standard work-in-process. All are necessary. On work time, both takt time and current cycle time (i.e. the time taken for one cycle of the process) should be recorded.

At the outset it should be said that standards are not the rigid, work-study imposed, job specifications associated with classic mass production. Such standards have no place in the world of Lean. They lead to industrial sabotage and absenteeism. Beware of the human-relations based reaction against 'work standards' that is often confused with work-study. Allowing loose standards may lead to no standards, which in turn lead to decreased safety and productivity.

Also, beware of thinking that standards have no place in non-repetitive work such as maintenance, service, design, or senior management. Good, flexible maintenance and service work is built by combining various small standard work elements. Good design comes out of creativity combined with standard methods and materials, adhering to standard procedures and gateways. Management standards should exist for meetings, communications, budgets, and many other activities.

Spear and Bowen in a classic article discuss the apparent paradox of TPS that activities, communications and flows at Toyota are at once rigidly scripted yet enormously flexible and adaptable. They conclude that that it is the rigid specification of standards and communications that gives the system the ability to make huge numbers of controlled changes. Without standards and the scientific method, change would amount to little more than trial and error.

Despite what some people think about Frederick Taylor, there remains "one best way" to do any task that will minimise effort and maximise safety, quality and productivity, with available technology. To some this may sound like boring repetition, but the "new" standards are about participation in developing the best and safest way, mastery of several jobs, and the ability to adapt to changes in rate and mix in the short term.

Ohno realised that the achievement of standardised work, with minimum variance, was the essential ingredient to allow one-piece flow and JIT production. Deming, in proposing the PDCA cycle, saw improvement moving from standard to standard. Juran emphasised the importance of "holding the gains" by establishing standards following a process improvement, rather than allowing them to drift back to the old ways. Recently the "Learning Organisation" has become fashionable, including "knowledge harvesting" from everyone in the organisation. How is this to be achieved? By documenting experience; in other words by establishing standards from which others may learn. Supervisors should have prime responsibility for maintaining and improving standard work.

At Toyota, emphasis is placed on workers documenting their own standards, and in mastering both a wider range of work tasks and greater responsibility for supporting tasks. Operators themselves establish work cycles within the specified takt time. It may be that they are assisted in this task by industrial engineers and supervisors, but the operators must write up the final documentation of work standards themselves. This achieves four goals. First, there can be no question that work standards are not understood. Second, the operator is forced to think about the best way in which he or she should do the work within the takt time. A trained operator will frequently do a better job than an uninvolved work-study officer. Third, the responsibility for setting the standard and then maintaining it is clearly up to the operator. There is motivation to update the standard when improved ways are found. And, fourth, because the standards reflect what actually happens rather than what might happen, learning can take place particularly when operators change jobs. In other words this is job enrichment and job mastery. The Toyota way takes time to train operators to do the analysis and standardisation themselves - they need to not only learn basic work-study principles but also to appreciate the reasons why they should do it. Toyota regards work standardisation as one of its most challenging management tasks. Robert Hall believes that this worker-oriented standardisation, requiring high levels of operator skill and motivation, takes much time but pays huge dividends.

Too many operations-based organisations delude themselves on standards. It is tempting to simply impose work standards by getting industrial engineers or work-study people to do the work and to post standards at workstations, or worse to keep them in a file. Then of course, there is no buy-in, no foundation for continuous improvement, and worst of all a great likelihood of large process variance. So the quick way turns out to be the least effective way and often a total waste. Traditional "Taylorism", is suitable only the sweat shop.

However, do not attempt to write a standard before you have taken out waste. Failure demand and special cause variation must be removed first. Do not lock in wast by standardising Failure Demand and special cause variation.

Today good standards make extensive use of digital photos, with close-ups of any operation requiring clarification, and specifying tools, quality checks, and a note on any special operation that is required to be carried out periodically. A standard operating procedure can be colour coded to match the product that carries a label of matching colour. When an engineering change occurs, a number on the product should match the number on the standard procedure. Often, a standard should cover not only what to do when things are normal, but also what to do if things go wrong. Consider health and safety. There must be own responsibility for the standard, for publishing it, for keeping it at the workplace, and for keeping it up to date. At Intel where consistency is an absolute requirement, operators audit one another using the standard instructions. Jaguar makes videos of the same operation on different shifts, and then gets operators to critique one another.

Three forms are common. The Standard Work Combination Chart is a Gantt-type chart detailing the sequence of steps against time bars joined by 'squiggles' to indicate walk times. The takt time is shown as a vertical bar, and the longest accumulation of job element times should be within this takt time. The Standard Work Analysis Chart gives a birds-eye view (plan view) of the cell showing the standard route that operators follow when carrying out a standard cycle, and the standard locations and quantities of inventory.

When cellular manufacturing is established or when takt times change, operators in the cell are encouraged to rebalance the line themselves or to change their own work standards to the new takt time. This is referred to as the 'Yamazumi' board.

Finally, especially in service orgsanisations, note the later secton on Failue demand and Value demand. Failure demand should not be standardised – it should be eliminated.

Further reading:
Robert W Hall, "Standard Work: Holding the Gains", *Target*, Fourth Quarter, 1998, pp 13- 19
Taiichi Ohno, *Toyota Production System*, Productivity Press, Portland, OR, 1988
Charles Standard and Dale Davis, *Running Today's Factory*, Hanser Gardner, 1999
Spear and Bowen, 'Decoding the DNA of the Toyota Production System', *Harvard Business Review*, Sept/Oct 1999
Fred Owen James, *How can standard operations be sustained on a short cycle manual assembly line?* MSc Dissertation, Cardiff Business School, 2001

Window Analysis

Window Analysis and the Johari Window (next section) share common features.

The purpose of Window Analysis is to categorise the practice or non-practice of standards. This approach is particularly appropriate to assembly operations where assembling to standard operations is crucial to achieving world class quality.

The categories for standaards adherence are alpha, beta, gamma and delta (α, β, and γ, δ,) and this method looks to understand if the symptom of unpractised standards is a result of a failure to establish the standard, communicate the standard or adhere to the standard.

In a similar way to the Johari window, this approach seeks to understand whether the issue identified is confined to one person or group, or is wide spread. It tackles this by referring to party 1 (1 person or group) and party 2 (a separate person or group).

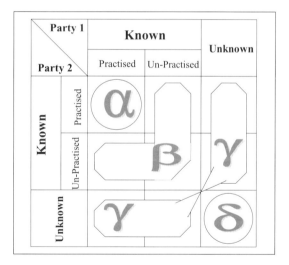

Known and unknown. If the correct methods to achieve excellent quality are established and known to everyone who needs to know, the window state is 'known'.

Practised and un-practiced. Only if the correct methods are practised 100% of the time by all parties can we say we have an ideal Alpha condition.

There are 3 conditions when there may not be 100% practised methods. These are:

Condition β, Adherence Problem, when a method is established and understood, but not practised by all parties.

Condition γ Communication Problem, when a method is established, but some individuals or groups are not informed of it.

Category δ Standardisation Problem, when the right method is not established.

By understanding which is the prevalent condition causing the standard to be un-practiced (adherence, communication or established) the necessary management action can be taken quickly to address the problem.

The Johari Window

The Johari Window (named after its inventors Joe Lufts and Harry Ingham) is useful in fostering clearer understanding and better communication on an interpersonal basis. Teams may also use it. Communication and understanding are of course keys for better quality. The window also helps in building trust.

The idea is that there are things (concepts, facts, assumptions, behaviours etc.) that are known to you and there are things that are not known to you. Likewise there are things known the other person (or team) and things unknown. This leads to a two by two matrix, as shown. The greater the "Arena", and the smaller the other quadrants, the better. To reduce the Blind Spot requires you to solicit feedback from the other person, or the other person to disclose information to you. To reduce the Façade requires either you to give feedback to the other person, or to self disclose formerly unknown information. This has to be done actively. So disclosure and feedback are central characteristics.

Just knowing about the Johari Window helps both sides. Poor communication and knowledge are at the heart of many organisational, quality, and human problems. I always assumed that you had been trained in CNC programming! Did you know

that press operator is a model builder whose skills could be of great benefit? Did you know that you have an annoying characteristic of sucking on your teeth that disturbs team concentration? I did not realise that you were nervous about being team leader! So there are obligations to both listen (" seek to understand before seeking to be understood" says Stephen Covey), and to provide appropriate information. Often there is a feedback loop at work – the more you tell me, the more I will tell you, and vice versa. Think in terms of the other person – what would be useful for him to know that I know. Give people the opportunity and time to speak and tell. Ask. Have patience. Don't assume that what you have to say is more important than what others have to say; don't interrupt to add your own (irrelevant?) anecdote. Gently remind others to do the same.

Use the phrase "Remember Johari" whenever necessary.

A variation on the Johari window is to do with attitudes and relationships. Scholtes, for instance, has suggested that the axes are then, "I am OK, I am not OK" and "You are OK, You are not OK". Here the object is get to the Trust quadrant where both sides believe and trust in the other. You are OK, but I am not OK indicates insecurity. If we are both not OK then there is serious mistrust and disruption. If I am OK but you are not, then there is suspicion and "theory Y" type behaviour.

JOHARI WINDOW

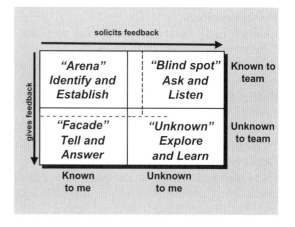

Total Productive Maintenance (TPM)

TPM can be regarded as integral to Lean and Six Sigma. Certainly no Lean implementation can be a success with a high level of breakdowns. TPM goes well beyond breakdown issues to cover availability, performance, quality, as well as safety and capital investment through making best use of, and extending the life of, equipment.

TPM has much in common with Total Quality. Everyone has a role to play, not just experts. In total quality there is the concept of 'the chain of quality'; the TPM equivalent is the equipment life cycle. Both aim at prevention. Both widen the scope to include the operator, the product, the process, and the environment. Both aim to 'spread the load' by getting front line staff to take over as much responsibility as possible thereby directing authority to where it is most effective and freeing up specialists to do more complex tasks (thereby creating a positive feedback loop). Both use 'management by fact'.

TPM can be viewed in relation to the 'Bathtub Curve', below.

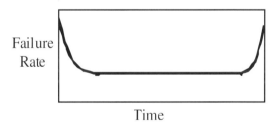

TPM addresses all parts of the curve. It reduces breakdowns in the burn-in period by early equipment maintenance and by improved understanding of equipment usage. It reduces breakdowns during the plateau period by autonomous maintenance and the 9 step programme. The 9 step programme also extends the life of equipment. The upturn point is addressed through predictive and planned maintenance. Failures during the wear-out period are also reduced.

Six Sigma Control Plan

A Control Plan is a management control document which serves to maintain process performance above an agreed level after the Six Sigma project closure.

The key purpose of having a Control Plan is to define the measured characteristics, their capability, how they are measured and a method of troubleshooting and repair if the process becomes out-of-control.

Quentin Brook proposes a tabular format for a Control Plan which records the process step, the measures, specifications, capability, measurement details (historical GR&R results and subsequent sampling plan), and response when required.

Brook also makes the useful comparison between the Control Plan and FMEA. The FMEA is used to identify and assess risks, and document existing controls. A Control Plan provides increased detail on the measurement controls which are required to maintain performance levels after the Six Sigma closure.

The Control Plan goes further than the operational measurements. It includes a Reliability Centred Maintenance (RCM) plan and future Gauge R&R requirements. It provides a clear action plan to identify process drift and recovery methodology, incorporating decision rules and references to Standard Operating Procedures and pokayoke warning systems.

The Control Plan must have agreement and buy-in at the point of the Six Sigma project closure. Although produced by the Project Manager, it should be contributed to by the Process Owner and team members and agreed to by the project Champion.

A useful example of a Plan is suggested in the 'The Black Belt Memory Jogger'. The structure is likely to be similar which ever template is used. The criteria are likely to include the following:

Process Step
KPIV
KPOV
Specification (LSL – Target – UPL)
Capability
RCM plan
GR&R (historical result and future plan)
Measurement plan
What (to measure)
When (to measure)
How (to perform, how many and how often)
Where (to measure)
Who (is responsible)
Decision Gate
Response

Note the similarity to the Six Sigma detailed process map.

Story Board

A Six Sigma Story Board is a graphical or pictorial account of the Six Sigma project as it progresses through the DMAIC methodology. It is the main record by which the project steps are communicated and is used in both project reviews with the Champion and also as a communication tool to support project closure.

The Storyboard is useful in maintaining project momentum and is also useful as a reference for future projects to see what tools were employed and what performance improvements resulted.

Completed Storyboards should be displayed close to the process to which they refer, and text should be kept brief, with the main communication served through graphics.

Storyboards come in many forms, but should contain the following:

- A statement of the problem (DEFINE)
- The name of all team members
- A photograph (or photos) of the problem or area
- A data history. (History is often a clue to the present problem)
- A project charter sheet (see page 15), probably enclosed in a plastic folder)

- A fishbone diagram. It is useful to show by means of coloured note, which aspects are outstanding (red), and which have addressed (green)
- The stagexs of sub-projects (or the DMAIC stages) each with a PDCA circle to indicate progress
- The savings in Quantity, Cost, Delivery, etc. A storyboard should be located at "Gemba", and should remain in place for (perhaps) 3 months after the project is complete

Further Reading on Control:

Stephen R. Schmidt, Mark J. Kiemele, Ronald J.Berdine, *Knowledge Based Management*, Air Academy Press & Associates, Colorado Springs, 1996.

Mark J. Kiemele, Stephen R. Schmidt, Ronald J.Berdine, *Basic Statistics*, Air Academy Press & Associates, Fourth Edition, Colorado Springs, 1997.

Stephen R.Schmidt and Robert G.Launsby (Air Academy Associates), *Understanding Industrial Designed Experiments*, Air Academy Press & Associates, Fourth Edition, Colorado Springs, 1997.

Quentin Brook, *Six Sigma and Minitab, 2004*. QSB Consulting Ltd, www.QSBC.co.uk.

Michael Brassard, Lynda Finn, Dana Ginn, Diane Ritter, *The Six Sigma Memory Jogger II*, Goal/QPC, New Hampshire, 2002.

Six Sigma Academy, *The Black Belt Memory Jogger*, Goal/QPC, New Hampshire, 2002.

Dana Ginn and Evelyn Varner, *The Design For Six Sigma Memory Jogger*, Goal/QPC, New Hampshire, 2004.

Rath & Strong, *Six Sigma Pocket Guide*, Fifth Printing, MA, 2001.

B.Cauldwell, *All Change*, IEE Manufacturing Engineer, pp16,17, June 2004.

John Bicheno, *The New Lean Toolbox*, PICSIE Books, Buckinghamshire, 2003.

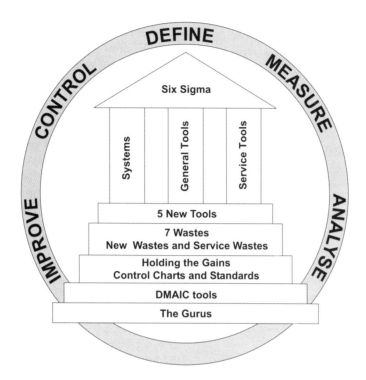

The 7 Wastes

Overproduction
Waiting
Transporting
Inappropriate Processing or "Overprocessing"
Unnecessary Inventory
Unnecessary Motion
Defects

New Wastes
Making the Wrong Product Correctly
Untapped Human Potential
Inappropriate Systems and Information
Waste Energy

Service Wastes
Delay
Duplication
Movement
Unclear Communication
Wrong Inventory
Lost Customer Opportunities
Errors

The 7 Wastes

Henry Ford and W. Edwards Deming both spoke about waste but it was Toyota's chief engineer Taiichi Ohno that identified the 7 wastes. Identification of waste is the first stage to its elimination. Now we recognize that use of the 7 wastes extends into service and distribution. Deming pointed out that to improve quality it is necessary to reduce waste. Continually.

The 7 wastes are productivity- rather than quality-related. But quality and productivity are closely linked. Improved productivity leads to leaner operations which make quality problems more visible. And better quality improves productivity by cutting out wasteful practices such as rework, extra inspection, and all the activities associated with doing an operation for the second time. So a systematic attack on wastes is also a systematic attack on some of the underlying causes of poor quality. By reducing waste we get to work "smarter" rather than "harder". More for less: its got to be good!

The opposite of waste is value adding. By definition, any activity that does not add value for the customer is waste and should be a candidate for reduction or elimination. We can classify activities into value adding, non value adding, and non value adding but temporarily necessary. The last two are waste. Value adding activities may be to do with the present or the future.

The 7 wastes are a set rather than individual entities. As a set they form the core of the just-in-time or lean philosophy, and as such they have been the subject of awareness training for operators in manufacturing. Checklists have often been developed from them. At Toyota there are waste checklists for manufacturing, distribution, and clerical operations.

You can remember the seven wastes by asking, "Who is TIM WOOD?" Answer: Transport, Inventory, Motion, Waiting, Overproduction, Over-processing, and Defects. (This idea came from the Lean Office at Cooper Standard, Plymouth, UK.)

The Waste of Overproduction

Ohno believed that the waste of overproduction was the most serious of all the wastes because it was the root of so many problems. Overproduction is making too much, too early or "just-in-case". It is working ahead of the production schedule, which in turn should be linked to the customer's rate of demand. The aim should be to make exactly what is required, no more and no less, just-in-time and with perfect quality. Overproduction discourages a smooth flow of goods or services. "Lumpiness" (i.e. making products or working in erratic bursts) is a force against quality and productivity. By contrast, regularity encourages a "no surprises" atmosphere which may not be very exciting but is much better management.

Overproduction leads directly to excessive lead time and storage time and storage cost. As a result defects may not be detected early, products may deteriorate, and artificial pressures on work rate may be generated. All these increase the chances of defects. Taking it further, overproduction leads to excessive work-in-process inventories which lead to the physical separation of operations and the discouragement of communication.

Yet overproduction is often the natural state. People do not have to be encouraged to overproduce; they often do so "just to be safe". Often this is reinforced by a bonus system that encourages output that is not needed. By contrast, the Kanban system prevents unplanned overproduction by allowing work to move forwards only when the next work area is ready to receive it. Although kanban was made famous in manufacturing, it was originally developed from the supermarket restocking procedure and certainly has application in the service industry. (Hamburgers are only made at a rate in line with demand and clerical operations are most effective when there is a uniform flow of work.) The motto "sell daily? make daily!" is as relevant in an office as it is in a factory. In Lean we talk about "EPE" - every product every - to emphasize regularity and avoid overproduction.

The Waste of Waiting

The waste of waiting occurs whenever time is not being used effectively. Time is an important element of competitiveness and quality. Customers do not appreciate being kept waiting but they may be prepared to pay a premium to be dealt with faster. Waiting involves a delay to value adding activities.

In a factory, any time that materials or components are seen to be not moving (or not having value added) is an indication of waste. Waiting is the enemy of smooth flow. Although it may be very difficult to reduce waiting to zero, the goal remains. Whether the waiting is of parts in a factory or customers in a bank there should always be an awareness of a non-ideal situation and a questioning of how the situation can be improved. Waiting interrupts the rhythm of work.

When operators and employees are waiting for work or simply waiting for something to do, it is waste. Can the time not be better spent on another operation or on training, cleaning, maintaining, checking, practising changeovers or even deliberate relaxation? All of these are forces for improved quality and productivity. But they require management to have developed a contingency plan on the best use of time.

A bottleneck operation that is waiting for work is a waste. As Goldratt has pointed out in his book "The Goal", "an hour lost at a bottleneck is an hour lost for the whole plant". Effective use of bottleneck time is a key to regular production which in turn strongly influences productivity and quality.

And of course don't keep customers waiting. Sooner or later they will leave, and you will get to feel the pain.

The Waste of Transporting

Customers do not pay to have goods moved around (unless they have hired a removal service!). So any movement of materials in a factory is waste. It is a waste that can never be fully eliminated but it is also a waste that over time should be continually reduced. The number of transport and material handling operations is directly proportional to the likelihood of damage and deterioration. Double handling is a waste that affects productivity and quality.

Transporting is closely linked to communication. Where distances are long, communication is discouraged and quality may be the victim. Feedback on poor quality is inversely related to transportation length, whether in manufacturing or in services. There is increasingly the awareness that for improved quality in manufacturing or services, people from interacting groups need to be located physically closer together. For instance, the design office may be placed deliberately near the production area.

When this waste gains recognition by employees steps can be taken to reduce it. Measures include monitoring the flow lengths of products through a factory or paper through an office. The number of steps, and in particular the number of non value-adding steps, should be monitored. (This can be used as an input into various techniques such as value analysis, nominal group, or time charting.)

A very useful exercise is to do a "spaghetti" diagram, tracing movement on a diagram of the layout. This works in offices and factories. And don't forget to do a spaghetti diagram on customer movement.

The Waste of Inappropriate Processing or "Overprocessing"

Inappropriate processing refers to the waste of "using a hammer to crack a nut". Thinking in terms of one big machine instead of several smaller ones discourages operator "ownership", leads to pressure to run the machine as often as possible rather than only when needed, and encourages general purpose machines that may not be ideal for the need at hand. It also leads to poor layout, which as we have seen in the previous section, leads to extra transportation and poor communication. So the ideal is to use the smallest machine, capable of producing the required quality, distributed to the points of use.

Inappropriate processing refers to machines and processes that are not quality capable. In other words, a process that cannot help but make defects. (The concept of capability is dealt with more fully in the section on "holding the gains".) In general, a capable process requires to have the correct methods, training, and tools, as well as having the required standards clearly known.

Inappropriate processing also refers to people who are not "quality capable" of doing the job required of them. If that is so, why is it so? Is it due to motivation or inability or unclear communication?

The Waste of Unnecessary Inventory

Although having no inventory is a goal that can never be attained, inventory is the enemy of quality and productivity. This is so because inventory tends to increase leadtime, prevents rapid identification of problems, and increases space thereby discouraging communication. The true cost of extra inventory is very much in excess of the money tied up in it.

Lean (or JIT) manufacturing has taught that inventory deliberately hides problems by covering them up. So, perhaps, a quality problem is not considered important because there are always extra parts available if one is defective. Lean encourages deliberate inventory reduction to uncover this sort of problem. Perhaps the safety inventory is deliberately cut. If nothing happens - fine, you have learned to operate with a leaner system. If stoppage occurs - good, because the problem has been recognized and can now be attacked at its root cause. (See the 5 Why technique on how this is done.)

The Waste of Unnecessary Motions

Unnecessary motions refers to the importance of ergonomics for quality and productivity. If operators have to stretch, bend, pick-up, move in order to see better, or in any way unduly exert themselves, the victim is immediately the operator but ultimately quality and productivity.

This is why an awareness of the ergonomics of the workplace is not only ethically desirable, but economically sound. Toyota, famous for its quality, is known to place a high importance on "quality of work life". Toyota encourages all its employees to be aware of working conditions that contribute to this form of waste.

It is sometimes instructive to make videos of both operators and customers. For instance, in a bistro a video may reveal that an assistant could serve coffee and cake in half the time with a little thought. Hotter and more consistent coffee would result, and customers would enjoy faster service. Get the operators themselves to make the video and to watch it. And in a bank make a video of customers searching for forms and pens.

At work, in factory or office, this waste is strongly related to safety. Remove unsafe acts and unsafe conditions. Audit for "near misses".

The Waste of Defects

Last, but not least, is the waste of defects. This one was included by Ohno to complete the set, and is the "bottom line". Defects cost money. Just how much is discussed under the technique of Cost of Quality. The Toyota philosophy is that a defect should be regarded as a challenge, as an opportunity to improve, rather than something to be traded off against what is ultimately poor management. That a defect, any defect, is a waste has much in common with the uncompromising "zero defect" view of Phil Crosby.

Further reading:
Japan Management Association, Kanban : *Just-in-Time at Toyota*, Productivity Press, 1985
Maasaki Imai, *Gemba Kaizen*, McGraw Hill, 1997, Chapter 6
Goldratt and Cox, *The Goal*, STG

New Wastes

Various authors have extended Ohno's list. Here are a few:

*   The *Waste of Making the Wrong Product* (correctly). Womack and Jones have suggested this. It relates back to their first principle of Lean Thinking "The critical starting point for Lean Thinking is Value" and value "begins with the ultimate customer". Today this is also the starting point of ISO 9001:2000.

*   The *Waste of Untapped Human Potential*. Ohno was reported to have said that the real objective of the Toyota Production System was "to create thinking people". So this "new" waste links directly back to the original seven. Human potential does not just need to be set free. It requires clear communication, commitment, and support.

*   The *Waste of Inappropriate Systems and Information*. This also has its origins in Lean Thinking and Business Processes. Don't automate waste. Go for the most simple, visible system. As Michael Hammer has said, "don't automate, obliterate"

*   *Waste Energy*. This is not merely a question of being green, but reduction makes increasing economic sense. But beyond this, wasting energy such as leaving lights and printers switched on overnight is symptomatic of wider malaise.

Seven Service Wastes

Most of the above wastes are seen from the organisations perspective. What about the customer's perspective? Perhaps a quality improvement programme should begin with the service wastes:

*   *Delay:* on the part of customers waiting for service, for delivery, in queues, for response, not arriving as promised. The customer's time may seem free to the provider, but when she goes elsewhere the pain begins.

*   *Duplication:* having to re-enter data, repeat details on forms, copy information across, answer queries from several sources within the same organisation.

*   *Unnecessary Movement:* queuing several times, lack of one-stop, poor ergonomics in the service encounter.

*   *Unclear Communication,* and the wastes of seeking clarification, confusion over product or service use, wasting time finding a location which may result in misuse or duplication.

*   *Incorrect Inventory:* out-of-stock, unable to get exactly what was required, substitute products or services.

*   *Opportunity Lost* to retain or win customers, failure to establish rapport, ignoring customers, unfriendliness, rudeness.

*   *Errors:* in the service transaction, product defects in the product-service bundle, lost or damaged goods.

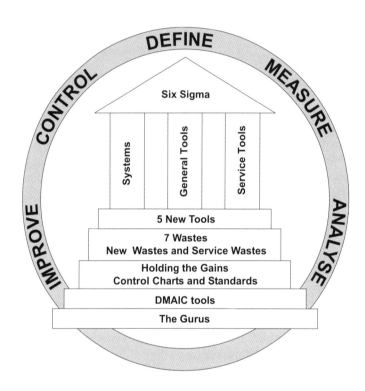

5 "New" Tools

**Affinity Diagram
Interrelationship or Network Diagram
Tree Diagram
Contingency Chart or Decision Tree
Matrix Analysis**

The New Tools

A working knowledge of the basic "7 Tools of Quality", described in a separate section, was considered by Ishikawa to be necessary for everyone. The "new" tools, described in this section, are not for everyone in the organisation, but should be useful to every manager, decision maker and team leader. The origin of the new tools is unclear. Several have been around for a long time. But it was Mizuno who collected up seven and assembled them in a book entitled "The 7 New Quality Tools for Managers and Staff". The five new tools presented here are almost the same as those assembled by Mizuno and concentrate on the most useful ones. Like the basic 7 tools, the new tools should be thought of as a set, working together for maximum effectiveness.

The Affinity Diagram

The Affinity Diagram is a brainstorming aid used in group situations. The concept is a simple, but very effective. First a problem or issue is selected. This may be a specific issue or gut desire to improve. Then an appropriate group is assembled. A facilitator is appointed, ideally not a usual member of the group. The group brainstorms out suggestions by writing them on cards in silent generation mode. The cards are stuck up on a board. The group, now in discussion or in silent mode, works on assembling the cards into sets having an "affinity" with one another. Having rearranged and assembled them, a new card is added for each set with a brief description summarising the essential features of the group. So the output is a set of Summary Cards, one for each set of ideas. The end result is a clearer understanding of the issues involved or approaches that are possible. This tool should be used for idea generation and grouping, but not for detailed problem solving; the facilitator has to watch for this.

There seem to be several advantages: it is a participative exercise which generates commitment, it identifies commonalities in thinking within the group, and it provides a wealth of ideas which can be refined by using other tools. It is excellent for preliminary planning purposes, particularly in addressing ill-defined areas where the problem is to identify the problems. The group undertaking an Affinity Diagram task will often be an established team, but for some situations a special purpose group, ideally comprising a "diagonal slice" through the organisation, is required.

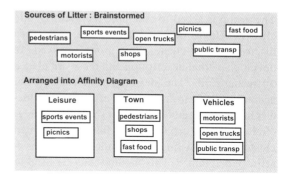

There is no one correct way, but a few suggestions follow :

- Use an external facilitator, with no "bones to pick"
- State the area clearly, even if it is not possible to state the problem
- Use 3M "Post-It" cards : one idea per card
- Have a silent generation period of 10 minutes
- Confine the card writing to a few words. Use verbs and nouns.
- Put the cards up on a flip chart in random order; don't preassemble
- Allow brief description of each idea but no discussion or criticism
- Let the facilitator assemble the first affinity sets without discussion
- Allow extra cards to be generated or cards to be rewritten
- In rearranging cards, don't allow arguments or long discussions
- It is worth spending time on the wording of Summary Cards
- Draw bold lines around the sets
- Keep the pace brisk; don't bog down in discussion.

Recently Gitlow has suggested the use of the "pictorial affinity diagram". Here, clusters of pictures rather than ideas are grouped. A leader develops a problem or mission. A suitable group is chosen. The group is given a set of pictures relating to a problem, product or service situation. The group is asked to assemble the pictures into clusters. This is done in silence. The group then discussses each cluster. The group is asked to develop a verbal description and these are placed on header cards. The idea is to name each cluster according to their "root cause effect". The clusters are transferred onto a large sheet of paper. A circle is drawn around each cluster and related clusters joined by lines. The result is the "pictorial affinity diagram". This method may be used to identify hitherto unrcognised themes, requirements or activities. For instance, what are the true attractions of a resort or theme park or university?

The Interrelationship or Network Diagram

An interrelationship diagram seeks to identify logical strings of connections between several problems or issues. The aim is to reach consensus about root causes, and about the sequence in which work should proceed. It helps prioritise areas to be tackled and avoids tackling inappropriate problems. People who have been involved with systems analysis will have already used this tool. So will project managers.

The tool can be used as a follow up from the generation of an Affinity Diagram. In this case, just begin where the team left off assembling the Affinity Diagram. There will already be logical groupings, so the task is to connect up the cards.

Alternatively, begin with a statement of the problem or issue or "Root Definition". Then brainstorm out the set of "minimum necessary activities" to address the problem or issue. Use a verb and noun in each activity. It's a good idea to use "Post-It" stickers; one per activity. Once again the task is to connect up the activities.

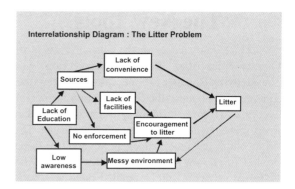

Yet another possibility is project management. First consider the major elements to be completed. (This is called "chunking"). Connect up the major chunks first. Then take each major chunk and consider the detailed activities for each. Where a project network is being considered there will be only one ending point, and usually one start point. This is not necessarily the case with interrelationship diagrams. Use with CPA - see Project Management.

Many connections will be obvious. There will be a logical sequence. But one can also tackle it in a more systematic way. For each activity ask
* which activities does the activity precede (draw an arrow to these activities)
* which activities does the activity follow (draw an arrow from these activities)
If the activities have been written on Post-It stickers, start a new diagram on a fresh sheet and reassemble stickers where the relationships exist.

Once you have completed the diagram examine it. Look out for activities where there are several arrows coming out. This would indicate an important root cause. These are obvious issues or problems to tackle first. Then look out for activities where there are several activities leading into them. This may indicate an important junction, milestone, or bottleneck that also requires serious attention.

Project managers know that the process of developing a network diagram is at least as important as doing the subsequent calculations to calculate the critical path (see the Project Network tool.) So it is with interrelationship diagrams in general. Having the team discuss the nature of the connections is a valuable educational task. Invariably the team will come away from the exercise feeling that they understand a lot more about the problem or issue. They will have much better ideas on how to tackle its solution or improvement. So for quality improvement in unstructured situations this is a very useful, but simple to use, tool.

The Tree Diagram

The Tree Diagram arranges goals, problems, or customer requirements in a hierarchy. It shows how a problem or goal is broken down into more detailed sub-problems or sub-goals. The breakdown into greater levels of detail can take place on several levels, until a manageable set of activities is achieved. It is similar to an organisation chart, or for those in manufacturing, like a bill of materials. That's it!

The Tree Diagram is another simple but effective tool. The only thing strange about it is the fact that it is not used more often. It helps to break down complex issues into sub issues. It is useful in planning a new program, a new service, or a new product. It is an essential part of constructing a Quality Function Deployment matrix (see the section on QFD) where it is used to assemble the "voice of the customer".

In constructing a Tree Diagram use a team. The same comments as for Affinity Diagrams apply. Start at the top, with the overriding goal or requirement. This is the first "parent" item. Then, layer by layer, consider what actions or activities or features are necessary to achieve the parent. What are the components (or child items) of the parent? When this is complete, consider each child item as a parent and repeat for the next layer. And so on. A rule of thumb is that there should no more than about 7 sub items (child items) for each parent item.

The Tree Diagram is related to the Affinity Diagram in as far as the statement of the original problem or issue may form the highest level item, the Summary Cards would be good candidates to form the first level, and a selection of cards from those brainstormed out would probably be used at various levels within a branch under each summary card.

The Tree Diagram is really another form of Interrelationship Diagram. The difference is that in a Tree Diagram each sub activity or goal has only one "parent" or main goal on the next highest level, whereas in the Interrelationship Diagram there is no such rule so that several interconnections are possible at each level. The Interrelationship Diagram is the spaghetti, but the Tree Diagram is a carefully layered dessert with the cherry on the top.

Perhaps the most difficult problem in assembling a tree diagram is to ensure that all items on each level are approximately at the same "level of resolution". So for example a "Total Quality Programme" would normally be found on a higher level than a "SPC Programme".

Contingency Chart or Decision Tree

The Contingency Chart helps to map the risks associated with the implementation of a plan. The chart looks similar to a Tree Diagram, except that on each layer all the alternatives to achieving the goal on the layer above are given. In the language used for the tree diagram, a parent is a statement of the goal and the child items are the alternatives. A child item on one level can also be a parent to levels below. Having established the tree, contingencies can be specifically considered.

Like much in project management the real value lies in the team-based process which considers alternatives beforehand. Too often project management concentrates on the mechanical aspects of activities and time, rather than on people and risk. The Contingency Chart helps to correct the balance. Both the Contingency Chart and the last of the new tools (discussed in the last section) are necessary for good project management.

Managers familiar with decision theory will recognise that we are talking about a "decision tree". In a proper decision tree, however, probabilities are assigned to each option, and a calculation made as to the path of least cost. This degree of sophistication is not considered necessary in a Contingency Chart; in fact more emphasis is placed on thinking through the alternatives than in doing the calculations.

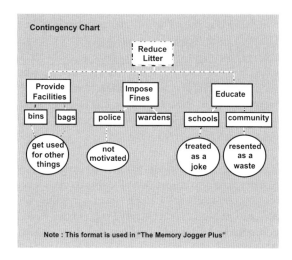

Note : This format is used in "The Memory Jogger Plus"

So the Contingency Chart amounts to sequential brainstorming followed by evaluation. Begin with the overall goal; write this at the top. Then the team brainstorms out alternative ways of getting there. These form the first level of the chart. Then each alternative is considered, and once again the team brainstorms out alternatives. These are written in under each major alternative. Continue in this way until the team considers that sufficient detail has been covered. This is normally two, or unusually three, levels down from the goal. An alternative to the first step is to list the major activities necessary to reach the goal. Thereafter the method proceeds as before.

After sufficient alternatives have been generated, a final level is brainstormed. This contains, for each alternative, a set of things that could go wrong or the more likely possibilities. Of course, there are many things that could go wrong, but the team should consider only major or most likely events. The difference between alternatives and things that can go wrong are that the former are choices under one's

own control, but the latter are chance events or uncertainties. (The same distinction is found in decision trees).

Now the team should consider the consequences of each branch. What are the risks? What are the advantages? There are no rules how to do this; the value lies in the discussion. After discussion the best alternative should emerge, but the real value is having thought through the alternatives and their risks in advance. There should be few major unexpected events, and however the uncertainty turns out, the Contingency Chart should have ensured that most eventualities have been covered. "Forewarned is forearmed".

Matrix Analysis

Typically, problems in quality management have several "dimensions" or interacting aspects. For instance, the problem of litter requires at least education, litter bin provision, enforcement, cleanup, and bin clearing. The problem is then to sort them out, to rank them, to separate the "vital few from the trivial many" (to quote Juran). So Matrix Analysis is a set of tools for analysing data and for decision making. There are several tools ranging from simple to quite complex. A few of the most useful versions are looked at here. Matrix analysis can be used in conjunction with several of other tools in this book, but notably QFD.

Relative Weighting
A common way to weight or indicate relative importance is to merely distribute points between the factors under consideration. This is a "gut feel" procedure, common in market research and in customer focus groups. When done with a good sample of people (say above 30) it is possible to assign confidence limits to the results. A simple and useful technique.

A Matrix for Ranking Priorities : Pairwise Comparison
Pairwise comparison forces a more systematic consideration to be made, and therefore could be regarded as more reliable than point distribution. Of

course, pairwise comparison merely has a relative ranking as its outcome, not a relative weighting. Pairwise comparison typically follows an Affinity exercise or Tree Diagram exercise. The starting point is a set of actions or factors which need to rearranged into ranked order. Simply arrange the actions or factors to be ranked along two sides of a square matrix, with each side having the same actions. Give each factor or action a letter, just to make data entry easier. Mark the diagonal, from top left to bottom right. Then cross out all squares on the diagonal and all squares below the diagonal. You will left with a set of squares which enables each action to be compared with each other action. Now compare each action with each other action, pair by pair. Ask, firstly, for each pair, which action is the most important. If it is action A then write A in the square, and so on. If there is no clear difference or priority, leave the square blank. Repeat for all squares. Then, secondly, for all filled in squares, ask by how much does the chosen factor have priority over the second factor. If significantly different, give a score of 9 points. If only marginally, give a score of 3. Write the numbers in the squares. When all squares have been completed, add up the scores associated with each letter. The resulting scores represent the ranking. Very often you would find one or two really dominant actions or factors, and several with lower scores. This is normal and desirable. A Pareto analysis.

Two Dimensional Weighting

In, for example, Quality Function Deployment, but also in many other areas of quality management it is necessary to relate means to ends or "whats" to "hows". In QFD the "whats" are customer requirements and the "hows" are product features. To start, there will typically be a set of weighted or ranked "whats", derived by a method such as relative weighting. As for "hows", many product characteristics serve more than one purpose, for instance the meat in a hamburger provides nutrition, flavour, and bulk. The same can be said for a training programme which may provide skills, motivation and retain staff.

The problem is how to give weights or a ranking to the "hows", so that they reflect the "whats". Begin by constructing a matrix : whats in rows against hows in columns. The whats will usually be weighted, so add an extra column to reflect these weights. Now go through the matrix, cell by cell. For each, ask to what extent the how is able to meet the what. (eg. To what extent does the meat in a hamburger meet the requirement for nutrition?). The answer is high (write in 9 points), medium (write in 3 points), low (write in 1 point), or not at all (write in zero). In some cases a negative is possible (write in minus 3). Then, for each cell, multiply the point score by the weight for that row (i.e. for that "what"). Write this figure in the top right hand of the cell. Lastly, add up the top right hand figures for each column (i.e. for each "how"). This gives a weighting which reflects the ability of each "how" to meet each "what".

Example : Design of a Hamburger to Customer preferences

Begin with a Focus Group to determine Customer Requirements and relative weightings. Then :

Customer Requirements	Customer preference weighting	Beef	Bun	Lettuce	
Moisture	1	0 / 0	0 / 0	1 / 1	9 / 9
Flavour	3	27 / 9	0 / 0	0 / 0	9 / 3
Nutrition	3	27 / 9	9 / 3	0 / 0	0 / 0
Visual Appeal	5	45 / 9	5 / 1	5 / 1	5 / 1
Value for Money	5	45 / 9	5 / 1	0 / 0	5 / 1
Weighted scores		144	19	6	28

Conclusion : Concentrate attention on Beef and Ketchup

Note : This is the analysis performed in a QFD Matrix

The applications of this method are very wide. Apart from product design through QFD, other applications are selecting what sub-programmes are to be implemented as part of a Six Sigma programme, selecting suppliers, and selecting between several locations for a new factory.

Multi Dimensional Matrices

Multi Dimensional Matrices are a whole class of matrices which allow data to be analysed in several dimensions. Of course, strictly a matrix can compare only two factors at a time, but the inclusion of additional factors can add insight.

Two Dimensional matrices can show, for example, defects against operator; or complaints against shift.

Three Dimensional matrices can show defects against operator and time; or complaints against shift and location.

Four Dimensional matrices can show defects against operator and time as well as giving additional data relating to products; or complaints against shift and location as well as giving additional data on tasks performed.

In all cases the cells of the matrices can contain numerical data or symbols to indicate high, medium, low or nil.

Further reading:
Shigeru Mizuno (ed), *Management for Quality Improvement : The 7 New QC Tools*, Productivity Press, 1988
Michael Brassard, *The Memory Jogger Plus*, GOAL/ QPC, 1989
Howard S. Gitlow, "Learning about a Loved One: The Quality Management Approach", *Quality Engineering*, 13(1), September 2000, pp 115-119 (about pictorial affinity diagrams).

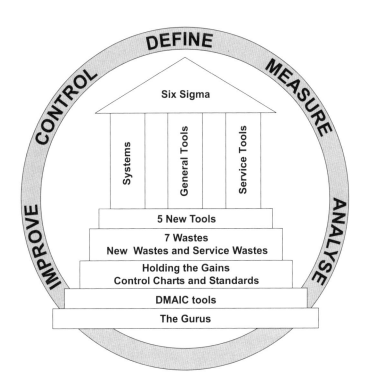

General Tools

5s, 5 Whys, 6 Honest Working Men, Benchmarking, Best Demonstrated Practice, Better Brainstorming, Cusum Charts, Force Field Analysis, Importance-Performance Matrix, Kaizen, Market Surveys and Customer Observation, Nominal Group Technique, Quality Function Development, Single Point Lessons, Supplier Partnerships

5S

5S is the basic housekeeping discipline for lean, quality and safety. It applies in office and on shop floor equally. Everyone has the experience of working better and feeling better in a tidy room. But it's also a mindset thing – changing attitudes from "I work in a dirty factory" to "I work in a manufacturing laboratory". The team should carry out the following steps with their supervisor. They should not be done by an outsider.

SORT

Throw out what is not used. The first step is to CLASSIFY literally everything by frequency. A good idea is to do this with the team and to touch every item systematically. If used every day, is the quantity correct? If used weekly can it be brought out weekly? If used monthly should it rather be located in the store? If never, or in doubt, then red tag or throw out. A Red Tag is a label with the date; if no one accesses it within a specified period it should be thrown out, recycled or auctioned. The sort stage should be done regularly – say once every six months, but as a regular activity not a re-launch of 5S.

SIMPLIFY (or Set in Order or Straighten)

Locate what is used in the best place. A place for everything (using shadow boards, inventory footprints, tools and dies on trolleys or at the right height, and colour matching to link associated tools). And everything in its place (if not in place and not in use, a problem is indicated). Personal toolboxes are discouraged because the tools for the job should be located at standardised locations. The standard is The "Dental Surgery". Why? Because all can relate to that standard of excellence, and know the consequences of failure. Try for 'One level' which means keeping dies, tools and parts at the same level as the workplace to minimise bending. Repeat this stage whenever products or parts change. Use a spaghetti diagram for analysis. Ergonomic principles should play a role here, and an ergonomic audit may help.

SWEEP (or Shine or Scrub)

Keep up the good work. This includes physical tidy up, on an ongoing basis, and "visual sweeping" whereby operators are always on the lookout for anything out of place, and try to correct it immediately. Some companies adopt a 5 minute routine whereby operators work out a 5 minute cleanup routine for each day of the week such that by week end everything has been covered the required number of times. Designate exactly who is responsible for what and what the standard is. The stage will require suitable cleaning equipment to be suitably located and renewed. There may be a sign-off chart for routine cleaning.

"Cleaning is Checking," means that these are integrated. You don't just clean up, you check for any abnormality and its root causes. The garage analogy is first clean up – this enables oil leakage to be identified. Continue to clean up any leakage that occurs. But then ask 'why is leakage occurring' and decide what should be done for prevention.

STANDARDISE (or Stabilize)

Only now is it possible to adopt standard work. This is the real bottom line for 5S. See the section on Standard Work. But 5S standards also need to be maintained. So develop standards for the first 3 S's.

SUSTAIN (or Self Discipline)

Everyone participates in 5S on an ongoing basis. Self-discipline is about participation and improvement. Carry out audits on housekeeping regularly. Some award a floating trophy for achievement.

Some companies add a sixth S – **SAFETY**. Although good to emphasize, a good 5S program should stress safety as an aspect of each of the five stages. It may confuse to list safety separately. Safety procedures and standards should also be developed, maintained and audited as part of the programme. Unsafe conditions should certainly be integral to 5S. Toyota and Ford, amongst others, do an ergonomic risk assessment exercise.

An alternative for 5S is CANDO – Cleanup, Arrange, Neatness, Discipline, and Ongoing improvement.

Some companies adopt regular walk about audits and competitions. The shift supervisor audits daily, the area manager weekly at random times, the production manager monthly – perhaps on the basis of drawing a number out of a hat in the presence of all cell leaders, whereupon all cell leaders and managers descend on the chosen area (office or factory) and give it a thorough evaluation. At weekly audit level, a floating trophy and wooden spoon are awarded.

Many companies now claim that they are doing 5S but are in fact doing 2S sporadically. Not completing all 5 means that sustainability will be low. This is waste. 5S will then require increasing effort to re-energise. The real productivity and quality benefits of 5S are in the later S's, particularly standardisation, not the relatively easy-to-do first two.

5S audit and scoring systems are becoming more common. The best do this regularly and display the result for all areas on a board showing comparisons with the last period.

The physical areas of responsibility must be clear. Display a layout diagram of the plant showing 5S boundaries.

Hirano suggests a host of activities including 5S days, 5S visits to outside companies. 5S model workplaces, 5S patrols, and a 5S month. Excessive?

Extending the 5S Concept.
5S can be applied more widely. Four areas are given in the table. There are probably many more applications.

REMEMBER THE PRIME REASON FOR 5S IS STANDARD WORK.

Further reading:
Productivity Press Development Team, *5S for Operators*, Productivity, 2002
Hiroyuki Hirano, *5 Pillars of the Visual Workplace*, Productivity, 1995

	Inventory	Suppliers	Computer Systems	Costing Systems
Sort	Throw out all dead and excessive stock	Select the best two suppliers in each category. Scrap the rest.	Delete all dead files and applications	Do you need all those costs and variances? Prune them!
Simplify	Arrange in the best positions	Cut all wasteful, duplicate transactions	Arrange files in logical folders, hierarchies	Cut transactions. Review report frequency. Incorporate o/head directly
Sweep	Regularly review dated stock and ABC category changes	Improve supplier performance by supplier assoc & kaizen	Clear out inactive files regularly	Audit the use made of costing reports and transaction size & frequency
Standardise	Footprint	Milkrounds, payments	Systems, formats	Adopt reporting standards
Sustain	Audit ABC, RRS	Audit performance	Audit perform & response	Review and reduce.

The "Five Whys" and Root Cause Problem Solving

The 5 whys is a technique to ensure that the root causes of problems are sought out. It simply requires that the user asks "why?" several times over. The technique is called the "5 whys" because it is the experience of its inventor, the Toyota company, that "why" needs to be asked successively five times before the root cause is established.

This simple but very effective technique really amounts to a questioning attitude. Never accept the first reason given; always probe behind the answer. It goes along with the philosophy that a defect or problem is something precious; not to be wasted by merely solving it, but taking full benefit by exposing the underlying causes that have led to it in the first place. Many (for instance the MIT study on the worldwide car industry) believe that it is this unrelenting seeking out of root causes that have given the Japanese motor industry the edge on quality, reliability and productivity.

An example follows: A door does not appear to close as well as it should. Why? Because the alignment is not perfect. Why? Because the hinges are not always located in exactly the right place. Why? Because, although the robot that locates the hinge has high consistency, the frame onto which it is fixed is not always resting in exactly the same place. Why? Because the overall unit containing the frame is not stiff enough. Why? Because stiffness of the unit during manufacture does not appear to have been fully accounted for. So the real solution is to look at the redesign of the unit for manufacture.

Perhaps there are even more whys. Why did this happen in the first place? (Insufficient cooperation between design and manufacturing.) Why so? (It was a rushed priority.) Why? (Marketing had not given sufficient notice.) Why? And so on.

A variation of the 5 Why technique is the "5 How" technique. This is often used in tracing the cause of a failure in a product or in service delivery. ("How did that happen?"....) The thinking and procedure is exactly the same.

Root Cause Problem Solving

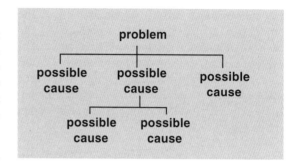

The emphasis on "root cause" problem solving is fundamental to the philosophies of JIT, lean manufacturing, continuous improvement, the Toyota production system, and TQM. It means solving problems at the root rather than at the superficial or immediately obvious levels. But how do you get to the root cause? In the following sections two technique are examined. But first, we should look at the whole concept of root cause analysis.

In a thoughtful article Finlow-Bates concludes that there are no ultimate root causes. Rather, root causes are dependent upon the problem owner; there can be more than one potential root cause and that the final choice of root cause cannot be made until the economics of possible solutions have been considered. He illustrates the point by the example of a delivery failure. The root cause for the customer is that the parcel is late. The root cause for the delivery company is that the problem delivery failure was due to the van not starting which can be traced to the root cause of a leaking underground tank. For the tank supplier the root cause was a failure in the solder. For the solder supplier the root cause was .... Each person along the chain is not interested in the problems of lower echelons. Each of these causes represents a failure in control or in communication. The real issue is therefore not what is the root cause, but how can the problem be (temporarily?) solved most economically and effectively to prevent recurrence.

Finlow-Bates suggests following **six steps:**
*   What is the unwanted effect? (Finlow-Bates suggests two words; subject and deviation, for example parcels late)

* What is the direct physical cause?
* Follow the direct physical line of the cause. For example, parcels late, van won't start, etc. This establishes the "staircase"
* Ask who owns the problem at each stage.
* Identify where should one intervene in the staircase to effect a long-term solutions.
* Identify the most cost-effective of the solutions.

Barrier Analysis

Barrier Analysis (Wilson et al) may be used where implementation problems are being experienced. It amounts to a straightforward set of questions that are addressed to an unwanted problem or event:

* What are the threats, hazards or potential problems that can influence the situation? Threats may be physical or psychological, or influence status, security, or self esteem.
* Who or what are the "Targets" for change? In any change there will be victims and beneficiaries, some perhaps unintended. It is useful to list these. The target may be human, animal, organisation, environment, group, team, family, or other.
* What are the barriers? These may be physical, geographic, communication, language, culture, administrative, organisational. Also, what are the safeguards that are supposed to be in place to make the change easier or more acceptable, and if they are not in place, why are they not. Should the threat be isolated, or should the target be isolated, or both?
* What is the "Trace". That is, what is the sequence of events or history that has lead up to this situation? Real or imaginary.

Further reading:
T Finlow-Bates, "The Root Cause Myth", *The TQM Magazine*, Volume 10 Number 1, 1998, pp10-15
The following book has some useful material in relation to the last section:
Paul Wilson, Larry Dell, Gaylord Anderson, *Root Cause Analysis: A Tool for Total Quality Management*, ASQC Quality Press, Milwaukee, WI, 1993

Six Honest Working Men and Is Is-not Analysis

Rudyard Kipling's "Six Honest Serving Men" remains, some 100 years after it was first written, one of the most useful problem analysis tools. The original verse is,

> "I knew six honest serving men, they taught me all I knew; their names are what and why and when, and where and how and who".

Such a simple little verse; so much wisdom – so often ignored!

The six men are a very useful way of defining customers, their requirements and what is really valued. In the opinion of the author it's a pity that the six men is not the first call of marketeers rather than the "marketing mix" or 4 P's (product, price, place, promotion).

The six men can also be usefully combined with Is Is-Not analysis first put forward (it is believed) by Kepner-Tregoe. This helps clarify what is, and what is not the issue, and so on:

	Is	Is Not	So...
What	Lectures	Tutorials	
(Why) **When**	Start Time	Finish Time	
Where	Too cold	Seats	
Who	John	Norman	
(How)			

Benchmarking

The Benchmarking Centre defines Benchmarking as "the continuous, systematic search for, and implementation of, best practices which lead to superior performance". In essence it aims to compare the performance of critical processes with leading achievers. It is a guideline to what is necessary in present performance and to future requirements if the organization is to be "world class". It is about knowing yourself and really knowing the competition - where they are weak, where they are strong, and where they are going. To an extent, benchmarking is an alternative to "cost plus" budgeting, and to productivity targeting by simply "matching inflation". It is outward looking rather than inward looking. It is concerned with tracking performance, not just taking snapshots. Think of the ongoing Deming Cycle. And like several other techniques discussed here it is equally applicable to products and to services.

Of course, benchmarking is not new. People and organizations have always compared themselves to others. Juran quotes the example of how, early in the 20th century, German generals visited the Barnum and Bailey circus to study the world-renowned methods it used to move materials and animals from city to city. But it was the Xerox corporation that appears to have pioneered "competitive benchmarking". It was the systematic and comprehensive way in which Xerox set about making benchmarking a competitive weapon that has brought this technique into prominence. Robert Camp of Xerox is responsible for much of the thinking, and has written the definitive book.

Types of benchmarking include Internal (where one branch is compared with others - see the section on Best Demonstrated Practice), Competitive (as per Xerox, comparing with the toughest competitors), Functional (where similar processes are compared inside of your industry but not with direct competitors - say room service in two non-competing hotels), Generic or Process (where basic processes found in any business, such as recruitment or billing, are compared), and Performance (where measures (typically on cost, quality, delivery, reliability, and response) are compared.

Benchmarking can be seen not just as a technique on its own, but as one of a mutually reinforcing family. The insights from benchmarking are useful if not necessary for quality function deployment. For value management it can help identify what is technically possible. It is powerful as a force for change when used in force field analysis. It identifies on which of Garvin's dimensions

of quality a competitor is competing. And systematic measurement is part of any quality improvement process, such as the Deming cycle or the Juran Trilogy.

We begin with the understanding that a single measure of performance is rarely adequate. Just as several instruments are necessary to monitor and control the performance of a car or plane, so it is with any organization. Now recognize that to be competitive in quality and productivity, steady inward-looking progress may not be enough. But of course one does not go out to benchmark everything possible. It must be a directed search. Robert Camp proposes using a process control model (involving inputs, process, outputs, feedback, and results) and suggests that all these are benchmarking candidates, and that "step zero", where time and care is spent considering the purpose of the exercise is most important. Camp has a 10 step approach covering planning (covering what, whom, and how), analysis (where the current and future gaps are determined), integration (involving communication and revision of goals), action (where actions are developed, then monitored, and benchmarks recalibrated).

What to measure

Robert Camp states that benchmarking is "first a goal setting process". You have to know what to benchmark, and, as with much of quality management, this brings you right back to the customer. Identify who are your customers, present and future. Now you can begin to assess their needs and the necessary core processes. These are the areas where the organization absolutely needs to perform well, and areas where unique advantages can be obtained. (Garvin's dimensions are useful as an aid). The areas can be assembled by a team using the nominal group technique (see the section on NGT) and the Affinity Diagram (see the New Tools).

There may be a particular interest in targeting areas that are known to be important, such as costs or complaints or geographical areas. Staff policies, salaries, and personnel policies on training, recruitment, and the use of people at work may be relevant. There may well be some standard productivity or quality measures in the industry. Beware of being too specific on what should be measured - there may be "more than one way to skin a cat". The idea is to concentrate on processes first and measures of performance second. With what it is you wish to benchmark now known, the next step is to identify who to benchmark.

It is a good idea to think through the information collection procedure, in particular who will be responsible and where will it be centred. The latter has to be clearly communicated so that if information is obtained from or by an unexpected source, it will still go to the right place. It will often be necessary to dedicate people, part time or short term, to information collection.

Who to measure
The aim of competitive benchmarking is to find the "industry best" performance, and where appropriate the "world best" performance. The toughest competitors now and in future are often known or easy to short-list, so a search can be more focused. But do not close minds to the possibility of world class performance from a new or unexpected source. Benchmarking is an ongoing process. In Xerox, benchmarking is known of throughout the company and a "little red book" on benchmarking has been widely issued. For non competitive benchmarking the services of organisations such as the Benchmarking Centre can be used to pinpoint benchmarking partners.

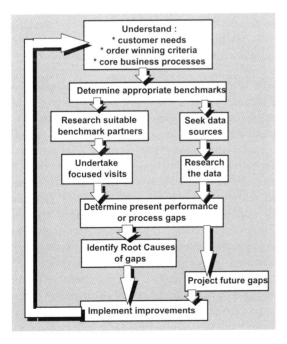

How to measure
Internal benchmark information is relatively easy to obtain. Now comes the external information. There is a huge number of potential sources of benchmark information. But it must be ethically collected and secured (The Benchmarking Centre has a code of conduct including legality, exchange (give and take, not just take), confidentiality (not publishing or passing on ideas to third party competitors), and use.) For competitive benchmarking some possibilities are: a library database search, commercial press cutting databases, specialist industry reviews in newspapers or journals, specialist surveys (e.g. by *The Economist Intelligence Unit*), trade magazines, conference papers and proceedings (managers love to tell of their achievements at such events), market research, special surveys, factory visits and evening meetings of relevant societies, annual financial reports and published accounts, trade and sales literature, quotations from the companies themselves, management consultants and academics (who may be prepared to disclose general information while disguising names). Several authors have made the point that benchmarking is not "industrial tourism" (just visiting), nor is there any point in visiting companies that are in such a totally different league of organisation or technology that there is no chance of catching up.

Many benchmarking exercises will involve actual use of competitor products, including one-way viewing through mirrors of customer usage, and full technical disassembly.

Using benchmarks
Benchmarking is not static. It aims at projecting future trends. So when the internal and external benchmarks are assembled, analysts can begin to assess the critical question of whether the "gap" between own and competitor performance is widening or narrowing. This leads to the establishment of areas for priority action. Competitive benchmarking can become a management philosophy in itself, with the attempt being to remain or achieve "industry best" position in the particular niches identified as important. As soon as one set of improvements has been implemented, it all begins again. It's the Deming cycle.

Benchmarking Beware!

To quote Womack and Jones in *Lean Thinking*: "to hell with benchmarking!". The only true benchmark is the zero waste operation. And Christensen warns of benchmarking yesterday's advantage.

Further reading:

Robert Camp, *Benchmarking*, ASQ Quality Press, 1989

Gregory Watson, *The Benchmarking Workbook*, Productivity Press, 1992

Robert C. Camp, *Business Process Benchmarking*, ASQ Quality Press, 1995

Best Demonstrated Practice

Best Demonstrated Practice (BDP) is a form of internal Benchmarking. It assembles the best features of several operations to create a benchmark of a theoretical operation comprising the best features of each. For instance, in an insurance company one branch may have the best life policy service, another branch the best walk-in service, a third the best postal response time. So the best theoretical branch could comprise the best demonstrated practice from each.

Assuming that an organisation has several similar operations, the steps are as follows :

* Establish the prime measure of interest. For quality, this may be response time or queue time, a customer satisfaction measure, or a defect level, error rate, or number of complaints. For costs the measure could be contribution level, a resource utilisation level, or a comparable cost such as personnel cost per square metre. The measures should be measurable without much controversy. These measures should be carefully chosen, often in association with representative staff from operations, and be related to corporate objectives.

* Establish a suitable measure or measures against which to analyse the prime measure. Examples may be number of customers or products, sales or turnover, or size or area of operation.

* Plot the graph and analyse with branch representatives. Examples are shown. Usually an envelope or lower bound will be formed. This represents the best demonstrated practice. These are the locations to learn from. And operations furthest from the line should get attention: What special problems do they have? What are the causes? After discussion the group may conclude that there are subgroups involved within which it is possible to learn, and that nothing can be learned by comparing some locations with others.

BDP is applicable in decentralised operations where there are several branches, offices or outlets providing approximately the same products or services. It is particularly useful where, in addition, there are no external benchmarks. The approach has been used for both quality improvement and cost reduction. A more sophisticated version of BDP known as Data Envelopment Analysis, which enables analysis beyond two dimensions to be undertaken, relies on linear programming. This mathematical technique is often not warranted because of data uncertainties when an approximation is good enough and has presentational difficulties. The real challenge lies in acceptance of the findings and participation in the analysis, both of which are inhibited by sophisticated mathematics.

BDP can be used in conjunction with several other techniques in this book, such as flowcharting (to better understand the process), SPC (to identify branches that are operating beyond the control limits), and Six Sigma. It should not be used as a "big stick" by management to chase apparent laggards but rather to explore reasons for deviation and opportunities for improvement and learning.

Further reading:
Michael Norman and Barry Stoker, *Data Envelopment Analysis,* Wiley, 1991

Better Brainstorming

Brainstorming is a vastly popular technique for idea generation. But beware!

Although a popular technique, research shows brainstorming to yield results that are often worse than obtained by the same number of individuals working alone. The Nominal Group Technique (NGT) is often superior – see the separate section on this. Yet brainstorming may still be worthwhile to do to focus the team on a common problem, to build up team spirit, and to improve communication. A mixed strategy is probably best – use brainstorming for some general aspects, but individual creativity for specialised aspects. Also use brainstorming in series – breaking an overall problem down into elements, and sequencing sessions appropriately. Certainly if brainstorming is used casually without planning, it can be a poor technique.

Several "rules of thumb" have been established for a good brainstorming session. These are

* The group size should be approximately 5 to 9
* Quantity rather than quality of ideas is emphasised; evaluation comes later
* No judgement or criticism is allowed.
* Participants should be stimulated by the ideas of others. This means they have to listen and develop.
* All ideas should be noted down. You may make use of a fishbone diagram
* No hierarchy. All ideas carry equal status. No person should dominate.
* The facilitator or recorder should not allow discussion, lengthy explanation or criticism.
* Humour and "way-out" ideas are encouraged. Having fun works.

* The final stage is grouping of ideas, perhaps using "affiliation diagrams" (see separate section)

The problems with brainstorming have been summarised by Furnham as

* "Social loafing" where a few participants exert less effort and allow others to carry the load. Apparently this is strongly influenced by the perceptions of the participants as to eventual use and importance, and their position.
* "Evaluation apprehension" where participation is influenced by the fear of looking foolish or of being criticised.
* "Production blocking" where ideas that are coming thick and fast have to queue up and are forgotten or are considered less relevant.

A good facilitator should be aware of these, and give gentle encouragement.

Furnham suggests that "Electronic Brainstorming" is far more effective, Here participants work independently via a computer but have access to the developing ideas of others. These have several benefits including shorter meetings, more and better ideas, easier to set up, better documentation, and cost savings.

Further reading:
Adrian Furnham, "The Brainstorming Myth", *Business Strategy Review*, Vol 11 No 4, Winter 2000, pp 21-28
Weatherall and J Nunamaker, *Introduction to Electronic Meetings*, Technical Graphics, Chichester, 1996

Cusum Charts

A "Cusum" or Cumulative Sum Chart is a type of control chart which is particularly useful for detecting small but significant changes in the process. Take a look at the conventional control chart shown and the corresponding cusum chart. Notice that the change is almost undetectable in the control chart, but is very clear on the cusum chart. A large change, on the other hand, is easy to detect on a conventional control chart.

Any situation where it is desirable to detect a sudden change quickly is a candidate for a cusum. Examples are customer enquiries, fuel consumption (cusums are an excellent indicator that something has gone wrong with a vehicle), yield from a chemical process, response times or failure rates.

data presented as a time series

same data presented as a cusum :
the change is clearly apparent

"Mask" used for determining if a significant shift has occurred

Force Field Analysis

The force field diagram is a simple but very effective tool to identify, in good time, the various "pressures" for and against change. A force field diagram is typically used early on in the implementation of quality programs such as SPC, may also be used for introducing change on a much smaller scale. Force field diagrams were introduced by an organizational analyst, Kurt Lewin, in the 1920s. Their beauty lies in their simplicity which enables any employee to grasp and use the concept in minutes.

Consider a change, any change, that is being introduced within the organization. This may be an attempt to reduce defects or improve service. The concept is simply that a chart is put up with a vertical line drawn on it. This represents the "status quo", or position at present. To the left of the line are listed the forces encouraging change to take place. To the right are the forces resisting the change. The pressures for change oppose the forces resisting change. In a service delivery case, where speed of delivery is the problem, the forces for change could include customer expectations. Staff fears over redundancy may be opposing the change. Whether change will actually come about is dependent upon whether the forces for change will become dominant. To identify the forces at an early stage is half the battle - the forces for change can be effectively utilized and the forces opposing change effectively tackled. That's it!

To plot a cusum, merely subtract the average (or target) value of the process from the actual measurement, add the resulting number to the previously accumulated number and plot it on the chart. It will be appreciated that if the average remains unchanged the resulting cusum will hover around a constant value, but if the average changes the graph will "take off" either up or down.

An extension of the basic force field diagram is to show the linkages between the opposing forces. An example is shown in the figure.

With conventional control charts, control limits are needed to detect if a real change has taken place. With a cusum, a "V Mask" is used. To construct a V Mask you need to calculate the standard deviation of the process measurements. This will require a minimum of 20 readings. Then draw the V Mask as shown in the figure on a transparent sheet. Lay the V Mask with point A (the head) over the latest reading, keeping the mask horizontal. A change is significant if the cusum line crosses one of the trailing arms.

The "trick" of using force field analysis is group participation and brainstorming. Not only does a group think of many factors which an individual would not, but the results become "their" analysis of the problem. Get the people concerned together and ask them, "What are the factors that are tending to push us to make this change?" Enter them on the diagram. Then ask, "OK, now let's think about the factors that are preventing us from making this change." Enter them too. Now ask "What can be done about these factors?". There

Further reading:

BS5703, *Guide to Data Analysis and Quality Control using Cusums*, Parts 1 to 4, British Standards Institution, Milton Keynes, 1982

J. Murdich, *Control Charts*, Macmillan, London, 1979

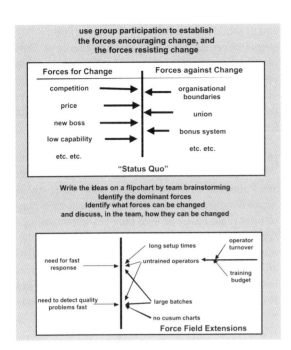

use group participation to establish
the forces encouraging change, and
the forces resisting change

Forces for Change — Forces against Change

competition

price

new boss

low capability

etc. etc.

organisational
boundaries

union

bonus system

etc. etc.

"Status Quo"

Write the ideas on a flipchart by team brainstorming
Identify the dominant forces
Identify what forces can be changed
and discuss, in the team, how they can be changed

need for fast
response

long setup times

untrained operators

operator
turnover

training
budget

need to detect quality
problems fast

large batches

no cusum charts

Force Field Extensions

are two sets of answers: encourage the 'good' forces and reduce the 'bad' forces. This should lead to a set of actions that the group has developed themselves, which can then be tackled. Force field analysis can be used in conjunction with several other techniques and tools. A common one is the cause and effect diagram, which can be used to explore alternatives to the barriers that have been identified.

The Importance Performance Matrix

When measuring performance or collecting survey information on service quality, it is important that a two-dimensional view be taken: performance along one axis and importance along the other. This was (probably) first suggested by Kotler in 1987, has appeared in several quality-related publications since then, with the latest variant by Slack et al. Collecting information along these two dimensions greatly improves the utility of the information. Thus a high score on performance may mean "overkill" or "achieving target", and a low score on performance may indicate urgent action or simply low priority. Often quality or

customer satisfaction surveys reflect only the dimension of satisfaction or performance but ignore the importance to the customer of the factor being surveyed. This can lead to misleading conclusions. It's a simple but powerful idea.

In a customer survey, using for instance a 1 to 5 rating scale, there should always be two scales for each question : one going from excellent to poor (or performed well to performed badly) to cover satisfaction or performance, and the other from important to not important. Then, when plotted on a matrix, the priority clusters become clear. See the figure.

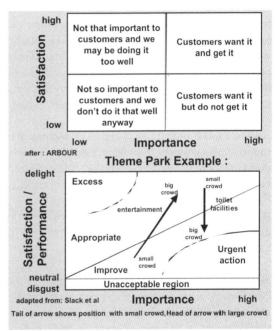

Tail of arrow shows position with small crowd, Head of arrow with large crowd

A further dimension is also possible : one could collect the performance importance data by category or market segment and show the variation on a performance importance matrix. For instance, one could categorise performance importance information at a theme park by the number of attendees and discover that some aspects might migrate from the high-low (overkill) quadrant to the low-high (priority) quadrant as the crowd size grows and facilities get pressed for capacity. See the lower figure.

Further reading:

Willard C Hom, "Making Customer Service Analysis a Little Easier with the PGCV Index", *Quality Progress*, Vol 30, No 3, March 1997, pp 89-93

Philip Kotler, *Marketing for Non-profit Organizations*, Prentice Hall, Englewood Cliffs, 1987, pp 635-636

Slack, N., Chambers, Harland, Harrison, Johnston, *Operations Management*, Pitman, London, 1995, p 740.

Kaizen

Kaizen is the Japanese name for continuous improvement. As such it is central to Quality and to Lean operations. It brings together several of the tools and techniques described in this book plus a few besides. The word originates from Maasaki Imai who wrote a book of the same name and made Kaizen popular in the West. Although a registered name of the Kaizen Institute, the word is now widely used and understood and has appeared in the English dictionary.

Kaizen can be thought of a series of incremental improvement projects. But a better thought is simply doing better today than yesterday. In a true Kaizen company everyone dedicates to doing this every day.

According to Imai, Kaizen comprises several elements. Kaizen is both a philosophy and a set of tools.

The Philosophy of Kaizen: Quality begins with the customer. But customers' views are continuously changing and standards are rising, so continuous improvement is required. Kaizen is dedicated to continuous improvement, in small increments, at all levels, forever (!). Everyone has a role, from top management to shop floor employees. Top management must allocate the resources and establish the strategy, systems, procedures and organisational structures necessary for Kaizen to work. Middle managers are responsible for implementing Kaizen. They must monitor performance of the continuous improvement programme, and ensure that employees are educated in the use of the necessary tools. Supervisors are responsible for applying Kaizen. They must maintain the rate of suggestions, coach, and improve communications at the workplace. And shop-floor employees must make suggestions, learn new jobs, use the tools, and generally participate in continuous improvement activities individually and in teams. Imai's book has several examples of how this philosophy works its way down the organisational hierarchy in Japanese companies.

John Shook and later Bill Sandras have made the point that there are two types of kaizen – Flow Kaizen and Point Kaizen. Flow kaizen is about value stream improvement and getting flow going on a cross plant or inter plant basis, or bold changes to streamline a service. Point kaizen are smaller scale opportunities often identified as constraints or low hanging fruit and coming out of mapping activities. Senior management should be more concerned with Flow Kaizen and middle management with point kaizen – however both types should be the concern of all levels.

The Kaizen Flag concept is that there are three activities: innovation (breakthrough), kaizen (ongoing improvement) and following standards. Each level of management needs to do all three but in different quantities. Operators need both to do kaizen and to follow standards. Imai believes that it is the central band of kaizen that makes the difference - but also the extent to which standards are followed. Imai believes that without active attention, the gains made will simply deteriorate (like the engineers' concept of entropy). But Imai goes further. Unlike Juran who emphasises "holding the gains", Kaizen involves building on the gains by continuing experimentation and innovation.

The authors believe there is another dimension: "passive" and "enforced" kaizen. Some organisations think they are doing kaizen, but their brand of kaizen is "passive" or left to chance. Improvements are left to the initiative of operators or industrial engineers or managers. If they make improvements - good. If they don't - "oh well, sometime". Passive incremental may also be termed "reactive". A reaction takes place in response to a crisis. By contrast, enforced improvement is proactive. "Crises" are actually engineered and the pressure kept on. For example, Intel brings out a new chip at regular, paced intervals and does not wait passively for technological breakthrough. 3M dictates that 30% of revenues will come from new products every year. Toyota has various "tricks" such as line stop and Andon, kanban withdrawal and waste checklists. This forces the pace.

According to Imai there are several guiding principles. These include:

* Questioning the rules (standards are necessary but work rules are there to be broken and must be broken with time)
* Developing resourcefulness (it is a management priority to develop the resourcefulness and participation of everyone)
* Try to get to the Root Cause (try not to solve problems superficially)
* Eliminate the whole task (question whether a task is necessary; in this respect Kaizen is similar to BPR),
* Reduce or change activities (be aware of opportunities to combine tasks).

The Tools of Kaizen: Kaizen incorporates several tools but the most well known are the Deming Cycle, "5 S", the "5 M Checklist", and the 5 Whys. Also central to Kaizen is the recognition and elimination of waste or Muda (see the section on the Wastes). 5 S and the 5 Whys are described in a separate sections. Visual management is a feature; making operations and quality visible through charts, displayed schedules, kanban, painted designated inventory and tool locations, and the like.

Standards are important in kaizen, to prevent slipping back to old ways. The Kaizen Institute believes there should be periods of consolidation to allow new ways to bed-in, rather than rushing ahead. This idea is absolutely compatible with Deming's "Standardise, Plan, Do, Check" sequence, or Juran's "holding the gains". Standards and Learning are inter-linked. The Joy Manufacturing Company, for instance, communicates value engineering improvements to sites around the world. At Toyota, engineers on new product development make extensive use of checklists. When an engineer learns something new, that knowledge is added to a checklist used for all future vehicles.

Recently, Imai has extended and elaborated on Kaizen in Gemba Kaizen. Gemba means going to the place of action and collecting the facts, rather than sitting in a remote office and collecting opinions.

Kate Mackle former head of the British Kaizen Institute and now with 'Thinkflow' promotes Kaizen through a bottom-up learning process, which eventually permeates the whole organisation. For this a good champion is needed, and Mackle has developed a methodology for identifying suitable people.

Yuso Yasuda has described the Toyota suggestion scheme or "Kaizen system". The scheme is co-ordinated by a "creative idea suggestion committee" whose chairmanship has included Toyota chairmen (Toyoda and Saito) as well as Taiichi Ohno. Rewards for suggestions are given at Toyota based on a points system. Points are scored for tangible and intangible benefits, and for adaptability, creativity, originality, and effort. The rewards are invariably small amounts, and are not based on a percentage of savings. However operators value the token reward and the presentation ceremony itself. Note the contrast with typical Western Suggestion Schemes. Toyota recognises that all suggestions or kaizen ideas may not be beneficial. The Pareto law certainly applies. There will be many ideas that are not really worthwhile, but at the other end of the distribution there will be few hugely beneficial ideas which make the whole scheme very worthwhile. One is reminded of the classic statement about advertising, "I waste half of the money I spend but the problem is I don't which half".

Further reading:
Maasaki Imai, *Kaizen: The Key to Japan's Competitive Success*, McGraw Hill, New York, 1986
Maasaki Imai, *Gemba Kaizen*, McGraw Hill, New York, 1997
Yuasa Yasuda, *40 Years, 20 Million Ideas*, Productivity Press, Cambridge MA, 1991

Market Surveys and Customer Observation

All organisations require information about customer needs, expectations, and satisfaction, so market research and surveys are vital. There are several types of market or customer survey but the real issue is to select the right mix and to make sure that information collected is used effectively. For instance, Hewlett Packard uses three linked approaches: A Customer Satisfaction Survey, a Customer Feedback System, and Customer Visits which are carefully integrated for comprehensiveness and efficiency.

But first, consideration needs to be given to which customers should be surveyed. This is not obvious, and depends on the questions you want answered. Candidates are current customers (by spending category, location, need ?), past customers, potential customers, competitor's customers, or customer's customer. Here we consider the major types of survey:

Focus Groups: A small group of customers or potential customers gathered to discuss open-ended questions. Powerful, and can lead down unexpected roads. Requires a skilled facilitator, and may not be representative of customer base, unless particular care is taken. Group members may stimulate one other, to produce further ideas.

Questionnaires: Answers to specific questions are sought. Inexpensive. Low response rate common, requires skilled questionnaire and sample design to be effective and representative. Temptingly easy, but to be meaningful should be first tested on a representative group, validated and statistically justified. Deming and Juran both emphasised that quality is in the eyes of the customer. Therefore a good satisfaction questionnaire should be a two stage process : the first a pilot to determine what it is that are important to customers, and the second to survey opinion. (See also the section on The Performance Importance Matrix).

Interviews: One-on-one talk seeking insights as to why a customer has or has not purchased, or has

"defected"; best done close after the event (a new customer, or with a customer where new business has failed to be gained or has been lost). Requires active follow up, skill with defecting customers, and assurance of confidentiality.

Mystery Shopping: A false or posed customer goes through the whole process with your company and with competitors. Not confined to shopping but can be used in any service. Valuable first hand documentation, but possibility of being accused of spying or mistrust.

Customer visits: To check on-site (for example, at a customer's home) on satisfaction levels, and on where and how a product is being used. Questioning users on-site may be very insightful, and may lead to unexpected opportunity. Requires customer goodwill, but is often appreciated by customers.

Debriefing of employees: Surveys show that perhaps three times as many complaints are registered with frontline staff as are received in writing. In many organisations, the views of customers picked up by front-line staff are simply lost. Debriefing must be done in a relaxed, supportive, no-blame atmosphere. Employees may also have good ideas as to new products or services.

Telephone surveys: See questionnaires. May get higher response than mail, but run a risk of greater annoyance.

Freephone (Toll free / Hotline): Making complaining easier. Effective because some problems can be solved immediately, or you are speaking to customers at the time they are actually experiencing problems. This is not the case with questionnaires, for example, and customers are prone to forget detail.

Customer Tours: Customers invited to visit the factory, service facility, bridge of ship or aeroplane. Can create goodwill with high-ticket items and can use the opportunity to discuss reasons for purchase, needs and expectations with captive customers. Confidence and loyalty building.

The Internet: A new source of customer satisfaction data is the internet. These sites have the advantage of assembling frank, uncensored, "from the hip" remarks and experiences. Some include photographs of products that have gone wrong - a well known 4WD vehicle is a case in point. Discussions and evaluations of consumer products and services appear in activity and hobby oriented web pages, and useful information can be obtained from newsgroups. Moreover, newsgroups can be continually monitored, automatically. You will need a search engine such as Google.

Observation: Observation has emerged as a most powerful way of creating innovative products and services, and is therefore particularly relevant for Kano "Performance" and "Delighter" factors. (See the section on the Kano model). Observation can also be combined with some of the previous survey methods, for instance during focus groups, mystery shopping, or customer tours. The method involves close observation, with or without video. Variations are a hidden camera, one-way mirrors, and sound recording. Observation can reveal hidden frustrations and anxieties and difficulties with products and services which customers are reluctant to reveal.

Imprint Analysis: This is a new way of conducting market research which aims at seeking out underlying emotions - the concept being that it is emotion that drives actions and emerging needs. Imprint analysis apparently uses "decoding workshops" involving discussion, word association and relaxation. The true meaning of words to customers and the emotions that result are explored. See Afors and Michaels.

Further reading:
Terry G Vavra, *Improving Your Measurement of Customer Satisfaction*, ASQ Quality Press, Milwaukee, WI,1997
Byron J Finch, "A New Way to Listen to the Customer", *Quality Progress*, May 1997, pp 73-76
Christina Åfors and Marilyn Zuckerman Michaels, "A Quick Accurate Way to Determine Customer Needs", *Quality Progress*, July 2001, pp 82-87

The Nominal Group Technique (NGT)

The nominal group technique (NGT) is a particular form of team brainstorming and creative problem identification. It is worth specific mention since it is now widely used in place of "classic" brainstorming. NGT is a well researched procedure that draws on both individual and group strengths, using each as appropriate, and which prevents domination by particular individuals. It is a technique that supplements most of the other techniques discussed, and can be used for issue identification, idea generation, and problem solving. NGT has been widely used in quality and productivity improvement and in organizational strategy formulation.

A team is the basic requirement; preferably a multi-level, multi-discipline team. Different disciplines bring different perspectives, and different levels cross the communication boundaries that exist in every organization. A team of between 8 and 12 is considered ideal and there is also a facilitator and perhaps an assistant. The facilitator usually explains to the team how NGT works before the actual process begins.

NGT begins with the facilitator reading out a **statement of the problem** to be tackled by the team. The statement must be carefully prepared and written out, not merely presented "off the cuff". After hearing the statement there are likely to be questions seeking clarification. The facilitator should not now try to revise the problem statement but should encourage the participants to restate the problem in their own words. The facilitator may even nominate two or three members to restate the problem. This is a deliberate stage which forces the team to think through the problem statement in their own words. The facilitator must prevent any team member from dominating, and must not allow the problem to be "hijacked". The original problem statement written out by the facilitator is not altered, it is merely a process of restating in the team's own terms. The facilitator allows discussion to continue until problem formulation, as expressed by the team, seems satisfactory.

The next stage is called **silent generation**. About 15 minutes is allowed for this, during which time silence is required. Each team member is asked to write out his or her responses, alternatives, or suggestions to the problem statement. The team should remain in one room for this purpose since the "atmosphere" of work encourages mental concentration. Team members who may finish early are still required to remain in the room without talking. The silent generation period is used because study has shown that this is the most effective initial way to generate a variety of viewpoints and ideas. The facilitator will discourage talking but may cut short the period if all seem to have completed the task. The facilitator would bring the period to an end, but emphasize that creativity has not stopped and that new ideas can be added to the team member's lists at any time.

Key: F = facilitator, I = individual, G = group

Now the **"round robin"** stage begins. Each team member is asked in turn to put forward an idea or suggestion. These will usually be taken from team member's lists but not necessarily so. Often, additional ideas will be stimulated by the ideas of others. When each idea is put forward, the facilitator may seek clarification from the team member, but should not change or develop the idea. Other team members are not allowed to participate in these

discussions but must wait their turn. No criticism is allowed by team members or the facilitator. As each idea is put forward or clarified is entered onto a chart by the facilitator or an assistant. Only one idea is put forward by each team member before passing onto the next member. Round robin continues until ideas begin to run out and team members say "pass". When there are no more ideas the stage ends.

With all ideas entered onto charts and displayed around the room , the next stage begins. This is called **clarification**. The stage encourages the power of group creativity. The facilitator goes through each suggestion in turn. Once again criticism is not allowed, and each idea is further explained as necessary. Team members may suggest modifications or additions. The team should also group ideas that they consider to be similar (See the section on the Affinity Diagram.) This may result in some deletions and rephrasing. It is important that this stage does not get bogged down in detail, so the facilitator must cut short any rambling discussion. Note: although not part of the original NGT theory, this is the stage at which various creative thinking concepts such as the de Bono "po" word or Roger van Oesch's "Creative Whack Pack" can be used.

The next stage is **selection and ranking**. Blank cards are now issued to all team members and, once again individually and in silence, each member is asked to select the top (say) six ideas. Each member writes the idea on a card together with the ranking at the top of the card. Use 6 for the best idea, and 1 for the lowest chosen idea. Often, team members are asked to alternate as follows. First the top idea of the chosen six is selected and a 6 entered on the card. Then the lowest ranking idea of the six is selected and a 1 written on its card. Then the second best idea is selected and a 5 written on its card, and so on.

The final stage involves the **final ranking**. This is done by the facilitator who gathers the cards and writes the results on a new chart. Next to each idea, transferred from the cards, is written the rankings as given by all the team members. The rankings are anonymous. Each idea will have a string of numbers being the rankings of the team members. There may be several zeros where a team member did not rank an idea in the top six. Now the scores are added up to five the final ranking. In the case of a tie, the idea having the highest number of team member rankings wins.

The result is a ranked set of ideas which , even though there may not be complete team consensus, at least come close to this ideal and which have been generated without dominance by any team member.

Quality Function Deployment (QFD)

Quality Function Deployment is a "meta" technique that has gown hugely in importance over the last decade and is now used in both product and service design. It is a meta technique because many other techniques described in this book can or should be used in undertaking QFD design or analysis. These other techniques include several of the "new tools", benchmarking, market surveys, the Kano model, the performance - importance matrix, and FMEA.

Customer needs are identified and systematically compared with the technical or operating characteristics of the product or service. The process brings out the relative importance of customer needs which, when set against the characteristics of the product leads to the identification of the most important or sensitive characteristics. These are the characteristics which need development or attention. Although the word "product" is used in the descriptions which follow, QFD is equally applicable in services. Technical characteristics then become the service characteristics.

Perhaps a chief advantage of QFD is that it is carried out by a multi-disciplinary team all concerned with the particular product. QFD acts as a forum for marketing, design, engineering, manufacturing, distribution and others to work together using a concurrent or simultaneous engineering approach. QFD is then the vehicle for these specialists to attack a problem together rather than by "throwing the design over the wall" to the next stage. QFD is therefore not only concerned with quality but with the simultaneous objectives of reducing overall development time, meeting customer requirements, reducing cost, and producing a product or service which fits together and works well the first time. The

mechanics of QFD are not cast in stone, and can easily be adapted to local innovation.

The first QFD matrix is also referred to as the "house of quality". This is because of the way the matrices in QFD fit together to form a house-shaped diagram. A full QFD exercise may deploy several matrix diagrams, forming a sequence which gradually translates customer requirements into specific manufacturing steps and detailed manufacturing process requirements. For instance, a complete new car could be considered at the top level but subsequent exercises may be concerned with the engine, body shell, doors, instrumentation, brakes, and so on. Thereafter the detail would be deployed into manufacturing and production. But the most basic QFD exercise would use only one matrix diagram which seeks to take customer requirements and to translate them into specific technical requirements.

The "House of Quality" Diagram

In the sections opposite the essential composition of the basic house of quality diagram is explained. Refer to the figure.

Customer requirements

The usual starting point for QFD is the identification of customer needs and benefits. This is also referred to as "the voice of the customer" or "the whats". Customers may be present or future, internal or external, primary or secondary. All the conventional tools of marketing research are relevant, as well as techniques such as complaint analysis and focus groups. Customers may include owners, users, and maintainers, all of whom have separate requirements. Refer to the section on market research. After collection comes the problem of how to assemble the information before entering it into the rows. In this the "new tools" of affinity and tree diagrams have been found to be especially useful. This results in a hierarchy; on the primary level are the broad customer requirements, with the secondary requirements adding the detail.

Marketing would have responsibility for assembling much of the customer information, but the team puts it together. Marketing may begin by circulating the results of surveys and by a briefing. It is important to preserve the "voice of the customer", but the team may group like requirements using the affinity diagram. The team must not try to "second guess" or to assume that they know best what is needed by customers.

Rankings or relative importance of customer requirements

When the customer requirements are assembled onto the matrix on the left of the house diagram, weightings are added on the right to indicate the importance of each requirement. Weightings are established by market research or focus groups or, failing these, the team may determine rankings by a technique such as "pairwise comparison". (In pairwise comparison, each requirement is compared with each other. The most important of the two requirements gains a point, and all scores are added up to determine final rankings.) The Kano model (see separate section) is very often used with QFD as an aid in determining appropriate weightings.

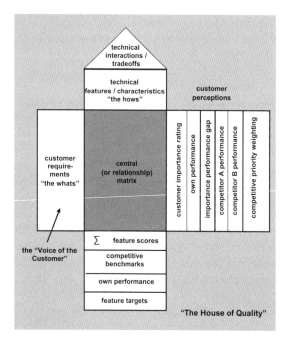

"The House of Quality"

Technical characteristics and associated rankings

Customer requirements and weightings are displayed in rows. The technical characteristics (or "hows" or "technical responses") form the columns. These characteristics are the features that the organisation provides in the design to respond to the customer requirements (For a kettle this may include power used, strength of the materials, insulation, sealing, materials used, and noise.) Once again these could be assembled into groups to form a hierarchy, using the Tree Diagram. Here the team will rely on its own internal expertise. There are at least two ways to develop technical characteristics. On way is go via measures that respond to customer needs. For instance a customer need for the kettle may be "quick boil". The measure is "minutes to boil" and the technical response is the power of the heating element. Another is to go directly to functions, based on the teams experience or on current technology.

The Planning Matrix

To the right of the central matrix is found the planning matrix. This is a series of columns which evaluate the importance, satisfaction, and goal for each customer need. (See the figure). The first column shows importance to the customer of each need. Here a group of customers may be asked to evaluate the importance of each need on a 1 to 5 scale (1=not important, 5=vital, of highest importance). In the next column the current performance of each product or service need, is rated by the group of customers. The difference between the columns is the gap - a negative number indicates possible overprovision, a positive number indicates a shortfall. The reader will recognise that here the QFD process is duplicating the importance-performance matrix (see separate section), or the SERVQUAL gaps. The next few columns give the competitors current performance on each customer need. The aim of this part of the exercise is to clearly identify the "SWOT" (strengths, weaknesses, opportunities, threats) of competitor products as against your own. For example, the kettle manufacturer may be well known for product sturdiness, but be weak on economy. If economy is highly ranked, this will point out an opportunity and, through the central matrix, show what technical characteristics can be used to make up this deficiency. The gap (if any) between own and competitors performance can then be determined. Since the QFD team now has detail on the gap for each need and of the importance of each need, they can then decide the desired goal for each customer need - normally expressed in the same units as the performance column. Deciding the goal for each need is an important task for the QFD team. These goals are the weights to be used in the relationship matrix. (Note: in some versions of QFD there are additional columns).

The Central (or Relationship) Matrix

The central matrix lies at the heart of the house of quality diagram. This is where customer needs are matched against each technical characteristic. The nature of the relationship is noted in the matrix by an appropriate symbol. The team can devise their own symbols; for instance, numbers may indicate the relative strength of the relationship or simply ticks may suffice. The strength of the relationship or impact is recorded in the matrix. These relationships may be nil, possibly linked, moderately linked or strongly linked. Corresponding weights (typically 0, 1, 3, 9) are assigned . Thereafter the scores for each technical characteristic are determined as in the "new tool" of Matrix Analysis (refer to the section in this book which details how a total score is determined for each characteristic). This matching exercise is carried out by the team based on their experience and judgement. The idea is to clearly identify all means by which the "whats" can be achieved by the "hows". It will also check if all "whats" can in fact be achieved (insufficient technical characteristics?), and if some technical characteristics are not apparently doing anything (redundancy?). A blank row indicates a customer requirement not met. A blank column indicates a redundant technical feature. In practice, matrix evaluation can be a very large task (a moderate size QFD matrix of 30 x 30 has 900 cells to be evaluated). The team may split the task between them.

Technical Matrix

Immediately below the relationship matrix appears one or more rows for rankings such as cost or technical difficulty or development time. The choice of these is dependent on the product. These will enable the team to judge the efficacy of various technical solutions. The prime row uses the customer weightings and central matrix to derive the relative technical characteristic rankings. A full example is given under Matrix Analysis in the New Tools section of this booklet.

Next below the relationship matrix comes one or more rows for competitive evaluation. Here, where possible, "hard" data is used to compare the actual physical or engineering characteristics of your product against those of competitors. In the kettle example these would include watts of electricity, mass, and thermal conductivity of the kettle walls. This is where benchmarking is done. By now the QFD team will know the critical technical characteristics, and these should be benchmarked against competitors (See the section on Benchmarking - especially competitive benchmarking). So to the right of the relationship matrix one can judge relative customer perceptions and below the relative technical performance.

The bottom row of the house, which is also the "bottom line" of the QFD process, are the target technical characteristics. These are expressed in physical terms and are decided upon after team discussion of the complete house contents, as described below. The target characteristics are, for some, the final output of the exercise, but many would agree that it is the whole process of information assembly, ranking, and team discussion that goes into QFD which is the real benefit, so that the real output is improved inter-functional understanding.

The roof of the house

The roof of the house is the technical interaction matrix. The diagonal format allows each technical characteristic to be viewed against each other one. This simply reflects any technical trade-offs that may exist. For example with the kettle two technical characteristics may be insulation ability and water capacity. These have a negative relationship; increasing the insulation decreases the capacity. These interactions are made explicit, using the technical knowledge and experience of the team. Some cells may highlight challenging technical issues - for instance thin insulation in a kettle, which may be the subject of R&D work leading to competitive advantage. The roof is therefore useful to highlight areas in which R&D work could best be focused.

Using the house as a decision tool

The central matrix shows what the required technical characteristics are that will need design attention. The costs of these can be seen with reference to the base rows. This may have the effect of shifting priorities if costs are important. Then the technical trade-offs are examined. Often there will be more than one technical way to impact a particular customer requirement, and this is clear from rows in the matrix. And it may also be that one technical alternative has a negative influence on another customer requirement. This is found out by using the roof matrix. Eventually, through a process of team discussion, a team consensus will emerge. This may take some time, but experience shows that time and cost is repaid many times over as the actual design, engineering and manufacturing steps proceed.

The bottom line is now the target values of technical characteristics. This set can now go into the next house diagram. This time the target technical characteristics become the "customer requirements" or "whats", and the new vertical columns (or "hows") are, perhaps, the technologies, the assemblies, the materials, or the layouts. And so the process "deploys" until the team feels that sufficient detail has been considered to cover all coordination considerations in the process of bringing the product to market.

Note: QFD may be used in several stages in order to "deploy" customer requirements all the way to the final manufacturing or procedural stages. Here the outcome of one QFD matrix (e.g. the technical specifications), becomes the input into the next matrix which may aim to look at process specifications to make the product.

Assembling the team
A QFD team should have up to a dozen members with representation from all sections concerned with the development and launch of the product. Team composition may vary depending on whether new products or the improvement of existing products is under consideration. The important thing is that there is representation from all relevant sections and disciplines. There may well be a case for bringing in outsiders to stimulate the creative process and to ask the "silly" questions. Team members must have the support of their section heads. These section heads may feel it necessary to form a steering group. QFD teams are not usually full time, but must be given sufficient time priority to avoid time clashes. The team leader may be full time for an important QFD. The essential characteristics are team leadership skills rather than a particular branch of knowledge.

Relationship with other techniques
As mentioned. QFD is a "meta" technique in that several other techniques can be fitted in with it. For example, value management may be used to explore some of the technical alternatives, costs and trade-offs in greater detail. Taguchi analysis is commonly used with QFD because it is ideally suited to examining the most sensitive engineering characteristics so as to produce a robust design. Failure mode and effect analysis (FMEA) can be used to examine consequences of failure, and so to throw more light on the technical interactions matrix. And mention has already been made of the use of various "New Tools". In the way the QFD team carries out its work, weights alternatives, generates alternatives, groups characteristics, and so on, there are many possibilities. QFD only provides the broad concept. There is much opportunity for adaptation and innovation.

Further reading:
Ronald G. Day, *Quality Function Deployment*, ASQ Quality Press, Milwaukee, WI, 1994
Lou Cohen, *Quality Function Deployment : How to make QFD work for you*, Addison Wesley, Reading MA, 1995
Jack B ReVelle et al., *The QFD Handbook*, ASQ Quality Press, 1998

Single Point Lessons
A single point lesson is a useful way to tackle short, specific issues of importance or persistent quality issues. It is a different form of education. A single point lesson is simply a chart, placed at the point of use (at "Gemba") to illustrate one single new procedure. Examples may be a start up procedure for a machine, a regular check that must be carried out, the right way to dispatch a parcel, to manage kanban, or do any other standard operation. Usually a picture is incorporated as well as the stages of learning the procedure. Instead of sitting in a classroom learning a whole host of new concepts, most of which are soon forgotten, a single point lesson aims to teach new things of short duration at the point of use, by repetition.

Learning and short duration are significant points. The procedure should take a maximum of 15 minutes, frequently far less. The chart acts as a reminder and reinforcer. After basic instruction is given the chart is placed at the point of use for staff or operators to refer to. An instructor or manager would occasionally come around and test for compliance. When staff has demonstrated repeated competence the chart is removed. Stages are marked on the chart, frequently using a colour-in pie to indicate beginner, early learner, competent, master.

A single point lesson is not a standard operating procedure which should remain at the point of use permanently and which does not aim at learning.

Supplier Partnerships

The concept of supplier partners developed strongly in the 1990's as a result of the movement towards lean manufacturing. Lean emphasises reduction in waste, shortening of lead times, improvement in quality, continuous improvement, and simplicity. These are the goals of supplier partnership, also. Today supplier partnerships are found both in service and manufacturing.

The philosophy is that, through cooperation rather than confrontation, both parties benefit. It is a longer term view, emphasising total cost rather than product price. Cost includes not only today's price of the part or product, but also its quality (ppm rate), delivery reliability, delivery frequency, the simplicity with which the transaction is processed, and the future potential for price reductions.

But partnership goes further: long term, stable relationships are sought rather than short term, adversarial, quick advantage transactions. The analogy of a marriage is often used. It may have its ups and downs, but commitment remains. In a partnership, contracts will be longer term to give the supplier confidence and the motivation to invest and improve. Both parties recognise that the game whereby low prices are bid and then argued up on contingencies once the contract is awarded, is wasteful and counterproductive. Instead, it may be possible for both parties to cooperate on price reduction, sharing the benefits between them. Such cooperation may be achieved through the temporary secondment of staff.

For partnership to work, there must of necessity be few or single suppliers per part. There is small risk of "being taken for a ride" because there is too much for a supplier to lose, and much to gain. There may however be a risk of disruption in supply. This should be a calculated risk; where the probability is very small the advantages of a single supplier may outweigh the risks. And there are ways around this too : having one supplier exclusively supplying a part to one plant, but another supplier exclusively supplying the same part to another plant. This spreads the risk whilst still achieving single supplier advantages. Alternatively there is the Japanese practice of cultivating several suppliers simultaneously but then awarding an exclusive contract to one supplier of a part for the life of the product, and selecting another supplier for a similar part going into another end product. The idea is to work with a few good, trusted suppliers who supply a wide range of parts. Partnership has therefore resulted in drastic reductions in many a company's supplier base. An objective is to remove the long tail of the supplier Pareto curve whereby perhaps 10% of parts are supplied by 80% of the suppliers. Often it will be found that a large number of suppliers supply a very small proportion of value. Then, exploration as to how to reduce or combine sourcing begins. Award business to those identified as potential partners, and gradually drop the rest. Supplier days are held, often annually, when company plans and objectives are explained, measures given, prizes for best performance given out, and factory tours held. For true partnership, director level meetings are held periodically, with much more frequent manager and engineer contact.

On quality, a partnership aims at zero receiving inspection and delivery directly to the point of use. Packaging and part orientation may be specifically designed to reduce waste. Delivery would often be subject to kanban call-off : the partner would be given long term forecasts of gross requirements far out, more detailed requirements close in, but the actual sequence and timing of delivery is controlled by kanban. Both sides need to work towards schedule stability and avoiding "demand amplification" and the "Forrester Effect". This requires communication of demand right along the supply chain, and coordinated schedules. The point is, there should be advantages for both sides : unstable schedules ultimately cost the customer in terms of money and risk, and reduce the possibility of productivity gain at the supplier.

Sometimes, the supplier is responsible for maintaining inventory levels at a customer, called VMI (vendor managed inventory) which is increasingly found for consumables. Other times, a manufacturer may write the production schedule of the supplier. As trust builds, self billing or reconciliation becomes possible ("we built 100 cars, so here is our cheque for the 500 tyres we must have used"). An advanced form is "JITII" (a registered mark of the Bose corporation) whereby a few major suppliers have full time representatives in the host plant, with access to company records and schedules, and whose responsibilities include writing purchase orders on their own company. Such reps also participate in design work and R&D, and attend company planning meetings. JITII is now beginning to be found outside of Bose in companies such as Hewlett Packard and Intel. These partnership arrangements stem from the interesting insight of Lance Dixon that it is actually more secure to have a supplier write purchase orders on himself than it is for one of your own staff to do so (because legal action can recover damages from a supplier resulting from negligence, but seldom can be recovered from your own employee!).

Improved communication links via EDI or EPOS further enhance partnership advantages. Delivery cooperation becomes possible either through "milkrounds" (whereby small quantities are collected from several firms in an area every day, rather than from one firm once per week), or , where more work is given to one supplier, mixed loads are sent every day rather than one-product loads once per week. This improves flow and reduces inventories.

Cooperation on design is part of partnership. The manufacturer recognises the supplier's ability to design the parts that it makes, rather than simply specifying. This policy of "open specs" or "black box" specs can lead to faster product development, lower cost, and more up to date part supply. The partnership idea encourages the concept of a company sticking to its core business, whilst putting out non-core business.

Generally, supplier partnership makes sense for "A" and possibly "B" parts; less so for commodity items. Part criticality and risk also influence the partnership decision; you would not risk partnership with a company having poor industrial relations, or weak finances, or poor quality assurance. This means that a team approach is necessary in supplier selection. The Purchasing Officer may coordinate, but throughout the partnership Design would talk to their opposite number in Design, Quality to Quality, Production control to Production control, and so on.

Disadvantages? Time, commitment, costs of establishment, risk of inappropriate choices of partner, and short term cost reduction opportunities foregone against medium term gains.

Value engineering is a technique that both parties may adopt for mutual advantage. VE/VA is a powerful technique for cost, quality and delivery. In advanced partnerships a "satellite plant" dedicated to a particular customer and located nearby, or "suppliers in residence" where the supplier's operation and or some of its staff are permanently located on the customer's site, may be worth consideration. Volkswagen's Brazilian plants are reported to use supplier's employees on the VW assembly line - is this the future of partnership, or a quest for flexibility?

In Japan, and increasingly in the rest of the world, supplier partnership is now expanding down from relationships with first tier suppliers, to second and even third tier. Supplier associations are being established. These are "clubs" established to share the strengths of members. The thought, in common with TQM, is that quality is only as good as the weakest link in the supply chain or network.

Further reading:
James Womack, Daniel Jones, Daniel Roos, *The Machine that Changed the World*, Rawson Associates, New York, 1990, Chapter 6.
Peter Hines and David Taylor, *Going Lean*, 2000, Available via www. cf.ac.uk/carbs/lerc
Peter Hines, *Creating World Class Suppliers : Unlocking mutual competitive advantage*, Pitman, London, 1994,
Richard Lamming, *Beyond Partnership*, Prentice Hall, Hemel Hempstead, 1993,
Lance Dixon and Anne Millen Porter, *JITII : Revolution in Buying and Selling*, Purchasing Magazine / Cahners, Newton, MA, 1994

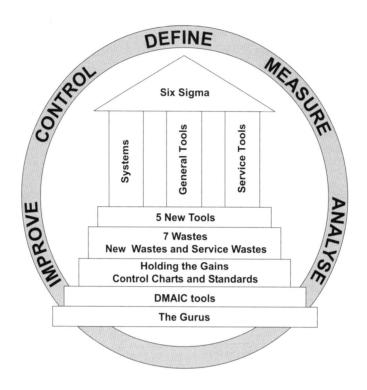

Service Quality Concepts

Service Mapping
Cycle of Service and Customer Processing Operation
Moments of Truth
Service Blueprinting

Other Service Tools
Customer Loyalty
Service Gaps, SERVQUAL, and Service Dimensions
Service Profit Chain
Service Recovery and Customer Retention
Zone of Tolerance
Value Demand and Failure Demand

Cycle of Service and Customer Processing Operation

Albrecht and Zemke originated the concept of a Cycle of Service, but the idea has been added to by Mahesh and by Vandermerwe. The Customer Processing concept is a variation, developed by Johnston.

A Cycle of Service (C of S) is much like a flowchart but has the important distinction of being written from the perspective of the customer, and is the sequence of events or "Moments of Truth" (MoT) (see section on this topic) experienced by the customer in dealing with the organisation. After all, as Vandermerwe suggests, value is associated with the customer, but providers only accumulate costs. As the name suggests, a C of S is normally shown on a circle. A flowchart shows the progress of a document or product, a cycle of service shows the events experienced by a customer. It is simple but effective.

The best way to draw up a cycle of service is to physically track a customer as he or she moves through a service process. Of course, not all customers will experience the same Moments of Truth, so several customer experiences may have to be combined. Where customer tracking is not possible, a team of front line employees should participate in drawing up the chart. It is best to use the verb plus noun rule in drawing up a C of S chart : for instance, "receive notice", "join queue", and the like.

Then analysis begins. Points of dissatisfaction are identified. The value of the C of S is that, perhaps for the first time, the complete sequence of events as experienced by the customer, is seen. A useful starting point is the "PETS" framework : ask, for each moment of truth, if the Procedure is known, if the Equipment is suitable or capable of doing the job, if Training has been adequate, and if Standards are in place. Some of the MoTs will be more important than others, and will require much more attention. Where necessary, any MoT can be further broken down into a greater level of detail. For instance, the MoT "receive bank balance", can be broken down into "wait for chit", "receive chit from teller", "open chit", "read balance and other information".

Thereafter the Kano model is extremely useful. (See the section on Kano.) Ask, for each MoT, what are the Basics, the Performance factors, and possible Delighters. This is a useful way of undertaking systematic analysis of weaknesses and of opportunities. The section on the Kano model emphasised that the identification of the three Kano factors is not necessarily trivial; good analysis and insight may only be gained by detailed observation.

In addition we can consider how or if each MoT can be failsafed (see the section on Shingo or Pokayoke). Recall the methods of failsafing : by contact (a height barrier in a car park), by fixed value (an airline meal tray with indentations), and by motion step (a customer number at a supermarket "deli" to ensure first come first serve).

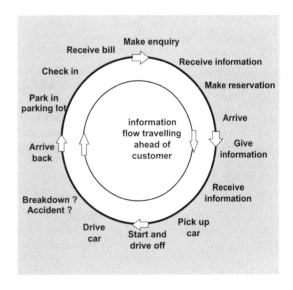

Sandra Vandermerwe's version of C of S is referred to as the Customer Activity Cycle (or CAC). This has the extension of considering "Pre", "During", and "Post" activities. Vandermerwe makes the point that customer's experiences span three stages : deciding what to do, doing it, and keeping it going and updating it. This is therefore a more powerful version because it is not limited to the actual service encounter itself. The tool acts as an agitation and educational device according to Vandermerwe. She refers to discontinuities in the flow of the cycle as "value gaps", a phrase which suggests that closing such gaps may find the framework suggested by Zeithaml et al (see the section on SERVQUAL) useful. As with the breakdown of the C of S into a hierarchy of detail, the CAC has "primary cycles", "dependent cycles" and "sub cycles".

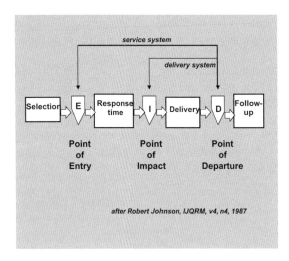

after Robert Johnson, IJQRM, v4, n4, 1987

The Johnston variation (known as the "customer processing operation" or CPO) is not shown as a cycle or a map but rather as a framework or checklist. The elements are useful in clarifying the stages, and could easily be incorporated in the previous C of S approaches. The elements are:

Selection:	when the customer decides between competing services.
Point of entry:	the initial assessment, the visual impact, possible confusion for a new customer.
Response time:	the time taken to respond, waiting, queuing
Point of Impact:	the first point of contact and initial impression
Delivery:	the actual events (MoTs?) of the service itself

Point of Departure:	any special events or opportunities when the customer leaves
Follow up:	obtaining feedback on satisfaction, or soliciting further business.

Further reading:

Lynn Shostack, "Designing Services that Deliver", *Harvard Business Review*, Vol 64, January / February 1984, pages 133-139

Vandermerwe, Sandra *The Eleventh Commandment*, Wiley, Chichester 1996, Chap 23

Mahesh, V.S. and Stanworth, James "Service Concept Delivery through System Design : The Case of Anglian Water Services", *Service Management : New perspectives, New initiatives*, C. Armistead and R. Teare (eds), Cassell, London, 1995

Robert Johnston, "A framework for delivering quality strategy in the customer processing operation", *Int Jnl of Quality and Reliability Mgmt*, 4, 4, 1987, pp 37-46

Moments of Truth (MoT)

Moments of truth (MoT) is a concept rather than a technique, apparently first articulated by Jan Carlzon, the head of the Scandinavian airline SAS. It is a powerful concept for quality management, and so deserves a place in any gallery of quality concepts. The concept was made even more popular by Albrect and Zemke in their book "Service America!"

A moment of truth is that moment in time when a customer comes into contact with the products, systems, people, or procedures of an organization and as a result is lead to make a judgement about the quality of that organization's products or services.

It is clear that scores, even hundreds, of MoTs are possible for a single customer in interaction with a company. Each one is a potential point of dissatisfaction where, as a result, the customer may be lost, or conversely where the customer can experience "delight" and become a loyal user. Some MoTs are critical, others less so, and here it is useful to bring in the Kano model concepts (see separate section). Moreover, the customer builds an impression of the organisation through the cumulative effect of MoT experiences. In many services (eg hotels, holidays, travel, parcel delivery, banking, consultancy) the customer has little or no tangible product that remains after the operation is complete. All that the customer is left with is a memory - of hundreds of moments of truth. That is why the proactive analysis of MoTs should be an important concern of management, particularly if they believe that it costs five times as much to regain a lost customer as it does to acquire a new one.

This leads to MoT analysis where the points of potential dissatisfaction can be proactively identified. MoT analysis begins with the assembly of process-type diagrams (these are referred to as "cycles of service"; see separate section). Every minute step taken by a customer in his or her dealings with company products, services or people is recorded. This begins when the customer first makes contact (perhaps by telephone, mail, or in person) to the last time the product or service is experienced. There would be a different chart for each type of customer service. Whether called a process chart or a cycle of service, the point is that the steps follow the experiences of the customer, irrespective of organizational boundaries or departments.

The problem from a quality management viewpoint is that most MoTs take place away from the eyes of management, but in interaction with the "front line" staff. All MoTs occur with either the visible product or with the front line - with the latter by far the predominant case in the case of service industry. That is why it is desirable to work through all possible MoTs in advance. It is said that, even if a product or service fails, if the backup service is good the customer will not be resentful and may even be grateful. One may argue that it is not possible to identify all MoTs, but at least if a systematic effort has been made the number and severity of unexpected failures will be minimized. In this respect MoT analysis has much in common with failure mode and effect analysis (FMEA).

Further reading:
Jan Carlzon, *Moments of Truth*, Harper and Row, 1987
Christian Grönroos, *Service Management and Marketing : Managing the Moments of Truth in Service Competition*, Lexinngton Books, MA, 1990

Service Blueprinting

Service blueprinting is the procedure of making a flowchart or map of a service process. This is one the longest established service mapping tools and was originally proposed by Shostack. The technique has much in common with industrial engineering flowcharts, except that customer links are specifically included. The aim is to identify points at which the service may fail to satisfy customers and to identify points where value may be added for customers. A service blueprint shows time horizontally, and the hierarchy of support vertically. In drawing up a blueprint, four areas are included :

* "customer actions" are the activities or interactions undertaken by the customer. These activities come into contact with two types of employee actions:
* "on stage" employee actions are visible to the customer and are separated in a service blueprint by a "line of interaction", drawn horizontally. Any vertical line crossing this line of interaction represents a direct contact or encounter between customer and front line employee.
* "backstage" employee actions are not visible to customers but are nevertheless in direct contact with customers (say by post or phone). These are separated from on stage activities by a "line of visibility", thus making clear what customers can see and possibly be influenced by.
* "support processes" are all those activities that support the front-line staff, whether visible or not. These are separated from backstage activities by a "line of internal interaction". Vertical lines crossing the line of internal interaction represent internal encounters.

A service blueprint can be read horizontally to focus on customer support activities and to answer questions such as how efficient, and how many points of contact are involved. Alternatively, a blueprint can be used to gain an overview or to understand the depth and nature of the support infrastructure, in which case it is read vertically. An immediate impression of the complexity of the service process is given by a blueprint, as are the steps that a customer faces in dealing with an organisation. An illustration is shown in the figure.

SERVICE BLUEPRINTING
Student Registration Example

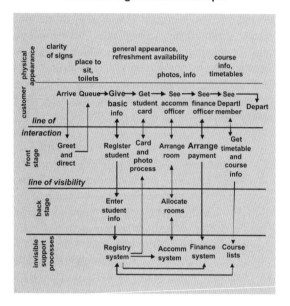

The power of service blueprints can be added to by including "pre", and "post" activities, pokayoke, and the Kano model. (See the section on Cycle of Service and Customer processing.) A service blueprint can be a particularly good device for training or standardisation purposes, where photos can be added. Service can be standardised by maintaining the up-to-date position on a computer service blueprint, possibly supported by digital photo or even video. Think of two accompanying charts. The first is the "Spaghetti Diagram" showing the physical movements of customers and servers (shown in different colours). The second chart lists, for each activity in the customer line, the Kano factors (Basics,

Performance, Delighters), and possible failsafing or pokayoke. See separate sections on each of these.

Further, service blueprinting can be the basis of "service positioning" using the SERVQUAL dimensions (see separate section) of "RATER". Thus a service interaction can be designed using a blueprint to specifically emphasise Reliability (say by providing computer-based maintenance backup), Assurance (say by emphasising care and security), Tangibles (giving particular emphasis to on stage activities and visibles), Empathy (say by emphasising individual care), and Responsiveness (say by providing extra capacity to enable staff to be flexible).

Further reading:
G. Lynn Shostack, "Designing Services that Deliver", *Harvard Business Review*, Jan / Feb 1984, pp 133-139
G. Lynn Shostack, "Service Positioning Through Structural Change", *Journal of Marketing*, Vol 51, January 1987, pp 34-43
Jane Kingman Brundage, "Service Mapping : Gaining a Concrete Perspective on Service System Design", in Eberhard Scheuing and William Christopher (eds), *The Service Quality Handbook,* Amacom, New York, 1993, pages 148-163
Szilvia Gyimothy, Odysseys: Analysing Service Journeys from the Customer's Perspective, *Managing Service Quality*, V10, N6, 2000, pp389-396

Customer Loyalty

Loyalty and retention have become big issues in service and manufacturing as evidence has mounted that loyal customers buy more products and services over time and become ever more profitable. Witness the growth of loyalty cards during the 1990s. Loyal customers are less expensive to advertise to, are early adopters of new products and services, and tend to give an increasing share of their business to their preferred suppliers. Loyal customers are also the source of word of mouth advertising – highly effective and free! However, the concepts are not without their critics.

This section relates closely to the section on the Service Profit Chain. The S-P-C established many of the linkages. Fred Reichheld, probably *the* guru of loyalty, was a student of Earl Sasser at Harvard. The feedback loop that is suggested is: Quality Service leads to Customer Satisfaction leads to Loyal Customers leads to Retained Customers leads to Increased Profit leads to improved Loyalty leads to better quality service.

Reichheld, Sasser and others at Harvard established the principle of the lifetime value of a customer. The lifetime value can be estimated by multiplying the average spend per period by the estimated period of retention. To this can be added additional purchases and profits from referrals, and subtracting the savings made by advertising to established customers. By contrast, Reichheld suggests (1996:2) that not managing retention may lose a company 50% of its customer base in five years, so he proposes retention as being as important a measure as profit or ROI.

TARP, a Boston based consultancy, has produced a often-quoted set of findings. (Goodman). These are:

* Problems decrease customer loyalty by 15% to 30%.
* Most customers encountering problems do not complain – hence the importance of actively soliciting complaints, because many complainants tell their friends.

* Quality of service can affect loyalty – perhaps a 50% gain in some industries. Customers who are completely satisfied with the resolution of a problem exhibit no less and sometimes more loyalty. "Mollified" complainants, by contrast, are only slightly more loyal than dissatisfied complainants.
* Service can affect word-of-mouth behaviour. Customers who are dissatisfied tell twice as many people about their experiences as do satisfied customers.

Building on these findings, TARP has developed a detailed methodology for costing customer loyalty. Refer to the article.

Reichheld identifies three categories of loyalty – customer, employee, and investor. Loyal employees are increasingly seen as being necessary for loyal customers.

Zeithaml and Bitner suggest that there are four types of retention strategy. (1) Financial bonds, for example, loyalty cards, pricing, and bundling; (2) Social Bonds, built through building personal relationships – these are more common in professional services; (3) Customisation bonds, whereby the provider seeks to understand the detailed requirements of customers through anticipation and customer knowledge – for example books provided with customer logo; and (4) Structural bonds where the service is designed specifically for the customer – for example by joint investment and in the book example by incorporating the specific chapters required. These four levels may be seen as successive- (2) building on (1) for example.

In his most recent writing Reichheld (2001) suggests that to really win loyal customers requires very senior managers to "walk that talk". He proposes six principles (1) Preach what you practice – the leader must articulate his views as well as practice them. (2) Win-win: this is building loyalty by making sure that both the company and the customer wins – it's no win if you take advantage. (3) Be picky – choose the customers to work with, don't accept all for short term gains. (4) Keep it simple – decentralise and delegate real authority to make service decisions rapidly. (5) Reward the right results – make sure that loyalty is rewarded, not short term gains. (6) "Listen hard, talk straight". This is really a restatement of one of Stephen Covey's 7 principles – "seek first to understand not to be understood"

Is Loyalty worth pursuing for all customers?

Apparently not. Some financial institutions now differentiate customers on a Pareto (ABC) basis. "A" class customers are cultivated with great attention, but "C" class are just not worth the effort. Worse, attention on "terrorist" customers may divert attention from good prospects. Some institutions have actively tried to discourage some customers from running high transaction, low balance accounts. This may be sensible and pragmatic, but beware because a few C class customers may eventually turn into A class. Dimensions other than current return are necessary.

Loyalty and Satisfaction

The relationship between customer satisfaction and customer loyalty remains a hot topic in service quality. Two concepts will be summarised here.

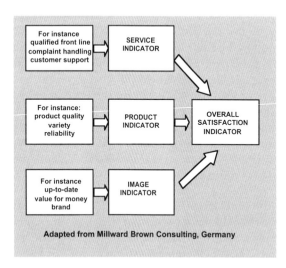

Adapted from Millward Brown Consulting, Germany

Millward Brown has suggested that an overall "satisfaction indicator" can be developed by combining several smaller indicators into one. Thus the task is to determine the quality dimensions that influence satisfaction. These are combined into area

indicators which lead in turn to an overall service indicator or OSI. Three "area indicators" are Service, Product, and Image. His model is shown in the figure.

Neely, working with BA, has used a model similar to the "expectancy model" of motivation. Three types of antecedants: Cognitive (e.g. accessibility, confidence), Affective (e.g. emotions, feelings), and Conative (e.g. switching costs, expectations) together drive Attitudes and Patronage. These are also affected by norms and situational influences. Attitudes and Patronage in turn drive the loyalty consequences, which in turn feed back to the antecedants.

Thus prior circumstances that a customer knows or is aware of, combine with prior feelings and with earlier factors that require effort to change, to create an attitude relative to other competitors. These, however, are modified by actual events and norms to produce loyalty-related consequences. There is feedback at work.

The relationship between loyalty and satisfaction is seldom linear. Biemans suggests the following relationships for different industries:

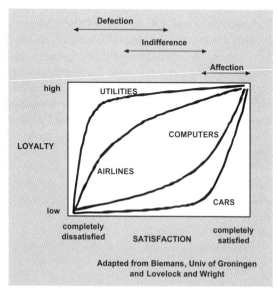

Adapted from Biemans, Univ of Groningen and Lovelock and Wright

The top lines indicate captive customers, so the bottom lines are more relevant. The shape indicates why for example Compac computer regards a satisfaction rating of 3.5 out of 5 as a failure.

On loyalty and repurchase, Stauss and Neuhaus suggest "five quality levels of satisfaction":

	Feeling	Repurchase
Demanding Satisfied	Optimism	Definitely
Stable Satisfied	Faith	Probably
Resigned Satisfied	Ignorance	Maybe
Stable Dissatisfied	Disappointment	Unlikely
Demanding Dissatisfied	Protest	No Way

After Stauss & Neuhaus, 1995

Complaint Handling
If TARP is to be believed managing complaints is important for retaining and even winning loyalty. Van Ossel and Stremersch suggest that complaints need to be handled rapidly but also that customers use three criteria: compensation, sincerity, and follow-up. Compensation is about fairness and can range from financial to replacement. Front-line staff may need special training in "sincerity" - real or perceived. And follow-up communication may be important with higher item services or purchases. It is the appropriate balance of all four which determines retention.

But beware, is much of this a myth? Henry warns of six common flaws about loyalty: Here, we build on his ideas (1) Retention is not the same as loyalty. (2) There may be many reasons for retention hiding under the heading of loyalty (geographically locked in, no alternative, switching costs, risk avoidance, other incentives such as frequent flyer schemes). For instance, you may take a package tour to Thailand because you are unsure of conditions. But this is not loyalty to the tour company. (3) Profitability may be ascribed to loyalty when in fact superior business design drives both. For instance, you may use an airline regularly because of convenient times but have no loyalty to it. (4) Managerial complacency. Perhaps there is no good competitor available yet. A good alternative would result in large scale defections. (5) Lifetime value is overstated. Today, it is a rare business that can maintain loyalty over several decades. Also, established customers may cost you more, not less, than new customers because they may demand loyalty rewards. (6) A competitor's apparently loyal customers discourage effort.

Further reading
John Goodman, Pat O'Brien and Eden Segal, "Turning CFOs into Quality Champions", *Quality Progress*, March 2000, pp 47-54

Frederick Reichheld, *The Loyalty Effect*, Harvard Business School Press, 1996

Reichheld, F and Sasser, W., "Zero Defections: Quality Comes to Services", *Harvard Business Review*, Sept-Oct 1990, pp 105 – 111

Frederick Reichheld, "Lead for Loyalty", *Harvard Business Review*, July-August 2001, pp 76 – 84

Biemans, W. *Satisfaction vs. Loyalty*, Lecture Notes of University of Groningen, Holland, 2000

Stauss, B and Neuhaus, P quoted in Finn v.Hammerstein, *MScThesis*, University of Buckingham, 2000

Andy Neely, *Measuring Business Performance – Why, What and How*, The Economist Books, London, 1998

Millward Brown Consulting, Germany

Christopher Lovelock and Lauren Wright, *Principles of Service Marketing and Management*, Prentice Hall, New York, 1999

Craig Douglas Henry, "Is Customer Loyalty a Pernicious Myth?", *Business Horizons*, July-August 2000, pp 13-16

Gino Van Ossel and Stefan Stremersch, "Complaint Management", in Van Looy et al, *Services Management*, FT - Pitman, London, 1998

Please refer to the very closely related section on Service Recovery, Retention and the 3 R's.

Service Gaps, "SERVQUAL" and Service Dimensions

Zeithaml, Parasuraman and Berry (or PZB as they are sometimes known) have, over several years, developed a well researched and tested methodology for identifying the dimensions of service quality and the causes of "gaps" that exist between the service that customers expect and the perceived service that is received. The methodology is presented in detail in their book, which includes questionnaires that can often be used directly with customers. These have been widely used in service industry.

The author's set of five "dimensions of service quality" can be compared with David Garvin's dimensions - see under "The Gurus". Customers in service make up their mind about the quality of service by considering each of these five, although an individual customer would have his or her own preferences or weightings between them. The five are (1) "Tangibles", which includes the physical appearance of people equipment and facilities (2) "Reliability", which is to do with ability to perform the service dependably and accurately (i.e. doing what they say they will do, on time and to specification), (3) "Responsiveness", which concerns willingness to help and to respond to individual requirements, (4) "Assurance", which is the possession of the required knowledge, the skill to perform the service, and to convey trust, confidence, and security, (5) "Empathy" which begins with an understanding of the customer's needs and the ability to provide an individualised service. (These can be remembered by the mnemonic RATER). Taken together the five are known as "SERVQUAL", a registered phrase which is widely known. Like Garvin's dimensions, these form a very useful checklist. The authors have found, in a wide variety of surveys in different service sectors, where customers are asked to allocate 100 points between the five factors to indicate relative importance, that the Reliability dimension is the one which is most highly valued. The next two highest valued dimensions are Responsiveness and Assurance.

SERVQUAL helps identify customer perceptions of service quality. The 'gaps' analysis takes this further and helps identify the causes of service quality

shortfalls in each or all of the dimensions. According to the authors, customers build an expectation of the service to be received depending on four factors. These are, firstly, word-of-mouth communications obtained from friends and acquaintances, secondly, personal needs, thirdly, past experience and, lastly, communications put out by the service company which create their own expectations. The authors refer to "Gap 5" as being the difference between expected service and the perceived service experienced. Gap 5 is the "customer gap" Gap 5 results from a combination of Gaps 1 to 4 (the "provider gaps"). These are :

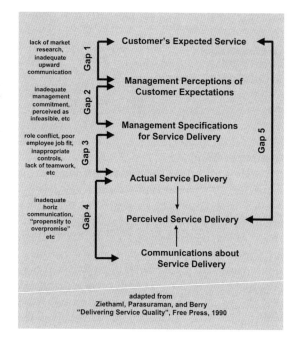

adapted from
Ziethaml, Parasuraman, and Berry
"Delivering Service Quality", Free Press, 1990

Gap 1 results from a difference between what customers expect and what management perceives these expectations to be. This can occur, for example, as a result of management not undertaking sufficient research or from communication failures within the company

Gap 2 results from a difference between management perceptions of what customers expect and the specifications that management draws up, or fails to draw up, spelling out what service quality delivery actions are required. This can result from inadequate management commitment and interest, from a perception that the company cannot actually meet customer requirements, from a failure to specify in detail what is required, or from a failure in the way in which the company sets its goals in relation to customers.

Gap 3 results from a mismatch between the service delivery specifications required by management and the actual service that is delivered by front line staff. There are many possible causes of this gap. Some include inappropriate technology, inappropriate staff or training, poor teamwork, and inappropriate control measures and methods. Gap 3 requires appropriate standards to be in place.

Finally Gap 4 results from a difference between the actual service that is delivered and messages that are put out to customers about what to expect. Clearly a major reason for this is poor internal communication and lack of familiarity with operations. There is also the often-found "propensity to overpromise". Clearly it is more desirable to under-promise and over-deliver.

Zeithaml and Bitner have written a whole text book around the closing of these gaps. Thus to close the customer gap requires all four provider gaps to be closed. So service quality, as we have heard before, begins with understanding customer expectations. These are "situational" - they vary by circumstance.

The fact that, under SERVQUAL, service quality is determined by the overall gap between what was expected and what was delivered, is important. It means that service quality is relative not absolute, and that different customers may perceive the level of service quality differently; that quality is determined by the customer who has "all the votes", not by the service provider; that service quality can be achieved by either meeting or exceeding expectations (see the Kano model), or by changing expectations (Gap 4, above).

Recent work has shown that the SERVQUAL dimensions and weightings do not necessarily apply in all parts of the world. For instance, Far East airline passengers seem to value respect above reliability.

Finland's Christian Grönroos views service quality as having 6 dimensions, the first four of which are roughly in line with those of PZB. These are Professionalism and Skills (assurance), Attitudes and Behaviour (empathy), Accessibility and Flexibility (responsiveness), and Reliability and Trustworthiness (reliability). Grönroos' additional two factors are Recovery and Problem Solving (the importance of which has been stressed by Reichheld and Sasser in their work on customer retention (see separate section), and Reputation and Credibility (to do with the image of the business in the mind of the customer, which overlaps with the concept of capability by Heskett, Sasser and Schlesinger (see the section on The Service Profit Chain).

Bienstock et al have suggested that the dimensions of timeliness, availability, and condition are also important dimensions in physical distribution and transport services.

Further reading:
Valerie Zeithaml, A. Parasuraman, and Leonard Berry, *Delivering Quality Service*, Free Press, New York, 1990.
Dick Schaaf, *Keeping the Edge : Giving Customers the Service They Demand*, Plume Penguin, New York, 1997, Part 2.
Valirie Zeithaml and Mary Jo Bitner, *Services Marketing*, Second edition, McGraw Hill, New York, 2000
Bienstock, Mentzer, and Bird, "Measuring Physical Distribution Service Quality", *Jnl Academy of Marketing Science*, V25, N1, 1997

The Service Profit Chain

The Service Profit Chain is a series of concepts developed by Heskett, Sasser and Schlesinger following years of research at Harvard Business School. It provides the foundation for work on Loyalty (see separate section). To quote the authors: "Service profit chain thinking maintains that there are direct and strong relationships between profit, growth, customer loyalty, customer satisfaction, the value of goods and services delivered to customers; and employee capability, satisfaction, loyalty, and productivity." In other words this is a systems approach to service quality, maintaining that there are a host of interacting factors and feedback loops at work. The book on the topic is a "tour de force" on service quality, with much relevance for manufacturing also.

The service profit chain model has been adapted by several others including the EFQM model and the Chris Voss studies. See the section on EFQM.

A central feature of the Service Profit Chain model is an equation for customer value which is

$$\text{Customer Value} = \frac{\text{Results} + \text{Process Quality}}{\text{Price} + \text{Customer Access Costs}}$$

In other words service quality includes both hard and soft factors, but is modified by price and influenced by ease of access. "Results" reminds us that customers buy benefits, not products or services. "Process Quality" is various service dimensions such as the RATER dimensions discussed under SERVQUAL. "Access" is to do with convenience in time and place of acquiring the service.

The service profit chain establishes the links between internal employee factors (loyalty, satisfaction, capability, service quality) which impact productivity and output quality. Variables here are factors such as workplace design, job design, selection, development, rewards, recognition, information and communication, and adequate "tools". Productivity and output quality impact value. Value impacts Customer satisfaction. Satisfaction impacts loyalty.

Loyalty impacts revenue and profitability.

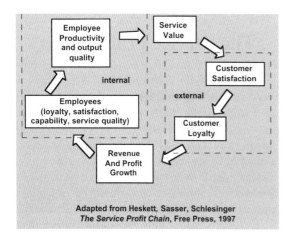

Adapted from Heskett, Sasser, Schlesinger
The Service Profit Chain, Free Press, 1997

On the customer side, the authors have identified and established links between the elements of the profit chain, as shown in the figure. Many of the linkages shown have been researched amongst leading companies, but much remains to be done. The service profit chain therefore provides a useful and interesting framework both for managers and for academic research. As such it is a very comprehensive work, the relevance of which can only grow.

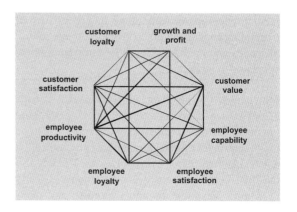

Further reading
James Heskett, W Earl Sasser, Leonard Schlesinger, *The Service Profit Chain*, The Free Press, New York, 1997

Service Recovery, Customer Retention and the "Three R's"

Two significant pieces of research are highlighted in this section which, when combined, have great significance for customer retention in service business.

The first is a study by Reichheld and Sasser. These researchers reported the powerful impact of customer defections on the "bottom line" . Several cases are quoted. (For example in a credit card company, priority was given to gathering information from defecting customers, adjusting products and services accordingly. As a result profits increased sixteen fold without acquisitions). Retained customers generate increasing profits the longer they stay : setup costs are paid, advertising costs decline, and prices may be increased. One rule of thumb is that it costs 5 times as much to acquire a new customer as it does to retain an existing one. As a result, Reichheld and Sasser maintain that customer retention is a more important determinant of profitability than market share.

The second is work by Technical Assistance Research Programs, Inc. a U.S. based research organisation which has produced some widely quoted, and very significant , findings which are especially important to service quality in general and "service recovery" (i.e. recovering from poor service delivery) in particular.

In response to the Question "How many of your unhappy customers will buy other products or services offered by your company?", TARP found that, for small and medium purchases:

* approximately 85% of customers who had experienced no problem would repurchase.
* only around 45% of customers who are dissatisfied and who complain, would repurchase.
* but, where the complaint is "mollified" the repurchase percentage rises to around 80%,
* and, where the complainant is satisfied, the percentage exceeds 90% (i.e. above the percentage who experienced no problem!).

TARP also found (U.S. figures) that only a small percentage of dissatisfied customers (perhaps 20%) actually complain, but even less (perhaps 4%) go to the trouble to write. The point is that many front line complaints are lost though employees not passing on the information. Worse though is the finding that dissatisfied customers do not complain to the company, but nevertheless tell an average of 9 to 10 other people. TARP also found that approximately one third of complaints relate to problems caused by customers themselves (for example, unclear instructions).

Customer retention should therefore be a high priority. Ways to go about this include the following:

* "Watching the Door", or identifying customers who have just "defected" or who are about to leave. Sometimes this can be easy where there are established accounts which have become

non-operative (or even where use has declined significantly), but may be more difficult where customers are nameless as in retailing. Here loyalty schemes such as store cards may be an answer. An efficient feedback process as to the reasons for defections is required. Of course, it should be kept up to date.

* Making complaining easier. Passive customer survey information collection is routinely attempted at hotels, but ways need to be found to make this more active by, for example, rewards. In any case have free phone or reply paid mail.
* A "no quibble" policy on returns.
* Key account management, including careful and regular monitoring.
* Trying to stay ahead of the game by identifying future expectations. One way is to work through so called "lead users" - the innovators who buy early.
* Eliminating any "climate of fear" as Deming would have called it, which prevents onward communication of poor performance. An attitude that a dissatisfied customer is an opportunity not a threat needs to pervade an organisation, but is especially important for first tier managers.
* Offer some compensation, even if small : a voucher or free meal. In Britain "service guarantees" are offered by telephone and water companies.
* Have a preplanned service recovery process : recognise that some service failures are predicable, others not, but that a routine should be worked out for the former category. This routine swings into place automatically when service failure occurs. Of course, such routines should not prevent seeking a failsafe solution.
* Explain what happened to the customer. TARP research suggests that a clear explanation is more effective than just fixing the problem.
* Giving employees the authority to solve customer problems right there and then; don't add to the problem by shifting responsibility.

Heskett, Sasser and Schlesinger have therefore proposed an extension to the traditional 4 P's of marketing (Product, Price, Place, Promotion), as being more appropriate to the service firm (but, no doubt, also very relevant to manufacturing firms that invariably bundle product and service). These are the Three R's : Retention, Referrals, and Related Products. Retention is the ability to hold on to valuable customers (whilst also identifying and dropping low loyalty, very dissatisfied customers - whom these authors refer to as "terrorists"). Referrals is the ability to gain from word of mouth recommendations - which are not only free but the have the highest credibility. And selling related products and services is made easier and more cost effective by the reputation for value and customer care from loyal customers.

On retention, loyalty and referrals, the final word goes to Marge Simpson who said, "Dear God, if you save us from the tornado I will be very grateful and will recommend you to all my friends."

Further readings:
Frederick Reichheld and W Earl Sasser Jr., "Zero Defections : Quality Comes to Services", *Harvard Business Review*, Vol 70, Sept./October 1990, pages 105-111.
Frederick Reichheld, *The Loyalty Effect*, Harvard Business School Press, Boston, 1996.
Technical Assistance Research Programs, *Consumer Complaint Handling in America : an Update Study*, U.S. Office of Consumer Affairs, March 1986.
Valerie Zeithaml and Mary Jo Bitner, *Services Marketing*, Mc Graw Hill, New York, 1996, Chapters 6 and 16.
James Heskett, W Earl Sasser, Leonard Schlesinger, *The Service Profit Chain*, The Free Press, New York, 1997

Zone of Tolerance

Statistical Process Control thinking has been extended into the service area by, amongst others, Berry, Zeithaml and Bitner and by Johnston and Clark. Both refer to a zone of customer tolerance of customer satisfaction located between zones of delight and dissatisfaction. Berry's zone of tolerance falls between zones of desired service and adequate service, so perhaps is more like "Pre Control" than SPC. These conceptual models are useful in thinking about the bounds of service quality.

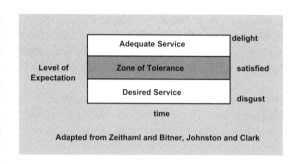

Adapted from Zeithaml and Bitner, Johnston and Clark

Both sets of authors make the point that the zone can shift depending on the importance of the factor and upon prior experience. Thus the zone is wider for first time buyers but narrows for service recovery situations. The size of the band may also be affected by the level of interest and commitment.

Johnston and Clark use the Zone of Tolerance concept much like an SPC control chart, maintaining that various "transactions" or moments of truth can be plotted in the chart. A succession of points plotted in the dissatisfied zone leads to the equivalent of out of control conditions (a dissatisfied customer) but several points above the zone result in delight. Presumably the SPC "out of control" apply - one very high (unsatisfactory) point or several successive more or less unsatisfactory points would both lead to an "out of control" condition (in SPC language). Some behaviour may be compensatory – a poor experience may be compensated by several satisfactory experiences. A poor experience may also shift the 'control limits' upwards making the customer even more demanding, but a great experience may lower the zone thus making it easier to achieve further delight. A great experience may lower the tolerances for subsequent events.

Adapted from Zeithaml and Bitner, Johnston and Clark

Zeithaml and Bitner have done interesting work identifying the factors that shift the control limits (although they don't use these terms). The upper limit of the zone (leading to desired service) is influenced by implicit and explicit service promises, by word of mouth and by past experience. The lower limit is influenced by:

* "service intensifiers" (where, for example, an anniversary dinner might imply reduced tolerance)
* by service alternatives (where there are fewer options there is more tolerance)
* the degree of influence that a customer has on the service provider
* factors that are perceived to be out of the service provider's control.
* the predicted service.

Although conceptual in nature, these are useful ideas particularly when used with service mapping, moments of truth, and the Kano model (See section on Service Blueprinting). Thus Kano Delighters more or less correspond to Adequate Service zone, and Performance factors to the Zone of Tolerance.

Further reading:
Valerie Zeithaml and Mary Jo Bitner, *Services Marketing*, McGraw Hill, Boston, 2000, Chapter 3
Leonard Berry, *Marketing Services: Competing through Quality*, Free Press, New York, 1991
Robert Johnston and Graham Clark, *Service Operations Management*, FT/Prentice Hall, Harlow, 2000, Chapter 4

Value Demand and Failure Demand

John Seddon of Vanguard consulting is the originator of the powerful Service Management concept of Value Demand and Failure Demand. Value demand is 'first time' demand for service. Failure demand is any demand that results from a failure to get something right the first time or of not doing something. Seddon maintains that analysis and quantification of these two types of demand is the essential starting point on any project concerned with improving service quality or productivity. Value demand can be made efficient for flow. Failure demand, however, requires different responses - namely a waste elimination procedure and a service recovery procedure. Different failure demands require to be classified and arranged in a Pareto, so that the biggest causes of failures or problems can be systematically tackled and eliminated. It is fundamentally wrong to include failure demand in a capacity calculation, call centre, computer system or value stream map. If you do so, you risk building in waste - a prime 'sin' of the Lean movement.

Worse, if failure demand is ignored, there is a real risk of a feedback loop being established, with more complaints driving out the time for good, first time demands, leading to even higher levels of failure. (Meanwhile a complacent manager thinks that they are doing well because demand is increasing.)

Think of a two by two matrix. On the one axis is value demand and failure demand. On the other axis is common cause and special cause variation. This gives four cells. Begin with a run diagram, and link this to specific demands. This will enable you to list various types of events being made on your system. You can design a good flow service system for common cause, value demand. The aim should be to drive all events into this category. Many managers assume, incorrectly, that most demand falls in this cell. It does not. Events falling in the common cause, failure demand represent institutionalized failure that is probably going unnoticed. They should not be built into systems. A systematic attack is called for, but one that can be planned. Events falling into special cause, value demand represent true demands that for some reason take an inordinate time or effort. Perhaps a new service, or procedure. They need to be isolated and streamlined. Events falling into the special cause, failure demand are expensive and wasteful, but are not routine. They require special attention.

Further reading:
John Seddon, *Freedom from Command and Control*, Vanguard, 2003.

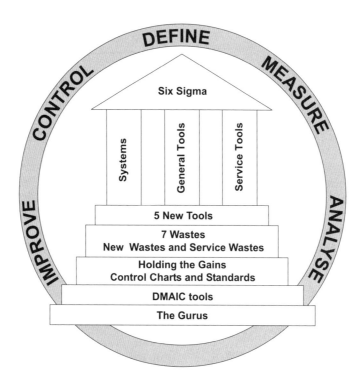

Systems

ISO 9001:2000
EFQM Excellence Model

ISO 9001:2000

ISO 9001:2000 is the new international standard on quality assurance, applicable to manufacturing and service. The new standard was published in December 2000. The previous version had accumulated some 350k registrations in 150 countries by January 2000. The 2000 version represents a considerable advance on the previous 1994 version which set down 20 clauses that organisations seeking accreditation had to demonstrate. ISO 9001 can be used by an organisation to both *demonstrate* its ability and to *assess* its ability to meet customer requirements. ISO 9001 sets the quality system standards, not the product standards. Quality is defined as the "degree to which a set of inherent characteristics fulfils requirements."

The 2000 version is based on eight Quality Management Principles that are an excellent guide to modern thinking on quality. The principles are:

* *Customer Focused Organisation.* It is customers, not the organisation that defines quality, so look outward rather than inward. Survival ultimately depends upon understanding customer needs.
* *Leadership* – is necessary to drive the organisation to meet customer needs and to improve.
* *Involvement of People.* It is the people in the organisation that makes for high quality products and services.
* *Process Approach.* It is linked (horizontal) processes, transforming inputs into outputs, which produce the requirements of customers. It is not functional departments or (vertical) 'silos'. (This is perhaps the most fundamental change to the previous standard which emphasised the responsibilities of functions). The continuous improvement process involves establishing objectives (a management responsibility), resource management, realising the product or service, and measurement and analysis.
* *Systems Approach:* The organisation is a system: it has inputs, outputs, information flows, goals, controls, and interactions. Processes come together to form purposeful systems.

* *Continual Improvement* – is necessary for survival. Everyone needs to participate. (This links with Kaizen)
* *Fact-based Approach.* As Deming said, 'In God we trust; all others must bring data". (This links with "Gemba")
* *Supplier Relationships.* A well known and valid saying is that 'companies don't compete, supply chains compete'. Ultimately quality depends upon the company and its suppliers.

The new standard has core sections which are broadly similar to the Deming PDCA cycle. Management must plan the system in relation to customers, the resources must be provided, the activities carried out, and then measured, analysed and improved. The standard provides fairly specific guidelines and advice on each. In the overview below, some important points are highlighted. For people not involved in quality certification, it is instructive to read through the following section to gain an impression of an integrated view of quality.

* *General Requirements.* Like the previous version, the phrase "say what you do and do what you say" still applies. You make up the rules for your own organisation following the guidelines. Then you are expected to follow them and be audited upon them. The organisation must identify the necessary processes, determine criteria, ensure the availability of resources, monitor and measure, and implement to achieve results and continual improvement. (In short, PDCA).
* *Management Responsibility.* Management must establish the quality policy, the policy must be communicated, and management must demonstrate and give evidence of its commitment. Senior management must ensure that customer needs and expectations are determined, and ensure that the organisation is able to fulfil the requirements. Processes must be identified. A quality management system must be established, documented, maintained, and improved. A management representative must promote an awareness of customer requirements. And a review process must take place to ensure that the quality system remains effective.

* *Resource Management.* This covers human resources, facilities, and the work environment. Management must determine and provide the necessary resources and facilities to implement the system and to address customer satisfaction. Records must be kept of experience, training, and qualifications. Training must be evaluated.

* *Product (or Service) Realisation.* This is a mini PDCA cycle within the broader quality system. The emphasis is on process. The steps of the process must be determined, say by flowcharts. Customer requirements must be clearly understood and orders not accepted until there is the ability to meet the requirements. Communication with the customer must take place. The process must be designed, reviewed, verified, and measured, all in relation to the customer. ISO requires a system for suppliers to be identified, selected, communicated with, and evaluated. Then the entire process needs to be controlled by having acceptance criteria, work standards, capable processes, and procedures for release, delivery and service. ISO also gives guidelines on traceability, customer property, preservation of product, process validation (for example SPC), and the control of measuring devices

* *Design and Development.* These requirements ensure that the process of design is planned and controlled. The organisation is expected to design the stages, review and validate, and clarify responsibilities.

* *Purchasing and Production and Service Provision.* Purchased product must conform to requirements and suppliers must be chosen and evaluated in relation to criteria that must be established. Production must be carried out under controlled conditions, including work standards, equipment, and monitoring and measurement. In short using standard operations and capable equipment.

* *Measurement, Analysis, Improvement.* Finally the system needs to be measured, monitored and controlled, and improved. Non-conformities need to be controlled. The new standard is more specific on improvement and on customer satisfaction which needs to be included in any performance measurement system. Processes and products need to be monitored. Importantly feedback needs to be given to Management Review thereby closing the loop.

ISO 9001 includes reduced requirements for documentation in comparison with the old standard. The organisation has greater freedom to specify its own documentation, but must nevertheless have documentation for the effective planning, operation and control of its processes. Six types of documentation are specifically required. For: control of documents, control of nonconforming products, corrective actions, preventive actions, control of records, and for internal quality audits.

Criticisms of the old standard cited its cost to implement, excessive "red tape", its unsuitability for particular kinds of industry (witness the emergence of the auto industry standard QS9000), and the possibility of management attention being diverted from real quality issues. On the positive side certification gives credibility, a reduction in the necessity for supplier audits, and may bring order to an undisciplined company. Hopefully the problems have been reduced, whilst benefits remain.

Further reading and Notes:
ISO 9001:2000 Quality Management Systems: Requirements. This is the standard for demonstrating conformity of a quality management system.
ISO 9004:2000. Guidelines for performance improvement. This is not for certification purposes but provides guidelines for both meeting customer requirements and improving performance.
ISO 9000:2000. This discusses the fundamental concepts and sets out definitions.

Charles Cianfrani, Joseph Tsiakals, John West, *ISO 9001:2000 Explained.* (Second edition), ASQ Quality Press, Milwaukee, 2001. This book contains the entire standard.
Web site: www.bsi.org.uk
The Quality Certification Bureau at www.qcbinc.com provides several comprehensive implementation and assessment guides on the standard which can be downloaded.

EFQM Excellence Model (and other models)

A European equivalent was started by the European Foundation for Quality Management (EFQM) in 1992. This is known as the Business Excellence Model. This is a "non-prescriptive framework which recognises there are many approaches to achieving sustainable excellence". It is a self-evaluation tool for organisations, large and small, public and private sector. The EFQM updates the model regularly. The model is shown in the Figure. Each of the nine boxes has sub-criteria for which there are a number of questions. Below each sub-criterion are lists of areas to consider. A full set of evaluation criteria is available from the EFQM website.

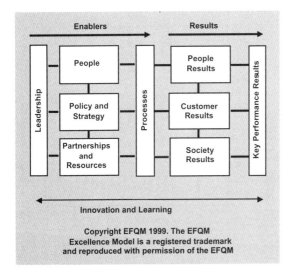

Copyright EFQM 1999. The EFQM Excellence Model is a registered trademark and reproduced with permission of the EFQM

The introductory section of this book gives the quality tools that may be relevant to each of the nine boxes of the EFQM model.

Some brief comments on the nine boxes follow:

Leadership
The importance of leadership is recognised, as is establishing vision and mission. EFQM defines leaders in wide terms, not limited to top management. Leaders are expected to be role models, and to improve their own performance. PDCA is not just for products and processes! EFQM is very much a Deming viewpoint on leadership ("constancy of purpose").

People
EFQM covers such "obvious" aspects as training and evaluation, but goes further requiring effective human resource development, teamworking, empowerment, and rewards and recognition.

Policy and Strategy
The EFQM is concerned not just with product and service quality, however important, but also with organisational policy and strategy. The "stakeholder" concept is used, and EFQM would expect a balanced consideration of all stakeholders. Policy deployment, to ensure that strategy is communicated, is important.

Partnerships and Resources
Active encouragement of supplier partnerships is given, with emphasis on mutually beneficial relationships. Interestingly EFQM talks about the use and development of knowledge. On resources, of course facilities need to be maintained for capability, but there is also mention of conservation of materials.

Processes
The focus of EFQM is on the key processes necessary to deliver the organisation's strategy. Of course quality processes are also important, such as Kaizen initiatives, and ISO 9001. Again a Deming viewpoint ("management by facts").

People Results
People are supposed to be adequately surveyed, with ideas such as team briefings and suggestion schemes incorporated.

Customer Results
This major box requires evaluation of customer satisfaction through surveys and interviews. Loyalty and market share are measures.

Society Results
EFQM asks the company to establish its impact on wider society, for example involvement in community activities.

Key Performance Results
EFQM requires a "balanced scorecard" type approach, as well as cost of quality, product and process measures.

It may be seen that EFQM goes well beyond a narrow definition of Quality. Perhaps what Juran would call "Big Q"?

EFQM and ISO 9001:2000.

Having said that EFQM interprets quality in a far wider sense, there are similarities and overlaps between the two. "Fundamental Concepts" underpin the EFQM model. These are broadly in line with the eight principles of ISO 9001, but with a much broader interpretation by EFQM in each case. The EFQM concepts are, with the corresponding ISO principle shown in brackets:

EFQM Concept	ISO Principle
Results orientation	(—)
Customer focus	(Customer focus)
Leadership and constancy of purpose	(Leadership)
Management by Process and Facts	(Process Approach) (Factual approach)
People development and involvement	(Involvement of people)
Continuous learning, innovation, improvement	(Continual improvement)
Partnership development	(Mutually beneficial supplier development)
Public responsibility	(—)
———	(System approach to management)

There are also similarities with the Service Profit Chain Model.

Service Excellence, Drivers, and Complacency

On business excellence, Chris Voss et al at London Business School undertook a survey of UK and US businesses. This used criteria based on the EFQM and on several other models. (It is possible to survey and benchmark your own organisation using these criteria via "Service Probe" marketed by the CBI, London – unfortunately not free like others).

Some interesting findings were

*   There is a good correlation between what the authors termed "Results" (market share, profit, customer and staff satisfaction) and "Drivers" (including process orientation, employees, measures, organisation structure)

*   In the UK there is a smaller proportion of "World Class" service companies than in the USA but the USA has a higher percentage of "laggards"

*   The "world class" companies tend to be much less complacent than the "laggards". In other words managers who regarded themselves as well above were often below average, and those who believe that they still have much to learn generally have above average results. (It's something to do with the Deming Cycle and the failure to check and learn!)

The Drivers that Voss et al use are in some ways similar to the Enablers in the Business Excellence model.

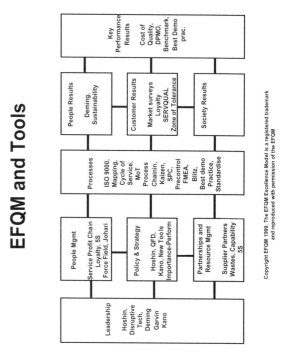

Further reading:

Web sites: www.efqm.org

Chris Voss, Kate Blackmon, Richard Chase et al, *Achieving World-Class Service*, London Business School, 1997.

Andrew Robson and Vas Prabhu, "What can we learn from leading service practitioners...", *Managing Service Quality*, V11, N4, 2001

Index

1.5 Sigma Shift 16
14 Points 26
14 Questions 43
3 R's 143
4 Absolutes 30
5 Whys 112, 130
5S 110, 121
6 Honest Men 113
7 Service Wastes 101
7 Tools 32, 41, 57
7 Wastes 98
ABC 60
Affinity Diagram 103, 114
Air Academy 7, 43, 83
ANOVA 77
Assurance 8, 148
Attribute 57, 71
Baldridge 31
Barrier Analysis 113
Basis Factors 38, 40
Benchmarking 114
Best Demonstrated Practice 116
Bhote 40
Black Belt 12, 20, 90
Blue - Service 136
Box and Whisker Chart 52
c Chart 71
Camp, Robert 114
CANDO 110
Capability 65, 67
Cause and Effect 60
CEDAC 60
Central Limit Theorem 74
Champion 12, 20
Charter 15, 47
Chase 36
Check Sheets 63
Circles 34
CNX 59
Complexity 88
Confidence Interval 75
Contingency Chart 105
Control 90
Control Plan 95
COPQ 17, 30, 33
Correlation Diagram 62

Costing 111
Covey 94
CPA 49
Cpk 66
CPO 133
Crosby 30
Cross Impact Analysis 64, 119
CTQ 49, 87
CUSUM 117
Cycle of Service 36, 39, 113
Data Envelopment 116
Deadly Disease 27
Decision Tree 105
Defect Waste 100
Delighter 38
Deming 25, 98, 121
Design of Experiments 37, 41, 83
Dimensions of Quality 34, 40
DMAIC 14, 43, 47
DOE 37, 41, 83
DPMO 16
Early Start 50
EFQM 149
Excellence Model 149
Explicit Quality 40
Failure Demand 92, 145
Feigenbaum 31
Fishbone 60
Flow Kaizen 120
FMEA 87
Force Field Analysis 118
Ford 91, 98
Full Factorial 83
Gantt Chart 50
Gaps - Service 140
Garvin 34
Gauge R&R 55
GE 7
Gitlow 104
Green Belt 13
Grönroos 40
Hall, Robert 92
Hinckley 88
Histogram 52, 61
House of Quality 125
Imai 43, 120

Importance-Performance	119	Philosophy	11
Improve	81, 120	Pokayoke	35, 88
Interaction Plot	85	PONC	30
Interrelationship Diagram	104	Process	48, 58
Inventory	111	Process Map	58
Inventory UnnecessaryIshikawa	100	Profit Chain	141
Ishikawa	32	Profound Knowledge	18, 25
Ishikawa Diagram	60	Project	49
ISO9000	31, 147	PZB Model	140
JIT II	130	QFD	39, 49, 87, 105, 125
Joharri	94	Radar Chart	52
Juran	27, 121	Range	53
Kaizen	43, 120	Ranking	124
Kano	38, 123	RATER	140
Key Variables	18	RCM	95
Kipling	48, 113	Recovery	142
LCL	65	Red X	40
Loss Function	11, 37, 49	Rees	18
Loyalty	137, 142, 149	Regression	82
Mahesh, V.S.	134	Reichheld	137
Map	134	Reproducibility	55
Mapping	57	Retention	142
Market Survey	38, 54, 122	Root Cause	112
Marketing	125	Run Diagram	62
Matrix	119, 129	Sampling	54, 74
Mean	53	Satisfaction	138, 142
Measels Chart	61	Seddon	145
Meduan	53	Service Profit Chain	131
Mistakes	35, 88	SERVQUAL	140
Mode	53	Shainin	40
Moment of Truth	134	Shingo	35
Motion Waste	100	Sholtes	94
Motorola	7, 14, 41	Single Point Lesson	128
MSA	55	SIPOC	47
Muda	59, 63, 98	SOP	59, 63, 91
Multi-Vari Chart	62	Sort	110
New Tools	103	SPC	67
NGT	123	SPC Limitations	72
Ohno	98, 121	Specification Limit	11
One Point Lesson	128	Standard Deviation	53,66
Orthogonal Array	86	Standard Work	63. 91
Out of Control	69	Statification	63
Overprocessing	99	Statistical Process Control	67
Overproduction	98	Story Board	96
p Chart	71	Suppliers	129
Pareto	28, 60	Sustainability	22
PDCA	26, 44, 90, 121, 147	t Distribution	76

Taguchi	36, 85
Tally Chart	63
TARP	137, 139, 143
Taylor, F.W.	92
TIM WOOD	98
Tolerance	38
Toyota	63, 92, 121
TPM	95
TPS	91
TQC	9
TQM	9, 32
Training	12
Transport Waste	99
Tree Diagram	105
UCL	65
Value	142
Value Demand	145
Variables	70
Variation	11, 16, 53, 88, 65
VMI	130
VOC	48, 65, 125
Waiting	99
Why	112
Wickens	91
Window Analysis	93
ZD	30
Zeithaml	137, 140
Zone of Tolerance	144